P9-AOW-936

MADNESS
AND
CIVILIZATION

A History of Insanity in the
Age of Reason

Translated from the French by
RICHARD HOWARD

Vintage Books
A DIVISION OF RANDOM HOUSE
New York

MADNESS

AND

CIVILIZATION

*A History of Insanity in the
Age of Reason*

MICHEL
FOUCAULT

FIRST VINTAGE BOOKS EDITION, April 1973

Copyright © 1965 by Random House, Inc.

All rights reserved under International and Pan-American Copyright Conventions. Published in the United States by Random House, Inc., New York, and simultaneously in Canada by Random House of Canada Limited, Toronto. Originally published in the United States by Pantheon Books, in 1965, and in France as *Histoire de la Folie* © 1961, by Librairie Plon. This translation is of the edition abridged by the author and published in the Plon 10/18 series. However, the author has added some additional material from the original edition, including the chapter "Passion and Delirium."

Library of Congress Cataloging in Publication Data

Foucault, Michel.
  Madness and civilization.

  Translation of Folie et déraison; histoire de la folie.
  Includes bibliographical references.
  1. Psychiatry—History.   2. Mental illness.
I. Title.
RC438.F613 1973   157'.2'09033   72–10582
ISBN 0–394–71914–x

Manufactured in the United States of America

INTRODUCTION

MICHEL FOUCAULT has achieved something truly creative in this book on the history of madness during the so-called classical age: the end of the sixteenth and the seventeenth and eighteenth centuries. Rather than to review historically the concept of madness, the author has chosen to re-create, mostly from original documents, mental illness, folly, and unreason as they must have existed in their time, place, and proper social perspective. In a sense, he has tried to re-create the negative part of the concept, that which has disappeared under the retroactive influence of present-day ideas and the passage of time. Too many historical books about psychic disorders look at the past in the light of the present; they single out only what has positive and direct relevance to present-day psychiatry. This book belongs to the few which demonstrate how skillful, sensitive scholarship uses history to enrich, deepen, and reveal new avenues for thought and investigation.

No oversimplifications, no black-and-white statements, no sweeping generalizations are ever allowed in this book; folly is brought back to life as a complex social phenomenon, part and parcel of the human condition. Most of the time, for the sake of clarity, we examine madness through one of its facets; as M. Foucault animates one facet of the problem after the other, he always keeps them related to each other. The end of the Middle Ages emphasized the comic, but just as often the tragic aspect of madness, as in *Tristan and Iseult*, for example. The Renaissance, with

Erasmus's *Praise of Folly*, demonstrated how fascinating imagination and some of its vagaries were to the thinkers of that day. The French Revolution, Pinel, and Tuke emphasized political, legal, medical, or religious aspects of madness; and today, our so-called objective medical approach, in spite of the benefits that it has brought to the mentally ill, continues to look at only one side of the picture. Folly is so human that it has common roots with poetry and tragedy; it is revealed as much in the insane asylum as in the writings of a Cervantes or a Shakespeare, or in the deep psychological insights and cries of revolt of a Nietzsche. Correctly or incorrectly, the author feels that Freud's death instinct also stems from the tragic elements which led men of all epochs to worship, laugh at, and dread folly simultaneously. Fascinating as Renaissance men found it—they painted it, praised it, sang about it—it also heralded for them death of the body by picturing death of the mind.

Nothing is more illuminating than to follow with M. Foucault the many threads which are woven in this complex book, whether it speaks of changing symptoms, commitment procedures, or treatment. For example: he sees a definite connection between some of the attitudes toward madness and the disappearance, between 1200 and 1400, of leprosy. In the middle of the twelfth century, France had more than 2,000 leprosariums, and England and Scotland 220 for a population of a million and a half people. As leprosy vanished, in part because of segregation, a void was created and the moral values attached to the leper had to find another scapegoat. Mental illness and unreason attracted that stigma to themselves, but even this was neither complete, simple, nor immediate.

Renaissance men developed a delightful, yet horrible way of dealing with their mad denizens: they were put on a ship and entrusted to mariners because folly, water, and sea, as everyone then "knew," had an affinity for each other. Thus, "Ships of Fools" crisscrossed the seas and canals of Europe with their comic and pathetic cargo of souls. Some of them found pleasure and even a cure in the changing surroundings, in the isolation of being cast off, while others withdrew further, became worse, or died alone and away from their families. The cities and villages which had thus rid themselves of their crazed and crazy, could now take pleasure in watching the exciting sideshow when a ship full of foreign lunatics would dock at their harbors. The seventeenth and eighteenth centuries saw much social unrest and economic depression, which they tried to solve by imprisoning the indigents with the criminals and forcing them to work. The demented fitted quite naturally between those two extremes of social maladjustment and iniquity.

A nice and hallowed tradition has labeled Tuke and Pinel as the saviors of the mentally ill, but the truth of the matter is not so simple. Many others had treated them with kindness, pleading that they belonged first and foremost with their families, and for at least two hundred years before the 1780s, legislation had been considered or passed to segregate criminals and indigents from fools. But this legislation was prompted, as often as not, by a desire to protect the poor, the criminal, the man imprisoned for debts, and the juvenile delinquent from the frightening bestiality of the madman. As the madman had replaced the leper, the mentally ill person was now a subhuman and beastly scapegoat; hence the need to protect others. While the Quaker Tuke applied his religious principles, first to demented "friends" and later to foes also, partly to convert them, the great Pinel was not sure at times that he was dealing with sick people; he often marveled at their unbelievable endurance of physical hardship, and often cited the ability of schizophrenic women to sleep naked in subfreezing temperatures without suffering any ill effects. Were not these people more healthy, more resistant than ordinary human beings? Didn't they have too much animal spirit in them?

Naturally, it is impossible to discuss a book as complex as *Madness and Civilization* without oversimplifying and doing it an injustice. It is a tale of nuances, relative values, and delicate shadings. Yet, it is an impressive monument: in a dispassionate manner it marshals overwhelming evidence to dispel more effectively than many previous attempts the myth of mental illness, and re-establishes folly and unreason in their rightful place as complex, human—too human—phenomena. The roots and symptoms of folly are being looked for today in psychology, medicine, and sociology, but they were and still are as present and important in art,* religion, ethics, and epistemology. Madness is really a manifestation of the "soul," a variable concept which from antiquity to the twentieth century covered approximately what came to be known, after Freud, as the unconscious part of the human mind.† Only time will tell how much better students of the psyche can look at the future, after reading this sobering re-creation of yesteryear's madness and the ineffective attempts of humanity to treat it by amputation, projections, prejudices, and segregation.

JOSÉ BARCHILON, M.D.

---

* My only quarrel with the book is the lack of emphasis on the humoristic elements in psychoses and neuroses: i.e., the patient laughs at himself, or laughs at the world through his illness.

† The fear and dread of madness is as real a factor in social and medical attitudes or measures as anxiety, symptoms, and resistance in coping with impulses from the individual unconscious; even though the author does not explicitly compare madness with the unconscious, he equates madness and dream activity so that the inference is clear enough.

PREFACE

Pascal: "Men are so necessarily mad, that not to be mad would amount to another form of madness." *And* Dostoievsky, *in his* DIARY OF A WRITER: "It is not by confining one's neighbor that one is convinced of one's own sanity."

We have yet to write the history of that other form of madness, by which men, in an act of sovereign reason, confine their neighbors, and communicate and recognize each other through the merciless language of non-madness; to define the moment of this conspiracy before it was permanently established in the realm of truth, before it was revived by the lyricism of protest. We must try to return, in history, to that zero point in the course of madness at which madness is an undifferentiated experience, a not yet divided experience of division itself. We must describe, from the start of its trajectory, that "other form" which relegates Reason and Madness to one side or the other of its action as things henceforth external, deaf to all exchange, and as though dead to one another.

This is doubtless an uncomfortable region. To explore it we must renounce the convenience of terminal truths, and never let ourselves be guided by what we may know of madness. None of the concepts of psychopathology, even and especially in the implicit process of retrospections, can play an organizing role. What is constitutive is the action that divides madness, and not the science elaborated once this division is made and calm restored. What is originative is the caesura that establishes the distance between reason and non-reason; reason's subjugation of non-reason, wrest-

ing from it its truth as madness, crime, or disease, derives explicitly from this point. Hence we must speak of that initial dispute without assuming a victory, or the right to a victory; we must speak of those actions re-examined in history, leaving in abeyance all that may figure as a conclusion, as a refuge in truth; we shall have to speak of this act of scission, of this distance set, of this void instituted between reason and what is not reason, without ever relying upon the fulfillment of what it claims to be.

Then, and then only, can we determine the realm in which the man of madness and the man of reason, moving apart, are not yet disjunct; and in an incipient and very crude language, antedating that of science, begin the dialogue of their breach, testifying in a fugitive way that they still speak to each other. Here madness and non-madness, reason and non-reason are inextricably involved: inseparable at the moment when they do not yet exist, and existing for each other, in relation to each other, in the exchange which separates them.

In the serene world of mental illness, modern man no longer communicates with the madman: on one hand, the man of reason delegates the physician to madness, thereby authorizing a relation only through the abstract universality of disease; on the other, the man of madness communicates with society only by the intermediary of an equally abstract reason which is order, physical and moral constraint, the anonymous pressure of the group, the requirements of conformity. As for a common language, there is no such thing; or rather, there is no such thing any longer; the constitution of madness as a mental illness, at the end of the eighteenth century, affords the evidence of a broken dialogue, posits the separation as already effected, and thrusts into oblivion all those stammered, imperfect words without fixed syntax in which the exchange between madness and reason was made. The language of psychiatry, *which is a monologue of reason about madness, has been established only on the basis of such a silence.*

I have not tried to write the history of that language, but rather the archaeology of that silence.

The Greeks had a relation to something that they called ὕβρις. *This relation was not merely one of condemnation; the existence of Thrasymachus or of Callicles suffices to prove it, even if their language has reached us already enveloped in the reassuring dialectic of Socrates. But the Greek Logos had no contrary.*

European man, since the beginning of the Middle Ages, has had a relation to something he calls, indiscriminately, Madness, Dementia, Insanity. Perhaps it is to this obscure presence that Western reason owes something of its depth, as the σωφροσυνή *of the Socratic reasoners owes something to the threat of* ὕβρις. *In any case, the Reason-Madness nexus constitutes for Western culture one of the dimensions of its originality; it already accompanied that culture long before Hieronymus Bosch, and will follow it long after Nietzsche and Artaud.*

What, then, is this confrontation beneath the language of reason? Where can an interrogation lead us which does not follow reason in its horizontal course, but seeks to retrace in time that constant verticality which confronts European culture with what it is not, establishes its range by its own derangement? What realm do we enter which is neither the history of knowledge, nor history itself; which is controlled by neither the teleology of truth nor the rational sequence of causes, since causes have value and meaning only beyond the division? A realm, no doubt, where what is in question is the limits rather than the identity of a culture.

The classical period—from Willis to Pinel, from the frenzies of Racine's Oreste to Sade's Juliette and the Quinta del Sordo of Goya—covers precisely that epoch in which the exchange between madness and reason modifies its language, and in a radical manner. In the history of madness, two events indicate this change with a singular clarity: 1657, the creation of the Hôpital Général and the "great confinement" of the poor; 1794, the liberation of the chained inmates of Bicêtre. Between these two unique and symmetrical events, something happens whose ambiguity has left the historians of medicine at a loss: blind repression in an absolutist regime, according to some; but according to others, the gradual discovery by science and philanthropy of madness in its positive truth. As a matter of fact, beneath these reversible meanings, a structure is forming which does not resolve the ambiguity but determines it. It is this structure which accounts for the transition from the medieval and humanist experience of madness to our own experience, which confines insanity within mental illness. In the Middle Ages and until the Renaissance, man's dispute with madness was a dramatic debate in which he confronted the secret powers of the world; the experience of madness was clouded by images of the Fall and the Will of God, of the Beast and the Metamorphosis, and of all the marvelous secrets of Knowledge. In our era, the experience of madness remains silent in the composure of a knowledge which, knowing too much about madness, forgets it. But from one of these experiences to the other, the shift has been made by a world without images, without positive character, in a kind of silent transparency which reveals— as mute institution, act without commentary, immediate knowledge—a great motionless structure; this structure is one of neither drama nor knowledge; it is the point where history is immobilized in the tragic category which both establishes and impugns it.

CONTENTS

MADNESS
AND
CIVILIZATION

*A History of Insanity in the
Age of Reason*

I

"STULTIFERA NAVIS"

At the end of the Middle Ages, leprosy disappeared from the Western world. In the margins of the community, at the gates of cities, there stretched wastelands which sickness had ceased to haunt but had left sterile and long uninhabitable. For centuries, these reaches would belong to the non-human. From the fourteenth to the seventeenth century, they would wait, soliciting with strange incantations a new incarnation of disease, another grimace of terror, renewed rites of purification and exclusion.

From the High Middle Ages to the end of the Crusades, leprosariums had multiplied their cities of the damned over the entire face of Europe. According to Mathieu Paris, there were as many as 19,000 of them throughout Christendom. In any case, around 1226, when Louis VIII established the lazar-house law for France, more than 2,000 appeared on the official registers. There were 43 in the diocese of Paris alone: these included Bourg-le-Reine, Corbeil, Saint-Valère, and the sinister Champ-Pourri (Rotten Field); included also was Charenton. The two largest were in the immediate vicinity of Paris: Saint-Germain and Saint-Lazare:[1] we shall hear their names again in the history of another sickness. This is because from the fifteenth century on, all were emptied; in the next century Saint-Germain became a reformatory for young criminals; and before the time of Saint Vincent there was only one leper left at Saint-Lazare, "Sieur Langlois, practitioner in the civil court." The lazar house of Nancy, which was among the largest in Europe, had only four inmates during the regency of Marie de Médicis. According to Catel's *Mémoires*, there were 29 hospitals in Toulouse at the end of the medieval period: seven were leprosariums; but at the beginning of the seventeenth century we find only three mentioned: Saint-Cyprien, Arnaud-Bernard, and Saint-Michel. It was a pleasure to celebrate the disappearance of leprosy: in 1635 the inhabitants of Reims formed a solemn procession to thank God for having delivered their city from this scourge.

For a century already, royal authority had undertaken the control and reorganization of the immense fortune represented by the endowments of the lazar houses; in a decree of December 19, 1543, François I had a census and inventory taken "to remedy the great disorder that exists at present in the lazar houses"; in his turn, Henri IV in an edict of 1606 prescribed a revision of their accounts and allotted "the sums obtained from this investigation to the sustenance of poor noblemen and crippled soldiers." The same request for regulation is recorded on October 24, 1612, but the excess revenues were now to be used for feeding the poor.

In fact, the question of the leprosariums was not settled in France before the end of the seventeenth century; and the problem's economic importance provoked more than one conflict. Were there not still, in the year 1677, 44 lazar houses in the province of Dauphiné alone? On February 20, 1672, Louis XIV assigned to the Orders of Saint-Lazare and Mont-Carmel the effects of all the military and hospital orders; they were entrusted with the administration of the lazar houses of the kingdom. Some twenty years later, the edict of 1672 was revoked, and by a series of staggered measures from March 1693 to July 1695 the goods of the lazar houses were thenceforth assigned to other hospitals and welfare establishments. The few lepers scattered in the 1,200 still-existing houses were collected at Saint-Mesmin near Orléans. These decrees were first applied in Paris, where the Parlement transferred the revenue in question to the establishments of the Hôpital Général; this example was imitated by the provincial authorities; Toulouse transferred the effects of its lazar houses to the Hôpital des Incurables (1696); those of Beaulieu in Normandy went to the Hôtel-Dieu in Caen; those of Voley were assigned to the Hôpital de Sainte-Foy. Only Saint-Mesmin and the wards of Ganets, near Bordeaux, remained as a reminder.

England and Scotland alone had opened 220 lazar houses for a million and a half inhabitants in the twelfth century. But as early as the fourteenth century they began to empty out; by the time Edward III ordered an inquiry into the hospital of Ripon—in 1342—there were no more lepers; he assigned the institution's effects to the poor. At the end of the twelfth century, Archbishop Puisel had founded a hospital in which by 1434 only two beds were reserved for lepers, should any be found. In 1348, the great leprosarium of Saint Albans contained only three patients; the hospital of Romenal in Kent was abandoned twenty-four years later, for lack of lepers. At Chatham, the lazar house of Saint Bartholomew, established in 1078, had been one of the most important in England; under Elizabeth, it cared for only two patients; it was finally closed in 1627.

The same regression of leprosy occurred in Germany, perhaps a little more slowly; and the same conversion of the lazar houses, hastened by the Reformation, which left municipal administrations in charge of welfare and hospital establishments; this was the case in Leipzig, in Munich, in Hamburg. In 1542, the effects of the lazar houses of Schleswig-Holstein were transferred to the hospitals. In Stuttgart a magistrate's report of 1589 indicates that for fifty years already there had been no lepers in the house provided for them. At Lipplingen, the lazar house was soon peopled with incurables and madmen.

A strange disappearance, which was doubtless not the long-sought effect of obscure medical practices, but the spontaneous result of segregation and also the consequence, after the Crusades, of the break with the Eastern sources of infection. Leprosy withdrew, leaving derelict these low places and these rites which were intended, not to suppress it, but to keep it at a sacred distance, to fix it in an inverse exaltation. What doubtless remained longer than leprosy, and would persist when the lazar houses had been empty for years, were the values and images attached to the figure of the leper as well as the meaning of his exclusion, the social importance of that insistent and fearful figure which was not driven off without first being inscribed within a sacred circle.

If the leper was removed from the world, and from the community of the Church visible, his existence was yet a constant manifestation of God, since it was a sign both of His anger and of His grace: "My friend," says the ritual of the Church of Vienne, "it pleaseth Our Lord that thou shouldst be infected with this malady, and thou hast great grace at the hands of Our Lord that he desireth to punish thee for thy iniquities in this world." And at the very moment when the priest and his assistants drag him out of the church with backward step, the leper is assured that he still bears witness for God: "And howsoever thou mayest be apart from the Church and the company of the Sound, yet art thou not apart from the grace of God." Brueghel's lepers attend at a distance, but forever, that climb to Calvary on which the entire people accompanies Christ. Hieratic witnesses of evil, they accomplish their salvation in and by their very exclusion: in a strange reversibility that is the opposite of good works and prayer, they are saved by the hand that is not stretched out. The sinner who abandons the leper at his door opens his way to heaven. "For which have patience in thy malady; for Our Lord hateth thee not because of it, keepeth thee not from his company; but if thou hast patience thou wilt be saved, as was the leper who died before the gate of the rich man and was carried straight to paradise." Abandonment is his salvation; his exclusion offers him another form of communion.

Leprosy disappeared, the leper vanished, or almost, from memory; these structures remained. Often, in these same places, the formulas of exclusion would be repeated, strangely similar two or three centuries later. Poor vagabonds, criminals, and "deranged minds" would take the part played by the leper, and we shall see what salvation was expected from this exclusion, for them and for those who excluded them as well. With an altogether new meaning and in a very different culture, the forms would remain—essentially that major form of a rigorous division which is social exclusion but spiritual reintegration.

Something new appears in the imaginary landscape of the Renaissance; soon it will occupy a privileged place there: the Ship of Fools, a strange "drunken boat" that glides along the calm rivers of the Rhineland and the Flemish canals.

The *Narrenschiff*, of course, is a literary composition, probably borrowed from the old Argonaut cycle, one of the great mythic themes recently revived and rejuvenated, acquiring an institutional aspect in the Burgundy Estates. Fashion favored the composition of these Ships, whose crew of imaginary heroes, ethical models, or social types embarked on a great symbolic voyage which would bring them, if not fortune, then at least the figure of their destiny or their truth. Thus Symphorien Champier composes a *Ship of Princes and Battles of Nobility* in 1502, then a *Ship of Virtuous Ladies* in 1503; there is also a *Ship of Health*, alongside the *Blauwe Schute* of Jacob van Oestvoren in 1413, Sebastian Brant's *Narrenschiff* (1494), and the work of Josse Bade: *Stultiferae naviculae scaphae fatuarum mulierum* (1498). Bosch's painting, of course, belongs to this dream fleet.

But of all these romantic or satiric vessels, the *Narrenschiff* is the only one that had a real existence—for they did exist, these boats that conveyed their insane cargo from town to town. Madmen then led an easy wandering existence. The towns drove them outside their limits; they were allowed to wander in the open countryside, when not entrusted to a group of merchants and pilgrims. The custom was especially frequent in Germany; in Nuremberg, in the first half of the fifteenth century, the presence of 63 madmen had been registered; 31 were driven away; in the fifty years that followed, there are records of 21 more obligatory departures; and these are only the madmen arrested by the municipal authorities. Frequently they were handed over to boatmen: in Frankfort, in 1399, seamen were instructed to rid the city of a madman who walked about the streets naked; in the first years of the fifteenth century, a criminal madman was expelled in the same manner from Mainz. Sometimes the sailors disembarked these bothersome passengers sooner than they had promised; witness a blacksmith of Frankfort twice expelled and twice returning before being taken to Kreuznach for good. Often the cities of Europe must have seen these "ships of fools" approaching their harbors.

It is not easy to discover the exact meaning of this custom. One might suppose it was a general means of extradition by which municipalities sent wandering madmen out of their own jurisdiction; a hypothesis which will not in itself account for the facts, since certain madmen, even before special houses were built for them, were admitted to hospitals and cared for as such; at the Hôtel-Dieu in Paris, their cots were set up in the dormitories. Moreover, in the majority of the cities of Europe there existed throughout the Middle Ages and the Renaissance a place of detention reserved for the insane; there was for example the Châtelet of Melun or the famous Tour aux Fous in Caen; there were the numberless *Narrtürmer* of Germany, like the gates of Lübeck or the Jungpfer of Hamburg. Madmen were thus not invariably expelled. One might then speculate that among them only foreigners were driven away, each city agreeing to care for those madmen among its own citizens. Do we not in fact find among the account books of certain medieval cities subsidies for madmen or donations made for the care of the insane? However, the problem is not so simple, for there existed gathering places where the madmen, more numerous than elsewhere, were not autochthonous. First come the shrines: Saint-Mathurin de Larchant, Saint-Hildevert de Gournay, Besançon, Gheel; pilgrimages to these places were organized, often supported, by cities or hospitals. It is possible that these ships of fools, which haunted the imagination of the entire early Renaissance, were pilgrimage boats, highly symbolic cargoes of madmen in search of their reason: some went down the Rhineland rivers toward Belgium and Gheel; others sailed up the Rhine toward the Jura and Besançon.

But other cities, like Nuremberg, were certainly not shrines and yet contained great numbers of madmen—many more, in any case, than could have been furnished by the city itself. These madmen were housed and provided for in the city budget, and yet they were not given treatment; they were simply thrown into prison. We may suppose that in certain important cities—centers of travel and markets—madmen had been brought in considerable numbers by merchants and mariners and "lost" there, thus ridding their native cities of their presence. It may have happened that these places of "counterpilgrimage" have become confused with the places where, on the contrary, the insane were taken as pilgrims. Interest in cure and in exclusion coincide: madmen were confined in the holy locus of a miracle. It is possible that the village of Gheel developed in this manner—a shrine that became a ward, a holy land where madness hoped for deliverance, but where man enacted, according to old themes, a sort of ritual division.

What matters is that the vagabond madmen, the act of driving them away, their departure and embarkation do not assume their entire significance on the plane of social utility or security. Other meanings much closer to rite are certainly present; and we can still discern some traces of them. Thus access to churches was denied to madmen, although ecclesiastical law did not deny them the use of the sacraments. The Church takes no action against a priest who goes mad; but in Nuremberg in 1421 a mad priest was expelled with particular solemnity, as if the impurity was multiplied by the sacred nature of his person, and the city put on its budget the money given him as a viaticum. It happened that certain madmen were publicly whipped, and in the course of a kind of a game they were chased in a mock race and driven out of the city with quarterstaff blows. So many signs that the expulsion of madmen had become one of a number of ritual exiles.

Thus we better understand the curious implication assigned to the navigation of madmen and the prestige attending it. On the one hand, we must not minimize its incontestable practical effectiveness: to hand a madman over to sailors was to be permanently sure he would not be prowling beneath the city walls; it made sure that he would go far away; it made him a prisoner of his own departure. But water adds to this the dark mass of its own values; it carries off, but it does more: it purifies. Navigation delivers man to the uncertainty of fate; on water, each of us is in the hands of his own destiny; every embarkation is, potentially, the last. It is for the other world that the madman sets sail in his fools' boat; it is from the other world that he comes when he disembarks. The madman's voyage is at once a rigorous division and an absolute Passage. In one sense, it simply develops, across a half-real, half-imaginary geography, the madman's *liminal* position on the horizon of medieval concern—a position symbolized and made real at the same time by the madman's privilege of being *confined* within the city *gates:* his exclusion must enclose him; if he cannot and must not have another *prison* than the *threshold* itself, he is kept at the point of passage. He is put in the interior of the exterior, and inversely. A highly symbolic position, which will doubtless remain his until our own day, if we are willing to admit that what was formerly a visible fortress of order has now become the castle of our conscience.

Water and navigation certainly play this role. Confined on the ship, from which there is no escape, the madman is delivered to the river with its thousand arms, the sea with its thousand roads, to that great uncertainty external to everything. He is a prisoner in the midst of what is the freest, the openest of routes: bound fast at the infinite crossroads. He is the Passenger *par excellence:* that is, the prisoner of the passage. And the land he will come to is unknown—as is, once he disembarks, the land from which he comes. He has his truth and his homeland only in that fruitless expanse between two countries that cannot belong to him. Is it this ritual and these values which are at the origin of the long imaginary relationship that can be traced through the whole of Western culture? Or is it, conversely, this relationship that, from time immemorial, has called into being and established the rite of embarkation? One thing at least is certain: water and madness have long been linked in the dreams of European man.

Already, disguised as a madman, Tristan had ordered boatmen to land him on the coast of Cornwall. And when he arrived at the castle of King Mark, no one recognized him, no one knew whence he had come. But he made too many strange remarks, both familiar and distant; he knew too well the secrets of the commonplace not to have been from another, yet nearby, world. He did not come from the solid land, with its solid cities; but indeed from the ceaseless unrest of the sea, from those unknown highways which conceal so much strange knowledge, from that fantastic plain, the underside of the world. Iseut, first of all, realized that this madman was a son of the sea, and that insolent sailors had cast him here, a sign of misfortune: "Accursed be the sailors that brought this madman! Why did they not throw him into the sea!"[2] And more than once in the course of time, the same theme reappears: among the mystics of the fifteenth century, it has become the motif of the soul as a skiff, abandoned on the infinite sea of desires, in the sterile field of cares and ignorance, among the mirages of knowledge, amid the unreason of the world—a craft at the mercy of the sea's great madness, unless it throws out a solid anchor, faith, or raises its spiritual sails so that the breath of God may bring it to port. At the end of the sixteenth century, De Lancre sees in the sea the origin of the demoniacal leanings of an entire people: the hazardous labor of ships, dependence on the stars, hereditary secrets, estrangement from women—the very image of the great, turbulent plain itself makes man lose faith in God and all his attachment to his home; he is then in the hands of the Devil, in the sea of Satan's ruses.[3] In the classical period, the melancholy of the English was easily explained by the influence of a maritime climate, cold, humidity, the instability of the weather; all those fine droplets of water that penetrated the channels and fibers of the human body and made it lose its firmness, predisposed it to madness. Finally, neglecting an immense literature that stretches from Ophelia to the Lorelei, let us note only the great half-anthropological, half-cosmological analyses of Heinroth, which interpret madness as the manifestation in man of an obscure and aquatic element, a dark disorder, a moving chaos, the seed and death of all things, which opposes the mind's luminous and adult stability.

But if the navigation of madmen is linked in the Western mind with so many immemorial motifs, why, so abruptly, in the fifteenth century, is the theme suddenly formulated in literature and iconography? Why does the figure of the Ship of Fools and its insane crew all at once invade the most familiar landscapes? Why, from the old union of water and madness, was this ship born one day, and on just that day?

Because it symbolized a great disquiet, suddenly dawning on the horizon of European culture at the end of the Middle Ages. Madness and the madman become major figures, in their ambiguity: menace and mockery, the dizzying unreason of the world, and the feeble ridicule of men.

First a whole literature of tales and moral fables, in origin, doubtless, quite remote. But by the end of the Middle Ages, it bulks large: a long series of "follies" which, stigmatizing vices and faults as in the past, no longer attribute them all to pride, to lack of charity, to neglect of Christian virtues, but to a sort of great unreason for which nothing, in fact, is exactly responsible, but which involves everyone in a kind of secret complicity. The denunciation of madness (*la folie*) becomes the general form of criticism.

In farces and *soties*, the character of the Madman, the Fool, or the Simpleton assumes more and more importance. He is no longer simply a ridiculous and familiar silhouette in the wings: he stands center stage as the guardian of truth—playing here a role which is the complement and converse of that taken by madness in the tales and the satires. If folly leads each man into a blindness where he is lost, the madman, on the contrary, reminds each man of his truth; in a comedy where each man deceives the other and dupes himself, the madman is comedy to the second degree: the deception of deception; he utters, in his simpleton's language which makes no show of reason, the words of reason that release, in the comic, the comedy: he speaks love to lovers, the truth of life to the young, the middling reality of things to the proud, to the insolent, and to liars. Even the old feasts of fools, so popular in Flanders and northern Europe, were theatrical events, and organized into social and moral criticism, whatever they may have contained of spontaneous religious parody.

In learned literature, too, Madness or Folly was at work, at the very heart of reason and truth. It is Folly which embarks all men without distinction on its insane ship and binds them to the vocation of a common odyssey (Van Oestvoren's *Blauwe Schute*, Brant's *Narrenschiff*); it is Folly whose baleful reign Thomas Murner conjures up in his *Narrenbeschwörung;* it is Folly which gets the best of Love in Corroz's satire *Contre fol amour*, or argues with Love as to which of the two comes first, which of the two makes the other possible, and triumphs in Louise Labé's dialogue, *Débat de folie et d'amour*. Folly also has its academic pastimes; it is the object of argument, it contends against itself; it is denounced, and defends itself by claiming that it is closer to happiness and truth than reason, that it is closer to reason than reason itself; Jakob Wimpfeling edits the *Monopolium philosophorum*, and Judocus Gallus the

Monopolium et societas, vulgo des lichtschiffs. Finally, at the center of all these serious games, the great humanist texts: the *Moria rediviva* of Flayder and Erasmus's *Praise of Folly.* And confronting all these discussions, with their tireless dialectic, confronting these discourses constantly reworded and reworked, a long dynasty of images, from Hieronymus Bosch with *The Cure of Madness* and *The Ship of Fools,* down to Brueghel and his *Dulle Griet;* woodcuts and engravings transcribe what the theater, what literature and art have already taken up: the intermingled themes of the Feast and of the Dance of Fools. Indeed, from the fifteenth century on, the face of madness has haunted the imagination of Western man.

A sequence of dates speaks for itself: the *Dance of Death* in the Cimetière des Innocents doubtless dates from the first years of the fifteenth century, the one in the Chaise-Dieu was probably composed around 1460; and it was in 1485 that Guyot Marchant published his *Danse macabre.* These sixty years, certainly, were dominated by all this grinning imagery of Death. And it was in 1494 that Brant wrote the *Narrenschiff;* in 1497 it was translated into Latin. In the very last years of the century Hieronymus Bosch painted his *Ship of Fools.* The *Praise of Folly* dates from 1509. The order of succession is clear.

Up to the second half of the fifteenth century, or even a little beyond, the theme of death reigns alone. The end of man, the end of time bear the face of pestilence and war. What overhangs human existence is this conclusion and this order from which nothing escapes. The presence that threatens even within this world is a fleshless one. Then in the last years of the century this enormous uneasiness turns on itself; the mockery of madness replaces death and its solemnity. From the discovery of that necessity which inevitably reduces man to nothing, we have shifted to the scornful contemplation of that nothing which is existence itself. Fear in the face of the absolute limit of death turns inward in a continuous irony; man disarms it in advance, making it an object of derision by giving it an everyday, tamed form, by constantly renewing it in the spectacle of life, by scattering it throughout the vices, the difficulties, and the absurdities of all men. Death's annihilation is no longer anything because it was already everything, because life itself was only futility, vain words, a squabble of cap and bells. The head that will become a skull is already empty. Madness is the *déjà-là* of death.[4] But it is also its vanquished presence, evaded in those everyday signs which, announcing that death reigns already, indicate that its prey will be a sorry prize indeed. What death unmasks was never more than a mask; to discover the grin of the skeleton, one need only lift off something that was neither beauty nor truth, but only a plaster and tinsel face. From the vain mask to the corpse, the same smile persists. But when the madman laughs, he already laughs with the laugh of death; the lunatic, anticipating the macabre, has disarmed it. The cries of Dulle Griet triumph, in the high Renaissance, over that *Triumph of Death* sung at the end of the Middle Ages on the walls of the Campo Santo.

The substitution of the theme of madness for that of death does not mark a break, but rather a torsion within the same anxiety. What is in question is still the nothingness of existence, but this nothingness is no longer considered an external, final term, both threat and conclusion; it is experienced from within as the continuous and constant form of existence. And where once man's madness had been not to see that death's term was approaching, so that it was necessary to recall him to wisdom with the spectacle of death, now wisdom consisted of denouncing madness everywhere, teaching men that they were no more than dead men already, and that if the end was near, it was to the degree that madness, become universal, would be one and the same with death itself. This is what Eustache Deschamps prophesies:

> We are cowardly and weak,
> Covetous, old, evil-tongued.
> Fools are all I see, in truth.
> The end is near,
> All goes ill . . .

The elements are now reversed. It is no longer the end of time and of the world which will show retrospectively that men were mad not to have been prepared for them; it is the tide of madness, its secret invasion, that shows that the world is near its final catastrophe; it is man's insanity that invokes and makes necessary the world's end.

In its various forms—plastic or literary—this experience of madness seems extremely coherent. Painting and text constantly refer to one another—commentary here and illustration there. We find the same theme of the *Narrentanz* over and over in popular festivals, in theatrical performances, in engravings and woodcuts, and the entire last part of the *Praise of Folly* is constructed on the model of a long dance of madmen in which each profession and each estate parades in turn to form the great round of unreason. It is likely that in Bosch's *Temptation of Saint Anthony* in Lisbon, many figures of the fantastic fauna which invade the canvas are borrowed from traditional masks; some perhaps are transferred from the *Malleus maleficarum*. As for the famous *Ship of Fools*, is it not a direct translation of Brant's *Narrenschiff*, whose title it bears, and of which it seems to illustrate quite precisely canto XXVII, also consecrated to stigmatizing "drunkards and gluttons"? It has even been suggested that Bosch's painting was part of a series of pictures illustrating the principal cantos of Brant's poem.

As a matter of fact, we must not be misled by what appears to be a strict continuity in these themes, nor imagine more than is revealed by history itself. It is unlikely that an analysis like the one Émile Mâle worked out for the preceding epochs, especially apropos of the theme of death, could be repeated. Between word and image, between what is depicted by language and what is uttered by plastic form, the unity begins to dissolve; a single and identical meaning is not immediately common to them. And if it is true that the image still has the function of speaking, of transmitting something consubstantial with language, we must recognize that it already no longer says the *same thing;* and that by its own plastic values painting engages in an experiment that will take it farther and farther from language, whatever the superficial identity of the theme. Figure and speech still illustrate the same fable of folly in the same moral world, but already they take two different directions, indicating, in a still barely perceptible scission, what will be the great line of cleavage in the Western experience of madness.

The dawn of madness on the horizon of the Renaissance is first perceptible in the decay of Gothic symbolism; as if that world, whose network of spiritual meanings was so close-knit, had begun to unravel, showing faces whose meaning was no longer clear except in the forms of madness. The Gothic forms persist for a time, but little by little they grow silent, cease to speak, to remind, to teach anything but their own fantastic presence, transcending all possible language (though still familiar to the eye). Freed from wisdom and from the teaching that organized it, the image begins to gravitate about its own madness.

Paradoxically, this liberation derives from a proliferation of meaning, from a self-multiplication of significance, weaving relationships so numerous, so intertwined, so rich, that they can no longer be deciphered except in the esoterism of knowledge. Things themselves become so burdened with attributes, signs, allusions that they finally lose their own form. Meaning is no longer read in an immediate perception, the figure no longer speaks for itself; between the knowledge which animates it and the form into which it is transposed, a gap widens. It is free for the dream. One book bears witness to meaning's proliferation at the end of the Gothic world, the *Speculum humanae salvationis,* which, beyond all the correspondences established by the patristic tradition, elaborates, between the Old and the New Testament, a symbolism not on the order of Prophecy, but deriving from an equivalence of imagery. The Passion of Christ is not prefigured only by the sacrifice of Abraham; it is surrounded by all the glories of torture and its innumerable dreams; Tubal the blacksmith and Isaiah's wheel take their places around the Cross, forming beyond all the lessons of the sacrifice the fantastic tableau of savagery, of tormented bodies, and of suffering. Thus the image is burdened with supplementary meanings, and forced to express them. And dreams, madness, the unreasonable can also slip into this excess of meaning. The symbolic figures easily become nightmare silhouettes. Witness that old image of wisdom so often translated, in German engravings, by a long-necked bird whose thoughts, rising slowly from heart to head, have time to be weighed and reflected on; a symbol whose values are blunted by being overemphasized: the long path of reflection becomes in the image the alembic of a subtle learning, an instrument which distills quintessences. The neck of the *Gutemensch* is endlessly elongated, the better to illustrate, beyond wisdom, all the real mediations of knowledge; and the symbolic man becomes a fantastic bird whose disproportionate neck folds a thousand times upon itself—an insane being, halfway between animal and thing, closer to the charms of an image than to the rigor of a meaning. This symbolic wisdom is a prisoner of the madness of dreams.

A fundamental conversion of the world of images: the constraint of a multiplied meaning liberates that world from the control of form. So many diverse meanings are established beneath the surface of the image that it presents only an enigmatic face. And its power is no longer to teach but to fascinate. Characteristic is the evolution of the famous gryllos already familiar to the Middle Ages in the English psalters, and at Chartres and Bourges. It taught, then, how the soul of desiring man had become a prisoner of the beast; these grotesque faces set in the bellies of monsters belonged to the world of the great Platonic metaphor and denounced the spirit's corruption in the folly of sin. But in the fifteenth century the gryllos, image of human madness, becomes one of the preferred figures in the countless *Temptations*. What assails the hermit's tranquillity is not objects of desire, but these hermetic, demented forms which have risen from a dream, and remain silent and furtive on the surface of a world. In the Lisbon *Temptation*, facing Saint Anthony sits one of these figures born of madness, of its solitude, of its penitence, of its privations; a wan smile lights this bodiless face, the pure presence of anxiety in the form of an agile grimace. Now it is exactly this nightmare silhouette that is at once the subject and object of the temptation; it is this figure which fascinates the gaze of the ascetic—both are prisoners of a kind of mirror interrogation, which remains unanswered in a silence inhabited only by the monstrous swarm that surrounds them. The gryllos no longer recalls man, by its satiric form, to his spiritual vocation forgotten in the folly of desire. It is madness become Temptation; all it embodies of the impossible, the fantastic, the inhuman, all that suggests the unnatural, the writhing of an insane presence on the earth's surface—all this is precisely what gives the gryllos its strange power. The freedom, however frightening, of his dreams, the hallucinations of his madness, have more power of attraction for fifteenth-century man than the desirable reality of the flesh.

What then is this fascination which now operates through the images of madness?

First, man finds in these fantastic figures one of the secrets and one of the vocations of his nature. In the thought of the Middle Ages, the legions of animals, named once and for all by Adam, symbolically bear the values of humanity. But at the beginning of the Renaissance, the relations with animality are reversed; the beast is set free; it escapes the world of legend and moral illustration to acquire a fantastic nature of its own. And by an astonishing reversal, it is now the animal that will stalk man, capture him, and reveal him to his own truth. Impossible animals, issuing from a demented imagination, become the secret nature of man; and when on the Last Day sinful man appears in his hideous nakedness, we see that he has the monstrous shape of a delirious animal; these are the screech owls whose toad bodies combine, in Thierry Bouts's *Hell*, with the nakedness of the damned; these are Stephan Lochner's winged insects with cats' heads, sphinxes with beetles' wing cases, birds whose wings are as disturbing and as avid as hands; this is the great beast of prey with knotty fingers that figures in Matthias Grünewald's *Temptation*. Animality has escaped domestication by human symbols and values; and it is animality that reveals the dark rage, the sterile madness that lie in men's hearts.

At the opposite pole to this nature of shadows, madness fascinates because it is knowledge. It is knowledge, first, because all these absurd figures are in reality elements of a difficult, hermetic, esoteric learning. These strange forms are situated, from the first, in the space of the Great Secret, and the Saint Anthony who is tempted by them is not a victim of the violence of desire but of the much more insidious lure of curiosity; he is tempted by that distant and intimate knowledge which is offered, and at the same time evaded, by the smile of the gryllos; his backward movement is nothing but that step by which he keeps from crossing the forbidden limits of knowledge; he knows already—and that is his temptation—what Jérôme Cardan will say later: "Wisdom, like other precious substances, must be torn from the bowels of the earth." This knowledge, so inaccessible, so formidable, the Fool, in his innocent idiocy, already possesses. While the man of reason and wisdom perceives only fragmentary and all the more unnerving images of it, the Fool bears it intact as an unbroken sphere: that crystal ball which for all others is empty is in *his* eyes filled with the density of an invisible knowledge. Brueghel mocks the sick man who tries to penetrate this crystal sphere, but it is this iridescent bubble of knowledge—an absurd but infinitely precious lantern—that sways at the end of the stick Dulle Griet bears on her shoulder. And it is this sphere which figures on the reverse of the Garden of Delights. Another symbol of knowledge, the tree (the forbidden tree, the tree of promised immortality and of sin), once planted in the heart of the earthly paradise, has been uprooted and now forms the mast of the Ship of Fools, as seen in the engraving that illustrates Josse Bade's *Stultiferae naviculae*; it is this tree, without a doubt, that sways over Bosch's *Ship of Fools*.

What does it presage, this wisdom of fools? Doubtless, since it is a forbidden wisdom, it presages both the reign of Satan and the end of the world; ultimate bliss and supreme punishment; omnipotence on earth and the infernal fall. The Ship of Fools sails through a landscape of delights, where all is offered to desire, a sort of renewed paradise, since here man no longer knows either suffering or need; and yet he has not recovered his innocence. This false happiness is the diabolical triumph of the Antichrist; it is the

End, already at hand. Apocalyptic dreams are not new, it is true, in the fifteenth century; they are, however, very different in nature from what they had been earlier. The delicately fantastic iconography of the fourteenth century, where castles are toppled like dice, where the Beast is always the traditional dragon held at bay by the Virgin, in short where the order of God and its imminent victory are always apparent, gives way to a vision of the world where all wisdom is annihilated. This is the great witches' Sabbath of nature: mountains melt and become plains, the earth vomits up the dead and bones tumble out of tombs; the stars fall, the earth catches fire, all life withers and comes to death. The end has no value as passage and promise; it is the advent of a night in which the world's old reason is engulfed. It is enough to look at Dürer's Horsemen of the Apocalypse, sent by God Himself: these are no angels of triumph and reconciliation; these are no heralds of serene justice, but the disheveled warriors of a mad vengeance. The world sinks into universal Fury. Victory is neither God's nor the Devil's: it belongs to Madness.

On all sides, madness fascinates man. The fantastic images it generates are not fleeting appearances that quickly disappear from the surface of things. By a strange paradox, what is born from the strangest delirium was already hidden, like a secret, like an inaccessible truth, in the bowels of the earth. When man deploys the arbitrary nature of his madness, he confronts the dark necessity of the world; the animal that haunts his nightmares and his nights of privation is his own nature, which will lay bare hell's pitiless truth; the vain images of blind idiocy—such are the world's *Magna Scientia;* and already, in this disorder, in this mad universe, is prefigured what will be the cruelty of the finale. In such images—and this is doubtless what gives them their weight, what imposes such great coherence on their fantasy—the Renaissance has expressed what it apprehended of the threats and secrets of the world.

During the same period, the literary, philosophical, and moral themes of madness are in an altogether different vein. The Middle Ages had given madness a place in the hierarchy of vices. Beginning with the thirteenth century, it is customarily ranked among the wicked soldiers of the psychomachy. It figures, at Paris as at Amiens, among the evil soldiery, and is among the twelve dualities that dispute the sovereignty of the human soul: Faith and Idolatry, Hope and Despair, Charity and Avarice, Chastity and Lust, Prudence and Folly, Patience and Anger, Gentleness and Harshness, Concord and Discord, Obedience and Rebellion, Perseverance and Inconstancy, Fortitude and Cowardice, Humility and Pride. In the Renaissance, Folly leaves this modest place and comes to the fore. Whereas according to Hugues de Saint-Victor the genealogical tree of the Vices, that of the Old Adam, had pride as its root, Folly now leads the joyous throng of all human weaknesses. Uncontested coryphaeus, she guides them, sweeps them on, and names them: "Recognize them here, in the group of my companions. . . . She whose brows are drawn is Philautia (Self-Love). She whom you see laugh with her eyes and applaud with her hands is Colacia (Flattery). She who seems half asleep is Lethe (Forgetfulness). She who leans upon her elbows and folds her hands is Misoponia (Sloth). She who is crowned with roses and anointed with perfume is Hedonia (Sensuality). She whose eyes wander without seeing is Anoia (Stupidity). She whose abundant flesh has the hue of flowers is Tryphé (Indolence). And here among these young women are two gods: the god of Good Cheer and the god of Deep Sleep."[5] The absolute privilege of Folly is to reign over whatever is bad in man. But does she not also reign indirectly over all the good he can do: over ambition, that makes wise politicians; over avarice, that makes wealth grow; over indiscreet curiosity, that inspires philosophers and men of learning? Louise Labé merely follows Erasmus when she has Mercury implore the gods: "Do not let that beautiful Lady perish who has given you so much pleasure."

But this new royalty has little in common with the dark reign of which we were just speaking and which communicated with the great tragic powers of this world.

True, madness attracts, but it does not fascinate. It rules all that is easy, joyous, frivolous in the world. It is madness, folly, which makes men "sport and rejoice," as it has given the gods "Genius, Beauty, Bacchus, Silenus, and the gentle guardian of gardens."[6] All within it is brilliant surface: no enigma is concealed.

No doubt, madness has something to do with the strange paths of knowledge. The first canto of Brant's poem is devoted to books and scholars; and in the engraving which illustrates this passage in the Latin edition of 1497, we see enthroned upon his bristling cathedra of books the Magister who wears behind his doctoral cap a fool's cap sewn with bells. Erasmus, in his dance of fools, reserves a large place for scholars: after the Grammarians, the Poets, Rhetoricians, and Writers, come the Jurists; after them, the "Philosophers respectable in beard and mantle"; finally the numberless troop of the Theologians. But if knowledge is so important in madness, it is not because the latter can control the secrets of knowledge; on the contrary, madness is the punishment of a disorderly and useless science. If madness is the truth of knowledge, it is because knowledge is absurd, and instead of addressing itself to the great book of experience, loses its way in the dust of books and in idle debate; learning becomes madness through the very excess of false learning.

> *O vos doctores, qui grandia nomina fertis*
> *Respicite antiquos patris, jurisque peritos.*

Non in candidulis pensebant dogmata libris,
Arte sed ingenua sitibundum pectus alebant.[7]

(O ye learned men, who bear great names,
Look back at the ancient fathers, learned in the law.
They did not weigh dogmas in shining white books,
But fed their thirsty hearts with natural skill.)

According to the theme long familiar to popular satire, madness appears here as the comic punishment of knowledge and its ignorant presumption.

In a general way, then, madness is not linked to the world and its subterranean forms, but rather to man, to his weaknesses, dreams, and illusions. Whatever obscure cosmic manifestation there was in madness as seen by Bosch is wiped out in Erasmus; madness no longer lies in wait for mankind at the four corners of the earth; it insinuates itself within man, or rather it is a subtle rapport that man maintains with himself. The mythological personification of madness in Erasmus is only a literary device. In fact, only "follies" exist—human forms of madness: "I count as many images as there are men"; one need only glance at states, even the wisest and best governed: "So many forms of madness abound there, and each day sees so many new ones born, that a thousand Democrituses would not suffice to mock them." There is no madness but that which is in every man, since it is man who constitutes madness in the attachment he bears for himself and by the illusions he entertains. Philautia is the first figure Folly leads out in her dance, but that is because they are linked by a privileged relation: self-attachment is the first sign of madness, but it is because man is attached to himself that he accepts error as truth, lies as reality, violence and ugliness as beauty and justice. "This man, uglier than a monkey, imagines himself handsome as Nereus; that one thinks he is Euclid because he has traced three lines with a compass; that other one thinks he can sing like Hermogenes, whereas he is the ass before the lyre, and his voice sounds as false as that of the rooster pecking his hen." In this delusive attachment to himself, man generates his madness like a mirage. The symbol of madness will henceforth be that mirror which, without reflecting anything real, will secretly offer the man who observes himself in it the dream of his own presumption. Madness deals not so much with truth and the world, as with man and whatever truth about himself he is able to perceive.

It thus gives access to a completely moral universe. Evil is not punishment or the end of time, but only fault and flaw. A hundred and sixteen cantos of Brant's poem are devoted to portraits of the insane passengers on the Ship: there are misers, slanderers, drunkards; there are those who indulge in disorder and debauchery; those who interpret the Scriptures falsely; those who practice adultery. Locher, Brant's translator, notes in his Latin preface the purpose and meaning of the work; it is concerned to teach "what evil there may be, what good; what vices; whither virtue, whither error may lead"; and this while castigating, according to the wickedness each man is guilty of, "the unholy, the proud, the greedy, the extravagant, the debauched, the voluptuous, the quick-tempered, the gluttonous, the voracious, the envious, the poisoners, the faith-breakers" . . . in short, all that man has been able to invent in the way of irregularities in his conduct.

In the domain of literary and philosophic expression, the experience of madness in the fifteenth century generally takes the form of moral satire. Nothing suggests those great threats of invasion that haunted the imagination of the painters. On the contrary, great pains are taken to ward it off; one does not speak of such things. Erasmus turns our gaze from that insanity "which the Furies let slip from hell, each time they release their serpents"; it is not these insane forms that he has chosen to praise, but the "sweet illusion" that frees the soul from "its painful cares and returns it to the various forms of sensuality." This calm world is easily mastered; it readily yields its naïve mysteries to the eyes of the wise man, and the latter, by laughter, always keeps his distance. Whereas Bosch, Brueghel, and Dürer were terribly earth-bound spectators, implicated in that madness they saw surging around them, Erasmus observes it from far enough away to be out of danger; he observes it from the heights of his Olympus, and if he sings its praises, it is because he can laugh at it with the inextinguishable laughter of the Gods. For the madness of men is a divine spectacle: "In fact, could one make observations from the Moon, as did Menippus, considering the numberless agitations of the Earth, one would think one saw a swarm of flies or gnats fighting among themselves, struggling and laying traps, stealing from one another, playing, gamboling, falling, and dying, and one would not believe the troubles, the tragedies that were produced by such a minute animalcule destined to perish so shortly." Madness is no longer the familiar foreignness of the world; it is merely a commonplace spectacle for the foreign spectator; no longer a figure of the *cosmos*, but a characteristic of the *aevum*.

But a new enterprise was being undertaken that would abolish the tragic experience of madness in a critical consciousness. Let us ignore this phenomenon for the moment and consider indiscriminately those figures to be found in *Don Quixote* as well as in Scudéry's novels, in *King Lear* as well as in the theater of Jean de Rotrou or Tristan l'Hermite.

Let us begin with the most important, and the most durable—since the eighteenth century will still recognize its only just erased forms: *madness by romantic identification*. Its features have been fixed once and for all by Cervantes. But the theme is tirelessly repeated: direct adaptations (the

Don Quichotte of Guérin de Bouscal was performed in 1639; two years later, he staged *Le Gouvernement de Sancho Pança*), reinterpretations of a particular episode (Pichou's *Les Folies de Cardenio* is a variation on the theme of the "Ragged Knight" of the Sierra Morena), or, in a more indirect fashion, satire on novels of fantasy (as in Subligny's *La Fausse Clélie,* and within the story itself, as in the episode of *Julie d'Arviane*). The chimeras are transmitted from author to reader, but what was fantasy on one side becomes hallucination on the other; the writer's stratagem is quite naïvely accepted as an image of reality. In appearance, this is nothing but the simple-minded critique of novels of fantasy, but just under the surface lies an enormous anxiety concerning the relationships, in a work of art, between the real and the imaginary, and perhaps also concerning the confused communication between fantastic invention and the fascinations of delirium. "We owe the invention of the arts to deranged imaginations; the *Caprice* of Painters, Poets, and Musicians is only a name moderated in civility to express their *Madness.*"[8] Madness, in which the values of another age, another art, another morality are called into question, but which also reflects—blurred and disturbed, strangely compromised by one another in a common chimera—all the forms, even the most remote, of the human imagination.

Immediately following this first form: *the madness of vain presumption.* But it is not with a literary model that the madman identifies; it is with himself, and by means of a delusive attachment that enables him to grant himself all the qualities, all the virtues or powers he lacks. He inherits the old *Philautia* of Erasmus. Poor, he is rich; ugly, he admires himself; with chains still on his feet, he takes himself for God. Such a one was Osuma's master of arts who believed he was Neptune.[9] Such is the ridiculous fate of the seven characters of Desmarets de Saint-Sorlin's *Les Vision-*

naires, of Chateaufort in Cyrano de Bergerac's *Le Pédant joué,* of M. de Richesource in *Sir Politik.* Measureless madness, which has as many faces as the world has characters, ambitions, and necessary illusions. Even in its extremities, this is the least extreme of madnesses; it is, in the heart of every man, the imaginary relation he maintains with himself. It engenders the commonest of his faults. To denounce it is the first and last element of all moral criticism.

To the moral world, also, belongs the *madness of just punishment,* which chastises, along with the disorders of the mind, those of the heart. But it has still other powers: the punishment it inflicts multiplies by nature insofar as, by punishing itself, it unveils the truth. The justification of this madness is that it is truthful. Truthful since the sufferer already experiences, in the vain whirlwind of his hallucinations, what will for all eternity be the pain of his punishment: Éraste, in Corneille's *Mélite,* sees himself already pursued by the Eumenides and condemned by Minos. Truthful, too, because the crime hidden from all eyes dawns like day in the night of this strange punishment; madness, in its wild, untamable words, proclaims its own meaning; in its chimeras, it utters its secret truth; its cries speak for its conscience. Thus Lady Macbeth's delirium reveals to those who "have known what they should not" words long uttered only to "dead pillows."

Then the last type of madness: that of *desperate passion.* Love disappointed in its excess, and especially love deceived by the fatality of death, has no other recourse but madness. As long as there was an object, mad love was more love than madness; left to itself, it pursues itself in the void of delirium. Punishment of a passion too abjectly abandoned to its violence? No doubt; but this punishment is also a relief; it spreads, over the irreparable absence, the mercy of imaginary presences; it recovers, in the paradox of innocent joy or in the heroism of senseless pursuits, the vanished form. If it leads to death, it is a death in which the lovers will never be separated again. This is Ophelia's last song, this is the delirium of Ariste in *La Folie du sage*. But above all, this is the bitter and sweet madness of *King Lear*.

In Shakespeare, madness is allied to death and murder; in Cervantes, images are controlled by the presumption and the complacencies of the imaginary. These are supreme models whose imitators deflect and disarm them. Doubtless, both testify more to a tragic experience of madness appearing in the fifteenth century, than to a critical and moral experience of Unreason developing in their own epoch. Outside of time, they establish a link with a meaning about to be lost, and whose continuity will no longer survive except in darkness. But it is by comparing their work, and what it maintains, with the meanings that develop among their contemporaries or imitators, that we may decipher what is happening, at the beginning of the seventeenth century, in the literary experience of madness.

In Shakespeare or Cervantes, madness still occupies an extreme place, in that it is beyond appeal. Nothing ever restores it either to truth or to reason. It leads only to laceration and thence to death. Madness, in its vain words, is not vanity; the void that fills it is a "disease beyond my practice," as the doctor says about Lady Macbeth; it is already the plenitude of death; a madness that has no need of a physician, but only of divine mercy. The sweet joy Ophelia finally regains reconciles her with no happiness; her mad song is as close to the essential as the "cry of women" that announces through the corridors of Macbeth's castle that "the Queen is dead." Certainly Don Quixote's death occurs in a peaceful landscape, which at the last moment has rejoined reason and truth. Suddenly the Knight's madness has grown conscious of itself, and in his own eyes trickles out in nonsense. But is this sudden wisdom of his folly anything but "a new madness that had just come into his head"? The equivocation is endlessly reversible and cannot be resolved, ultimately, except by death itself. Madness dissipated can be only the same thing as the imminence of the end; "and even one of the signs by which they realized that the sick man was dying, was that he had returned so easily from madness to reason." But death itself does not bring peace; madness will still triumph —a truth mockingly eternal, beyond the end of a life which yet had been delivered from madness by this very end. Ironically, Don Quixote's insane life pursues and immortalizes him only by his insanity; madness is still the imperishable life of death: "Here lies the famous hidalgo who carried valor to such lengths that it was said death could not triumph over life by his demise."

But very soon, madness leaves these ultimate regions where Cervantes and Shakespeare had situated it; and in the literature of the early seventeenth century it occupies, by preference, a median place; it thus constitutes the knot more than the denouement, the peripity rather than the final release. Displaced in the economy of narrative and dramatic structures, it authorizes the manifestation of truth and the return of reason.

Thus madness is no longer considered in its tragic reality, in the absolute laceration that gives it access to the other world; but only in the irony of its illusions. It is not a real punishment, but only the image of punishment, thus a pretense; it can be linked only to the appearance of a crime or to the illusion of a death. Though Ariste, in Tristan l'Hermite's *La Folie du sage*, goes mad at the news of his daughter's death, the fact is that she is not really dead; when Éraste, in *Mélite*, sees himself pursued by the Eumenides and dragged before Minos, it is for a double crime which he *might* have committed, which he might have *wanted* to commit, but which in fact has not occasioned any real death. Madness is deprived of its dramatic seriousness; it is punishment or despair only in the dimension of error. Its dramatic function exists only insofar as we are concerned with a false drama; a chimerical form in which only supposed faults, illusory murders, ephemeral disappearances are involved.

Yet this absence of seriousness does not keep madness from being essential—even more essential than it had been, for if it brings illusion to its climax, it is from this point that illusion is undone. In the madness in which his error has enveloped him, the character involuntarily begins to unravel the web. Accusing himself, he speaks the truth in spite of himself. In *Mélite*, for example, all the stratagems the hero has accumulated to deceive others are turned against himself, and he becomes their first victim, believing that he is guilty of the deaths of his rival and his mistress. But in his delirium, he blames himself for having invented a whole series of love letters; the truth comes to light, in and through madness, which, provoked by the illusion of a denouement, actually resolves the real imbroglio of which it is both cause and effect. To put it another way, madness is the false punishment of a false solution, but by its own virtue it brings to light the real problem, which can then be truly resolved. It conceals beneath error the secret enterprise of truth. It is this function of madness, both ambiguous and central, that the author of *L'Ospital des fous* employs when he portrays a pair of lovers who, to escape their pursuers, pretend to be mad and hide among madmen; in a fit of simulated dementia, the girl, who is dressed as a boy, pretends to believe she is a girl—which she really is— thus uttering, by the reciprocal neutralization of these two pretenses, the truth which in the end will triumph.

Madness is the purest, most total form of *qui pro quo;* it takes the false for the true, death for life, man for woman, the beloved for the Erinnys and the victim for Minos. But it is also the most rigorously necessary form of the *qui pro quo* in the dramatic economy, for it needs no external element to reach a true resolution. It has merely to carry its illusion to the point of truth. Thus it is, at the very heart of the structure, in its mechanical center, both a feigned conclusion, pregnant with a secret "starting over," and the first step toward what will turn out to be the reconciliation with reason and truth. It marks the point toward which converge, apparently, the tragic destinies of the characters, and from which, in reality, emerge the lines leading to happiness regained. In madness equilibrium is established, but it masks that equilibrium beneath the cloud of illusion, beneath feigned disorder; the rigor of the architecture is concealed beneath the cunning arrangement of these disordered violences. The sudden bursts of life, the random gestures and words, the *wind of madness* that suddenly breaks lines, shatters attitudes, rumples draperies—while the strings are merely being pulled tighter—this is the very type of baroque *trompe-l'oeil*. Madness is the great *trompe-l'oeil* in the tragicomic structures of preclassical literature.

This was understood by Georges de Scudéry, who made his *Comédie des comédiens* a theater of theater, situating his play, from the start, in the interacting illusions of madness. One group of actors takes the part of spectators, another that of actors. The former must pretend to take the decor for reality, the play for life, while in reality these actors are performing in a real decor; on the other hand, the latter must pretend to play the part of actors, while in fact, quite simply, they are actors acting. A double impersonation in which each element is doubled, thus forming that renewed exchange of the real and the illusory which is itself the dramatic meaning of madness. "I do not know," Mondory says in the prologue to Scudéry's play, "what extravagance has today come over my companions, but it is so great that I am forced to believe that some spell has robbed them of their reason, and the worst of it is that they

are trying to make me lose mine, and you yours as well.
They wish to persuade me that I am not on a stage, that
this is the city of Lyons, that over there is an inn, and
there an innyard where actors who are not ourselves, yet
who are, are performing a Pastoral." In this extravaganza,
the theater develops its truth, which is illusion. Which is,
in the strict sense, madness.

The classical experience of madness is born. The great
threat that dawned on the horizon of the fifteenth century
subsides, the disturbing powers that inhabit Bosch's painting have lost their violence. Forms remain, now transparent
and docile, forming a cortège, the inevitable procession of
reason. Madness has ceased to be—at the limits of the
world, of man and death—an eschatological figure; the
darkness has dispersed on which the eyes of madness were
fixed and out of which the forms of the impossible were
born. Oblivion falls upon the world navigated by the free
slaves of the Ship of Fools. Madness will no longer proceed
from a point within the world to a point beyond, on its
strange voyage; it will never again be that fugitive and
absolute limit. Behold it moored now, made fast among
things and men. Retained and maintained. No longer a ship
but a hospital.

Scarcely a century after the career of the mad ships, we
note the appearance of the theme of the "Hospital of Madmen," the "Madhouse." Here every empty head, fixed and
classified according to the true reason of men, utters contradiction and irony, the double language of Wisdom:
". . . the Hospital of incurable Madmen, where are recited
from end to end all the follies and fevers of the mind, by
men as well as women, a task no less useful than enjoyable,
and necessary for the acquisition of true wisdom."[10] Here
each form of madness finds its proper place, its distinguishing mark, and its tutelary divinity: frenzied and ranting

madness, symbolized by a fool astride a chair, struggles beneath Minerva's gaze; the somber melancholics that roam the countryside, solitary and avid wolves, have as their god Jupiter, patron of animal metamorphoses; then come the "mad drunkards," the "madmen deprived of memory and understanding," the "madmen benumbed and half-dead," the "madmen of giddy and empty heads" . . . All this world of disorder, in perfect order, pronounces, each in his turn, the Praise of Reason. Already, in this "Hospital," *confinement* has succeeded *embarkation*.

Tamed, madness preserves all the appearances of its reign. It now takes part in the measures of reason and in the labor of truth. It plays on the surface of things and in the glitter of daylight, over all the workings of appearances, over the ambiguity of reality and illusion, over all that indeterminate web, ever rewoven and broken, which both unites and separates truth and appearance. It hides and manifests, it utters truth and falsehood, it is light and shadow. It shimmers, a central and indulgent figure, already precarious in this baroque age.

Let us not be surprised to come upon it so often in the fictions of the novel and the theater. Let us not be surprised to find it actually prowling through the streets. Thousands of times, François Colletet has met it there:

> I see, in this thoroughfare,
> A natural, followed by children.
> . . . Consider this unhappy wretch;
> Poor mad fool, what will he do
> With so many rags and tatters? . . .
> I have seen such wild lunatics
> Shouting insults in the streets . . .

Madness traces a very familiar silhouette in the social landscape. A new and lively pleasure is taken in the old confraternities of madmen, in their festivals, their gather-

ings, their speeches. Men argue passionately for or against
Nicolas Joubert, better known by the name of Angoule-
vent, who declares himself Prince of Fools, a title disputed
by Valenti le Comte and Jacques Resneau: there follow
pamphlets, a trial, arguments; his lawyer declares and certi-
fies him to be "an empty head, a gutted gourd, lacking in
common sense; a cane, a broken brain, that has neither
spring nor whole wheel in his head." Bluet d' Arbères, who
calls himself Comte de Permission, is a protégé of the Cré-
quis, the Lesdiguières, the Bouillons, the Nemours; in 1602
he publishes—or someone publishes for him—his works,
in which he warns the reader that "he does not know how
to read or write, and has never learned," but that he is
animated "by the inspiration of God and the Angels."
Pierre Dupuis, whom Régnier mentions in his sixth satire,
is, according to Brascambille, "an archfool in a long robe";
he himself in his "Remontrance sur le réveil de Maître
Guillaume" states that he has "a mind elevated as far as the
antechamber of the third degree of the moon." And many
other characters present in Régnier's fourteenth satire.

This world of the early seventeenth century is strangely
hospitable, in all senses, to madness. Madness is here, at the
heart of things and of men, an ironic sign that misplaces the
guideposts between the real and the chimerical, barely re-
taining the memory of the great tragic threats—a life more
disturbed than disturbing, an absurd agitation in society,
the mobility of reason.

But new requirements are being generated:

A hundred and a hundred times have I taken up my lantern,
Seeking, at high noon . . .[11]

I I

THE GREAT
CONFINEMENT

Compelle intrare.

By a strange act of force, the classical age was to reduce to silence the madness whose voices the Renaissance had just liberated, but whose violence it had already tamed.

It is common knowledge that the seventeenth century created enormous houses of confinement; it is less commonly known that more than one out of every hundred inhabitants of the city of Paris found themselves confined there, within several months. It is common knowledge that absolute power made use of *lettres de cachet* and arbitrary measures of imprisonment; what is less familiar is the judicial conscience that could inspire such practices. Since Pinel, Tuke, Wagnitz, we know that madmen were subjected to the regime of this confinement for a century and a half, and that they would one day be discovered in the wards of the Hôpital Général, in the cells of prisons; they would be found mingled with the population of the work-houses or *Zuchthäusern*. But it has rarely been made clear what their status was there, what the meaning was of this proximity which seemed to assign the same homeland to the poor, to the unemployed, to prisoners, and to the insane. It is within the walls of confinement that Pinel and nineteenth-century psychiatry would come upon madmen; it is there —let us remember—that they would leave them, not with-out boasting of having "delivered" them. From the middle of the seventeenth century, madness was linked with this country of confinement, and with the act which designated confinement as its natural abode.

A date can serve as a landmark: 1656, the decree that founded, in Paris, the Hôpital Général. At first glance, this is merely a reform—little more than an administrative re-organization. Several already existing establishments are grouped under a single administration: the Salpêtrière, re-built under the preceding reign to house an arsenal; Bicêtre, which Louis XIII had wanted to give to the Commandery of Saint Louis as a rest home for military invalids; "the House and the Hospital of La Pitié, the larger as well as the smaller, those of Le Refuge, situated in the Faubourg Saint-Victor, the House and Hospital of Scipion, the House of La Savonnerie, with all the lands, places, gardens, houses, and buildings thereto appertaining."[1] All were now as-signed to the poor of Paris "of both sexes, of all ages and from all localities, of whatever breeding and birth, in what-ever state they may be, able-bodied or invalid, sick or con-valescent, curable or incurable." These establishments had to accept, lodge, and feed those who presented themselves or those by royal or judicial authority; it was also neces-sary to assure the subsistence, the appearance, and the gen-eral order of those who could not find room, but who might or who deserved to be there. This responsibility was entrusted to directors appointed for life, who exercised their powers, not only in the buildings of the Hôpital but throughout the city of Paris, over all those who came under their jurisdiction: "They have all power of authority, of direction, of administration, of commerce, of police, of jurisdiction, of correction and punishment over all the poor of Paris, both within and without the Hôpital Général." The directors also appointed a doctor at a salary of one thousand livres a year; he was to reside at La Pitié, but had to visit each of the houses of the Hôpital twice a week.

From the very start, one thing is clear: the Hôpital Général is not a medical establishment. It is rather a sort of semijudicial structure, an administrative entity which, along with the already constituted powers, and outside of the courts, decides, judges, and executes. "The directors having for these purposes stakes, irons, prisons, and dungeons in the said Hôpital Général and the places thereto appertaining so much as they deem necessary, no appeal will be accepted from the regulations they establish within the said hospital; and as for such regulations as intervene from without, they will be executed according to their form and tenor, notwithstanding opposition or whatsoever appeal made or to be made, and without prejudice to these, and for which, notwithstanding all defense or suits for justice, no distinction will be made."[2] A quasi-absolute sovereignty, jurisdiction without appeal, a writ of execution against which nothing can prevail—the Hôpital Général is a strange power that the King establishes between the police and the courts, at the limits of the law: a third order of repression. The insane whom Pinel would find at Bicêtre and at La Salpêtrière belonged to this world.

In its functioning, or in its purpose, the Hôpital Général had nothing to do with any medical concept. It was an instance of order, of the monarchical and bourgeois order being organized in France during this period. It was directly linked with the royal power which placed it under the authority of the civil government alone; the Grand Almonry of the Realm, which previously formed an ecclesiastical and spiritual mediation in the politics of assistance, was abruptly elided. The King decreed: "We choose to be guardian and protector of the said Hôpital Général as being of our royal founding and especially as it does not depend in any manner whatsoever upon our Grand Almonry, nor upon any of our high officers, but is to be totally exempt from the direction, visitation, and jurisdiction of the officers of the General Reform and others of the Grand Almonry, and from all others to whom we forbid all knowledge and jurisdiction in any fashion or manner whatsoever." The origin of the project had been parliamentary, and the first two administrative heads appointed were the first President of the Parlement and the Procurator General. But they were soon supplemented by the Archbishop of Paris, the President of the Court of Assistance, the President of the Court of Exchequer, the Chief of Police, and the Provost of Merchants. Henceforth the "Grand Bureau" had no more than a deliberative role. The actual administration and the real responsibilities were entrusted to agents recruited by co-optation. These were the true governors, the delegates of royal power and bourgeois fortune to the world of poverty. The Revolution was able to give them this testimony: "Chosen from the best families of the bourgeoisie, . . . they brought to their administration disinterested views and pure intentions."[3]

This structure proper to the monarchical and bourgeois order of France, contemporary with its organization in absolutist forms, soon extended its network over the whole of France. An edict of the King, dated June 16, 1676, prescribed the establishment of an *"hôpital général* in each city of his kingdom." Occasionally the measure had been anticipated by the local authorities; the bourgeoisie of Lyons had already organized in 1612 a charity establishment that functioned in an analogous manner. The Archbishop of Tours was proud to declare on July 10, 1676, that his "archepiscopal city has happily foreseen the pious intentions of the King and erected an *hôpital général* called La Charité even before the one in Paris, whose order has served as a model for all those subsequently established, within or outside the kingdom." The Charité of Tours, in fact, had been founded in 1656, and the King had endowed it with an income of four thousand livres. Over the entire face of France, *hôpitaux généraux* were opened; on the eve of the Revolution, they were to be found in thirty-two provincial cities.

Even if it had been deliberately excluded from the organization of the *hôpitaux généraux*—by complicity, doubtless, between royal power and bourgeoisie—the Church nonetheless did not remain a stranger to the movement. It reformed its own hospital institutions, redistributed the wealth of its foundations, even created congregations whose purposes were rather analogous to those of the Hôpital Général. Vincent de Paul reorganized Saint-Lazare, the most important of the former lazar houses of Paris; on January 7, 1632, he signed a contract in the name of the Congregationists of the Mission with the "Priory" of Saint-Lazare, which was now to receive "persons detained by order of His Majesty." The Order of Good Sons opened hospitals of this nature in the north of France. The Brothers of Saint John of God, called into France in 1602, founded first the Charité of Paris in the Faubourg Saint-Germain, then Charenton, into which they moved on May 10, 1645. Not far from Paris, they also operated the Charité of Senlis, which opened on October 27, 1670. Some years before, the Duchess of Bouillon had donated them the buildings and benefices of La Maladrerie, founded in the fourteenth century by Thibaut de Champagne, at Château-

Thierry. They administered also the Charités of Saint-Yon, Pontorson, Cadillac, and Romans. In 1699, the Lazarists founded in Marseilles the establishment that was to become the Hôpital Saint-Pierre. Then, in the eighteenth century, came Armentières (1712), Maréville (1714), the Good Savior of Caen (1735); Saint-Meins of Rennes opened shortly before the Revolution (1780).

The phenomenon has European dimensions. The constitution of an absolute monarchy and the intense Catholic renaissance during the Counter-Reformation produced in France a very particular character of simultaneous competition and complicity between the government and the Church. Elsewhere it assumed quite different forms; but its localization in time was just as precise. The great hospitals, houses of confinement, establishments of religion and public order, of assistance and punishment, of governmental charity and welfare measures, are a phenomenon of the classical period: as universal as itself and almost contemporary with its birth. In German-speaking countries, it was marked by the creation of houses of correction, the *Zuchthäusern;* the first antedates the French houses of confinement (except for the Charité of Lyons); it opened in Hamburg around 1620. The others were founded in the second half of the century: Basel (1667), Breslau (1668), Frankfort (1684), Spandau (1684), Königsberg (1691). They continued to multiply in the eighteenth century; Leipzig first in 1701, then Halle and Cassel in 1717 and 1720, later Brieg and Osnabrück (1756), and finally Torgau in 1771.

In England the origins of confinement are more remote. An act of 1575 covering both "the punishment of vagabonds and the relief of the poor" prescribed the construction of *houses of correction,* to number at least one per county. Their upkeep was to be assured by a tax, but the public was encouraged to make voluntary donations. It appears, however, that in this form the measure was scarcely ever applied, since, some years later, it was decided to authorize private enterprise: it was no longer necessary to obtain an official permit to open a hospital or a house of correction; anyone who pleased might do so. At the beginning of the seventeenth century, a general reorganization: a fine of five pounds was imposed on any justice of the peace who had not established one in the area of his jurisdiction; the houses were to install trades, workshops, and factories (milling, spinning, weaving) to aid in their upkeep and assure their inmates of work; a judge was to decide who was qualified to be sent there. The development of these "bridewells" was not too considerable; often they were gradually absorbed by the prisons to which they were attached; the practice never spread as far as Scotland. On the other hand, the workhouses were destined to greater success. They date from the second half of the seventeenth century. An act of 1670 defined their status, appointed officers of justice to oversee the collection of taxes and the administration of sums that would permit their functioning, and entrusted the supreme control of their administration to a justice of the peace. In 1697 several parishes of Bristol united to form the first workhouse in England, and to designate the corporation that would administer it. Another was established at Worcester in 1703, a third the same year at Dublin; then at Plymouth, Norwich, Hull, and Exeter. By the end of the eighteenth century, there were 126 of them. The Gilbert Act of 1792 gives the parishes facilities to create new ones; at the same time, the control and authority of the justice of the peace is reinforced; to keep the workhouses from becoming hospitals, it is recommended that all contagious invalids be turned away.

In several years, an entire network had spread across Europe. John Howard, at the end of the eighteenth century, undertook to investigate it; in England, Holland, Germany,

France, Italy, Spain, he made pilgrimages to all the chief centers of confinement—"hospitals, prisons, jails"—and his philanthropy was outraged by the fact that the same walls could contain those condemned by common law, young men who disturbed their families' peace or who squandered their goods, people without profession, and the insane. Proof that even at this period, a certain meaning had been lost: that which had so hastily, so spontaneously summoned into being all over Europe the category of classical order we call confinement. In a hundred and fifty years, confinement had become the abusive amalgam of heterogeneous elements. Yet at its origin, there must have existed a unity which justified its urgency; between these diverse forms and the classical period that called them into being, there must have been a principle of cohesion we cannot evade under the scandal of pre-Revolutionary sensibility. What, then, was the reality represented by this entire population which almost overnight found itself shut up, excluded more severely than the lepers? We must not forget that a few years after its foundation, the Hôpital Général of Paris alone contained six thousand persons, or around one per cent of the population. There must have formed, silently and doubtless over the course of many years, a social sensibility, common to European culture, that suddenly began to manifest itself in the second half of the seventeenth century; it was this sensibility that suddenly isolated the category destined to populate the places of confinement. To inhabit the reaches long since abandoned by the lepers, they chose a group that to our eyes is strangely mixed and confused. But what is for us merely an undifferentiated sensibility must have been, for those living in the classical age, a clearly articulated perception. It is this mode of perception which we must investigate in order to discover the form of sensibility to madness in an epoch we are accustomed to define by the privileges of Reason. The act which, by tracing the locus of confinement, conferred upon it its power of segregation and provided a new homeland for madness, though it may be coherent and concerted, is not simple. It organizes into a complex unity a new sensibility to poverty and to the duties of assistance, new forms of reaction to the economic problems of unemployment and idleness, a new ethic of work, and also the dream of a city where moral obligation was joined to civil law, within the authoritarian forms of constraint. Obscurely, these themes are present during the construction of the cities of confinement and their organization. They give a meaning to this ritual, and explain in part the mode in which madness was perceived, and experienced, by the classical age.

Confinement, that massive phenomenon, the signs of which are found all across eighteenth-century Europe, is a "police" matter. Police, in the precise sense that the classical epoch gave to it—that is, the totality of measures which make work possible and necessary for all those who could not live without it; the question Voltaire would soon formulate, Colbert's contemporaries had already asked: "Since you have established yourselves as a people, have you not yet discovered the secret of forcing all the rich to make all the poor work? Are you still ignorant of the first principles of the police?"

Before having the medical meaning we give it, or that at least we like to suppose it has, confinement was required by something quite different from any concern with curing the sick. What made it necessary was an imperative of labor. Our philanthropy prefers to recognize the signs of a benevolence toward sickness where there is only a condemnation of idleness.

Let us return to the first moments of the "Confinement," and to that royal edict of April 27, 1656, that led to the creation of the Hôpital Général. From the beginning, the institution set itself the task of preventing "mendicancy and idleness as the source of all disorders." In fact, this was the last of the great measures that had been taken since the Renaissance to put an end to unemployment or at least to begging.[4] In 1532, the Parlement of Paris decided to arrest beggars and force them to work in the sewers of the city, chained in pairs. The situation soon reached critical proportions: on March 23, 1534, the order was given "to poor scholars and indigents" to leave the city, while it was forbidden "henceforth to sing hymns before images in the streets." The wars of religion multiplied this suspect crowd, which included peasants driven from their farms, disbanded soldiers or deserters, unemployed workers, impoverished students, and the sick. When Henri IV began the siege of Paris, the city, which had less than 100,000 inhabitants, contained more than 30,000 beggars. An economic revival began early in the seventeenth century; it was decided to reabsorb by force the unemployed who had not regained a place in society; a decree of the Parlement dated 1606 ordered the beggars of Paris to be whipped in the public square, branded on the shoulder, shorn, and then driven from the city; to keep them from returning, an ordinance of 1607 established companies of archers at all the city gates to forbid entry to indigents. When the effects of the economic renaissance disappeared with the Thirty Years' War, the problems of mendicancy and idleness reappeared; until the middle of the century, the regular increase of taxes hindered manufactures and augmented unemployment. This was the period of uprisings in Paris (1621), in Lyons (1652), in Rouen (1639). At the same time, the world of labor was disorganized by the appearance of new economic structures; as the large manufactories developed, the guilds lost their powers and their rights, the "General Regulations" prohibited all assemblies of workers, all leagues, all "associations." In many professions, however, the guilds were reconstituted. They were prosecuted, but it seems that the Parlements showed a certain apathy; the Parlement of Normandy disclaimed all competence to judge the rioters of Rouen. This is doubtless why the Church intervened and accused the workers' secret gatherings of sorcery. A decree of the Sorbonne, in 1655, proclaimed "guilty of sacrilege and mortal sin" all those who were found in such bad company.

In this silent conflict that opposed the severity of the Church to the indulgence of the Parlements, the creation of the Hôpital was certainly, at least in the beginning, a victory for the Parlement. It was, in any case, a new solution. For the first time, purely negative measures of exclusion were replaced by a measure of confinement; the unemployed person was no longer driven away or punished; he was taken in charge, at the expense of the nation but at the cost of his individual liberty. Between him and society, an implicit system of obligation was established: he had the right to be fed, but he must accept the physical and moral constraint of confinement.

It is this entire, rather undifferentiated mass at which the edict of 1657 is aimed: a population without resources, without social moorings, a class rejected or rendered mobile by new economic developments. Less than two weeks after it was signed, the edict was read and proclaimed in the streets. Paragraph 9: "We expressly prohibit and forbid all persons of either sex, of any locality and of any age, of whatever breeding and birth, and in whatever condition they may be, able-bodied or invalid, sick or convalescent, curable or incurable, to beg in the city and suburbs of Paris, neither in the churches, nor at the doors of such, nor at the doors of houses nor in the streets, nor anywhere else in public, nor in secret, by day or night . . . under pain of being whipped for the first offense, and for the second condemned to the galleys if men and boys, banished if women and girls." The year after—Sunday, May 13, 1657 —a high mass in honor of the Holy Ghost was sung at the Church of Saint-Louis de la Pitié, and on the morning of Monday the fourteenth, the militia, which was to become, in the mythology of popular terror, "the archers of the Hôpital," began to hunt down beggars and herd them into the different buildings of the Hôpital. Four years later, La Salpêtrière housed 1,460 women and small children; at La Pitié there were 98 boys, 897 girls between seven and seventeen, and 95 women; at Bicêtre, 1,615 adult men; at La Savonnerie, 305 boys between eight and thirteen; finally, Scipion lodged 530 pregnant women, nursing women, and very young children. Initially, married people, even in need, were not admitted; the administration was instructed to feed them at home; but soon, thanks to a grant from Mazarin, it was possible to lodge them at La Salpêtrière. In all, between five and six thousand persons.

Throughout Europe, confinement had the same meaning, at least if we consider its origin. It constituted one of the answers the seventeenth century gave to an economic crisis that affected the entire Western world: reduction of wages, unemployment, scarcity of coin—the coincidence of these phenomena probably being due to a crisis in the Spanish economy. Even England, of all the countries of Western Europe the least dependent on the system, had to solve the same problems. Despite all the measures taken to avoid unemployment and the reduction of wages, poverty continued to spread in the nation. In 1622 appeared a pamphlet, *Grievous Groan for the Poor*, attributed to Thomas Dekker, which, emphasizing the danger, condemns the general negligence: "Though the number of the poor do daily increase, all things yet worketh for the worst in their behalf; . . . many of these parishes turneth forth their poor, yea, and their lusty labourers that will not work . . . to beg, filch, and steal for their maintenance, so that the country is pitifully pestered with them." It was feared that they would overrun the country, and since they could not, as on the Continent, cross the border into another nation, it was proposed that they be "banished and conveyed to the New-found Land, the East and West Indies." In 1630, the King established a commission to assure the rigorous observance of the Poor Laws. That same year, it published a series of "orders and directions"; it recommended prosecuting beggars and vagabonds, as well as "all those who live in idleness and will not work for reasonable wages or who spend what they have in taverns." They must be punished according to law and placed in houses of correction; as for those with wives and children, investigation must be made as to whether they were married and their children baptized, "for these people live like savages without being married, nor buried, nor baptized; and it is this licentious liberty which causes so many to rejoice in vagabondage." Despite the recovery that began in England in the middle of the century, the problem was still unsolved in Cromwell's time, for the Lord Mayor complains of "this vermin that troops about the city, disturbing public order, assaulting carriages, demanding alms with loud cries at the doors of churches and private houses."

For a long time, the house of correction or the premises of the Hôpital Général would serve to contain the unemployed, the idle, and vagabonds. Each time a crisis occurred and the number of the poor sharply increased, the houses of confinement regained, at least for a time, their initial economic significance. In the middle of the eighteenth century, there was another great crisis: 12,000 begging workers at Rouen and as many at Tours; at Lyons the manufactories closed. The Count d'Argenson, "who commands the department of Paris and the marshalseas," gave orders "to arrest all the beggars of the kingdom; the marshalseas will perform this task in the countryside, while the same thing is done in Paris, whither they are sure not to return, being entrapped on all sides."

But outside of the periods of crisis, confinement acquired another meaning. Its repressive function was combined with a new use. It was no longer merely a question of confining those out of work, but of giving work to those who had been confined and thus making them contribute to the prosperity of all. The alternation is clear: cheap manpower in the periods of full employment and high salaries; and in periods of unemployment, reabsorption of the idle and social protection against agitation and uprisings. Let us not forget that the first houses of confinement appear in England in the most industrialized parts of the country: Worcester, Norwich, Bristol; that the first *hôpital général* was opened in Lyons, forty years before that of Paris; that Hamburg was the first German city to have its *Zuchthaus*, in 1620. Its regulations, published in 1622, were quite precise. The internees must all work. Exact record was kept of the value of their work, and they were paid a fourth of it. For work was not only an occupation; it must be productive. The eight directors of the house established a general plan. The *Werkmeister* assigned a task to each, and ascertained at the end of the week that it had been accomplished. The rule of work would remain in effect until the end of the eighteenth century, since John Howard could still attest that they were "knitting and spinning; weaving stockings, linen, hair, and wool—and rasping logwood and hartshorn. The quota of a robust man who shreds such wood is forty-five pounds a day. Some men and horses labour at a fulling-mill. A blacksmith works there without cease." Each house of confinement in Germany had its specialty: spinning was paramount in Bremen, Brunswick, Munich, Breslau, Berlin; weaving in Hanover. The men shredded wood in Bremen and Hamburg. In Nuremberg they polished optical glass; at Mainz the principal labor was the milling of flour.

The first houses of correction were opened in England during a full economic recession. The act of 1610 recommended only joining certain mills and weaving and carding shops to all houses of correction in order to occupy the pensioners. But what had been a moral requirement became an economic tactic when commerce and industry recovered after 1651, the economic situation having been re-established by the Navigation Act and the lowering of the discount rate. All able-bodied manpower was to be used to the best advantage, that is, as cheaply as possible. When John Carey established his workhouse project in Bristol, he ranked the need for work first: "The poor of both sexes . . . may be employed in beating hemp, dressing and spinning flax, or in carding wool and cotton." At Worcester, they manufactured clothes and stuffs; a workshop for children was established. All of which did not always proceed without difficulties. It was suggested that the workhouses might enter the local industries and markets, on the principle perhaps that such cheap production would have a regulatory effect on the sale price. But the manufactories protested. Daniel Defoe noticed that by the effect of the too easy competition of the workhouses, poverty was created in one area on the pretext of suppressing it in another; "it is giving to one what you take away from another; putting a vagabond in an honest man's employment, and putting diligence on the tenters to find out some other work to maintain his family." Faced with this danger of competition, the authorities let the work gradually disappear. The pensioners could no longer earn even enough to pay for their upkeep; at times it was necessary to put them in prison so that they might at least have free bread. As for the bridewells, as Howard attested, there were few "in which any work is done, or can be done. The prisoners have neither tools, nor materials of any kind: but spend their time in sloth, profaneness and debauchery."

When the Hôpital Général was created in Paris, it was intended above all to suppress beggary, rather than to provide an occupation for the internees. It seems, however, that Colbert, like his English contemporaries, regarded assistance through work as both a remedy to unemployment and a stimulus to the development of manufactories. In any case, in the provinces the directors were to see that the houses of charity had a certain economic significance. "All the poor who are capable of working must, upon work days, do what is necessary to avoid idleness, which is the mother of all evils, as well as to accustom them to honest toil and also to earning some part of their sustenance."

Sometimes there were even arrangements which permitted private entrepreneurs to utilize the manpower of the asylums for their own profit. It was stipulated, for example, according to an agreement made in 1708, that an entrepreneur should furnish the Charité of Tulle with wool, soap, and coal, and in return the establishment would redeliver the wool carded and spun. The profit was divided between the entrepreneur and the hospital. Even in Paris, several attempts were made to transform the buildings of the Hôpital Général into factories. If we can believe the author of an anonymous *mémoire* that appeared in 1790, at La Pitié "all the varieties of manufacture that could be offered to the capital" were attempted; finally, "in a kind of despair, a manufacture was undertaken of a sort of lacing found to be the least costly." Elsewhere, such efforts were scarcely more fruitful. Numerous efforts were made at Bicêtre: manufacture of thread and rope, mirror polishing, and especially the famous "great well." An attempt was even made, in 1781, to substitute teams of prisoners for the horses that brought up the water, in relay from five in the morning to eight at night: "What reason could have determined this strange occupation? Was it that of economy or simply the necessity of busying the prisoners? If the latter, would it not have been better to occupy them with work more useful both for them and for the hospital? If for reasons of economy, we are a long way from finding any."[5] During the entire eighteenth century, the economic significance Colbert wanted to give the Hôpital Général continued to recede; that center of forced labor would become a place of privileged idleness. "What is the source of the disorders at Bicêtre?" the men of the Revolution were again to ask. And they would supply the answer that had already been given in the seventeenth century: "It is idleness. What is the means of remedying it? Work."

The classical age used confinement in an equivocal manner, making it play a double role: to reabsorb unemployment, or at least eliminate its most visible social effects, and to control costs when they seemed likely to become too high; to act alternately on the manpower market and on the cost of production. As it turned out, it does not seem that the houses of confinement were able to play effectively the double role that was expected of them. If they absorbed the unemployed, it was mostly to mask their poverty, and to avoid the social or political disadvantages of agitation; but at the very moment the unemployed were herded into forced-labor shops, unemployment increased in neighboring regions or in similar areas. As for the effect on production costs, it could only be artificial, the market price of such products being disproportionate to the cost of manufacture, calculated according to the expenses occasioned by confinement itself.

Measured by their functional value alone, the creation of the houses of confinement can be regarded as a failure. Their disappearance throughout Europe, at the beginning of the nineteenth century, as receiving centers for the indigent and prisons of poverty, was to sanction their ultimate failure: a transitory and ineffectual remedy, a social precaution clumsily formulated by a nascent industrialization. And yet, in this very failure, the classical period conducted an irreducible experiment. What appears to us today as a clumsy dialectic of production and prices then possessed its real meaning as a certain ethical consciousness of labor, in which the difficulties of the economic mechanisms lost their urgency in favor of an affirmation of value.

In this first phase of the industrial world, labor did not seem linked to the problems it was to provoke; it was regarded, on the contrary, as a general solution, an infallible panacea, a remedy to all forms of poverty. Labor and poverty were located in a simple opposition, in inverse proportion to each other. As for that power, its special characteristic, of abolishing poverty, labor—according to the classical interpretation—possessed it not so much by its productive capacity as by a certain force of moral enchantment. Labor's effectiveness was acknowledged because it was based on an ethical transcendence. Since the Fall, man had accepted labor as a penance and for its power to work redemption. It was not a law of nature which forced man to work, but the effect of a curse. The earth was innocent of that sterility in which it would slumber if man remained idle: "The land had not sinned, and if it is accursed, it is by the labor of the fallen man who cultivates it; from it no fruit is won, particularly the most necessary fruit, save by force and continual labor."[6]

The obligation to work was not linked to any confidence in nature; and it was not even through an obscure loyalty that the land would reward man's labor. The theme was constant among Catholic thinkers, as among the Protestants, that labor does not bear its own fruits. Produce and wealth were not found at the term of a dialectic of labor and nature. Here is Calvin's admonition: "Nor do we believe, according as men will be vigilant and skillful, according as they will have done their duty well, that they can make their land fertile; it is the benediction of God which governs all things." And this danger of a labor which would remain sterile if God did not intervene in His infinite mercy is acknowledged in turn by Bossuet: "At each moment, the hope of the harvest and the unique fruit of all our labors may escape us; we are at the mercy of the inconstant heavens that bring down rain upon the tender ears." This precarious labor to which nature is never obliged to respond—save by the special will of God—is nonetheless obligatory in all strictness: not on the level of natural syntheses, but on the level of moral syntheses. The poor man who, without consenting to "torment" the land, waits until God comes to his aid, since He has promised to feed the birds of the sky, would be disobeying the great law of Scripture: "Thou shalt not tempt the Lord thy God." Does not reluctance to work mean "trying beyond measure the power of God," as Calvin says? It is seeking to constrain the miracle,[7] whereas the miracle is granted daily to man as the gratuitous reward of his labor. If it is true that labor is not inscribed among the laws of nature, it is enveloped in the order of the fallen world. This is why idleness is rebellion—the worst form of all, in a sense: it waits for nature to be generous as in the innocence of Eden, and seeks to constrain a Goodness to which man cannot lay claim since Adam. Pride was the sin of man before the Fall; but the sin of idleness is the supreme pride of man once he has fallen, the absurd pride of poverty. In our world, where the land is no longer fertile except in thistles and weeds, idleness is the fault *par excellence*. In the Middle Ages, the great sin, *radix malorum omnium*, was pride, *Superbia*. According to Johan Huizinga, there was a time, at the dawn of the Renaissance, when the supreme sin assumed the aspect of Avarice, Dante's *cicca cupidigia*. All the seventeenth-century texts, on the contrary, announced the infernal triumph of Sloth: it was sloth which led the round of the vices and swept them on. Let us not forget that according to the edict of its creation, the Hôpital Général must prevent "mendicancy and idleness as sources of all disorder." Louis Bourdaloue echoes these condemnations of sloth, the wretched pride of fallen man: "What, then, is the disorder of an idle life? It is, replies Saint Ambrose, in its true meaning a second rebellion of the creature against God." Labor in the houses of confinement thus assumed its ethical meaning: since sloth had become the absolute form of rebellion, the idle would be forced to work, in the endless leisure of a labor without utility or profit.

It was in a certain experience of labor that the indissociably economic and moral demand for confinement was formulated. Between labor and idleness in the classical world ran a line of demarcation that replaced the exclusion of leprosy. The asylum was substituted for the lazar house, in the geography of haunted places as in the landscape of the moral universe. The old rites of excommunication were revived, but in the world of production and commerce. It was in these places of doomed and despised idleness, in this space invented by a society which had derived an ethical transcendence from the law of work, that madness would appear and soon expand until it had annexed them. A day was to come when it could possess these sterile reaches of idleness by a sort of very old and very dim right of inheritance. The nineteenth century would consent, would even insist that to the mad and to them alone be transferred these lands on which, a hundred and fifty years before, men had sought to pen the poor, the vagabond, the unemployed.

It is not immaterial that madmen were included in the proscription of idleness. From its origin, they would have their place beside the poor, deserving or not, and the idle, voluntary or not. Like them, they would be subject to the rules of forced labor. More than once, in fact, they figured in their singular fashion within this uniform constraint. In the workshops in which they were interned, they distinguished themselves by their inability to work and to follow the rhythms of collective life. The necessity, discovered in the eighteenth century, to provide a special regime for the insane, and the great crisis of confinement that shortly preceded the Revolution, are linked to the experience of madness available in the universal necessity of labor. Men did not wait until the seventeenth century to "shut up" the mad, but it was in this period that they began to "confine" or "intern" them, along with an entire population with whom their kinship was recognized. Until the Renaissance, the sensibility to madness was linked to the presence of imaginary transcendences. In the classical age, for the first time, madness was perceived through a condemnation of idleness and in a social immanence guaranteed by the community of labor. This community acquired an ethical power of segregation, which permitted it to eject, as into another world, all forms of social uselessness. It was in this *other world*, encircled by the sacred powers of labor, that madness would assume the status we now attribute to it. If there is, in classical madness, something which refers elsewhere, and to *other things*, it is no longer because the madman comes from the world of the irrational and bears its stigmata; rather, it is because he crosses the frontiers of bourgeois order of his own accord, and alienates himself outside the sacred limits of its ethic.

In fact, the relation between the practice of confinement and the insistence on work is not defined by economic conditions; far from it. A moral perception sustains and animates it. When the Board of Trade published its report on the poor in which it proposed the means "to render them useful to the public," it was made quite clear that the origin of poverty was neither scarcity of commodities nor unemployment, but "the weakening of discipline and the relaxation of morals." The edict of 1657, too, was full of moral denunciations and strange threats. "The libertinage of beggars has risen to excess because of an unfortunate tolerance of crimes of all sorts, which attract the curse of God upon the State when they remain unpunished." This "libertinage" is not the kind that can be defined in relation to the great law of work, but a moral libertinage: "Experience having taught those persons who are employed in charitable occupations that many among them of either sex live together without marriage, that many of their children are unbaptized, and that almost all of them live in ignorance of religion, disdaining the sacraments, and continually practicing all sorts of vice." Hence the Hôpital does not have the appearance of a mere refuge for those whom age, infirmity, or sickness keep from working; it will have not only the aspect of a forced labor camp, but also that of a moral institution responsible for punishing, for correcting a certain moral "abeyance" which does not merit the tribunal of men, but cannot be corrected by the severity of penance alone. The Hôpital Général has an ethical status. It is this moral charge which invests its directors, and they are granted every judicial apparatus and means of repression: "They have power of authority, of direction, of administration, of commerce, of police, of jurisdiction, of correction and punishment"; and to accomplish this task "stakes, irons, prisons, and dungeons"[8] are put at their disposal.

And it is in this context that the obligation to work assumes its meaning as both ethical exercise and moral guarantee. It will serve as *askesis*, as punishment, as symptom of a certain disposition of the heart. The prisoner who could and who would work would be released, not so much because he was again useful to society, but because he had

again subscribed to the great ethical pact of human existence. In April 1684, a decree created within the Hôpital a
section for boys and girls under twenty-five; it specified
that work must occupy the greater part of the day, and
must be accompanied by "the reading of pious books." But
the ruling defines the purely repressive nature of this work,
beyond any concern for production: "They will be made
to work as long and as hard as their strengths and situations
will permit." It is then, but only then, that they can be
taught an occupation "fitting their sex and inclination,"
insofar as the measure of their zeal in the first activities
makes it possible to "judge that they desire to reform."
Finally, every fault "will be punished by reduction of
gruel, by increase of work, by imprisonment and other
punishments customary in the said hospitals, as the directors shall see fit." It is enough to read the "general regulations for daily life in the House of Saint-Louis de la Salpêtrière" to understand that the very requirement of labor was
instituted as an exercise in moral reform and constraint,
which reveals, if not the ultimate meaning, at least the essential justification of confinement.

An important phenomenon, this invention of a site of
constraint, where morality castigates by means of administrative enforcement. For the first time, institutions of
morality are established in which an astonishing synthesis
of moral obligation and civil law is effected. The law of
nations will no longer countenance the disorder of hearts. To
be sure, this is not the first time in European culture that
moral error, even in its most private form, has assumed the
aspect of a transgression against the written or unwritten
laws of the community. But in this great confinement of
the classical age, the essential thing—and the new event—is
that men were confined in cities of pure morality, where
the law that should reign in all hearts was to be applied
without compromise, without concession, in the rigorous

forms of physical constraint. Morality permitted itself to be administered like trade or economy.

Thus we see inscribed in the institutions of absolute monarchy—in the very ones that long remained the symbol of its arbitrary power—the great bourgeois, and soon republican, idea that virtue, too, is an affair of state, that decrees can be published to make it flourish, that an authority can be established to make sure it is respected. The walls of confinement actually enclose the negative of that moral city of which the bourgeois conscience began to dream in the seventeenth century; a moral city for those who sought, from the start, to avoid it, a city where right reigns only by virtue of a force without appeal—a sort of sovereignty of good, in which intimidation alone prevails and the only recompense of virtue (to this degree its own reward) is to escape punishment. In the shadows of the bourgeois city is born this strange republic of the good which is imposed by force on all those suspected of belonging to evil. This is the underside of the bourgeoisie's great dream and great preoccupation in the classical age: the laws of the State and the laws of the heart at last identical. "Let our politicians leave off their calculations . . . let them learn once and for all that everything can be had for money, except morals and citizens."[9]

Is this not the dream that seems to have haunted the founders of the house of confinement in Hamburg? One of the directors is to see that "all in the house are properly instructed as to religious and moral duties. . . . The schoolmaster must instruct the children in religion, and encourage them, at proper times, to learn and repeat portions of Scripture. He must also teach them reading, writing and accounts, and a decent behaviour to those that visit the house. He must take care that they attend divine service, and are orderly at it."[10] In England, the workhouse regulations devote much space to the surveillance of morals and to religious education. Thus for the house in Plymouth, a schoolmaster is to be appointed who will fulfill the triple requirement of being "pious, sober, and discreet." Every morning and evening, at the prescribed hour, it will be his task to preside at prayers; every Saturday afternoon and on holidays, he will address the inmates, exhorting and instructing them in "the fundamental parts of the Protestant religion, according to the doctrine of the Church of England." Hamburg or Plymouth, *Zuchthäusern* and workhouses—throughout Protestant Europe, fortresses of moral order were constructed, in which were taught religion and whatever was necessary to the peace of the State.

In Catholic countries, the goal is the same but the religious imprint is a little more marked, as the work of Saint Vincent de Paul bears witness. "The principal end for which such persons have been removed here, out of the storms of the great world, and introduced into this solitude as pensioners, is entirely to keep them from the slavery of sin, from being eternally damned, and to give them means to rejoice in a perfect contentment in this world and in the next; they will do all they can to worship, in this world, Divine Providence. . . . Experience convinces us only too unhappily that the source of the misrule triumphant today among the young lies entirely in the lack of instruction and of obedience in spiritual matters, since they much prefer to follow their evil inclinations than the holy inspiration of God and the charitable advice of their parents."[11] Therefore the pensioners must be delivered from a world which, for their weakness, is only an invitation to sin, must be recalled to a solitude where they will have as companions only their "guardian angels" incarnate in the daily presence of their warders: these latter, in fact, "render them the same good offices that their guardian angels perform for them invisibly: namely, instruct them, console them, and procure their salvation." In the houses of La Charité, the greatest attention was paid to this ordering of life and conscience, which throughout the eighteenth century would more and more clearly appear as the *raison d'être* of confinement. In 1765, new regulations were established for the Charité of Château-Thierry; it was made quite clear that "the Prior will visit all the prisoners at least once a week, one after the other, and separately, to console them, to exhort them to better conduct, and to assure himself that they are treated as they should be; the subordinate officer will do this every day."

All these prisons of moral order might have borne the motto which Howard could still read on the one in Mainz: "If wild beasts can be broken to the yoke, it must not be despaired of correcting the man who has strayed." For the Catholic Church, as in the Protestant countries, confinement represents, in the form of an authoritarian model, the myth of social happiness: a police whose order will be entirely transparent to the principles of religion, and a religion whose requirements will be satisfied, without restrictions, by the regulations of the police and the constraints with which it can be armed. There is, in these institutions, an attempt of a kind to demonstrate that order may be adequate to virtue. In this sense, "confinement" conceals both a metaphysics of government and a politics of religion; it is situated, as an effort of tyrannical synthesis, in the vast space separating the garden of God and the cities which men, driven from paradise, have built with their own hands. The house of confinement in the classical age constitutes the densest symbol of that "police" which conceived of itself as the civil equivalent of religion for the edification of a perfect city.

Confinement was an institutional creation peculiar to the seventeenth century. It acquired from the first an importance that left it no rapport with imprisonment as practiced in the Middle Ages. As an economic measure and a social precaution, it had the value of inventiveness. But in the history of unreason, it marked a decisive event: the moment when madness was perceived on the social horizon of poverty, of incapacity for work, of inability to integrate with the group; the moment when madness began to rank among the problems of the city. The new meanings assigned to poverty, the importance given to the obligation to work, and all the ethical values that are linked to labor, ultimately determined the experience of madness and inflected its course.

A sensibility was born which had drawn a line and laid a cornerstone, and which chose—only to banish. The concrete space of classical society reserved a neutral region, a blank page where the real life of the city was suspended; here, order no longer freely confronted disorder, reason no longer tried to make its own way among all that might evade or seek to deny it. Here reason reigned in the pure state, in a triumph arranged for it in advance over a frenzied unreason. Madness was thus torn from that imaginary freedom which still allowed it to flourish on the Renaissance horizon. Not so long ago, it had floundered about in broad daylight: in *King Lear*, in *Don Quixote*. But in less than a half-century, it had been sequestered and, in the fortress of confinement, bound to Reason, to the rules of morality and to their monotonous nights.

III

THE INSANE

From the creation of the Hôpital Général, from the opening, in Germany and in England, of the first houses of correction, and until the end of the eighteenth century, the age of reason confined. It confined the debauched, spendthrift fathers, prodigal sons, blasphemers, men who "seek to undo themselves," libertines. And through these parallels, these strange complicities, the age sketched the profile of its own experience of unreason.

But in each of these cities, we find an entire population of madness as well. One-tenth of all the arrests made in Paris for the Hôpital Général concern "the insane," "demented" men, individuals of "wandering mind," and "persons who have become completely mad." Between these and the others, no sign of a differentiation. Judging from the registries, the same sensibility appears to collect them, the same gestures to set them apart. We leave it to medical archaeology to determine whether or not a man was sick, criminal, or insane who was admitted to the hospital for "derangement of morals," or because he had "mistreated his wife" and tried several times to kill himself.

Yet it must not be forgotten that the "insane" had as such a particular place in the world of confinement. Their status was not merely that of prisoners. In the general sensibility to unreason, there appeared to be a special modulation which concerned madness proper, and was addressed to those called, without exact semantic distinction, insane, alienated, deranged, demented, extravagant.

This particular form of sensibility traces the features proper to madness in the world of unreason. It is primarily concerned with scandal. In its most general form, confinement is explained, or at least justified, by the desire to avoid scandal. It even signifies thereby an important change in the consciousness of evil. The Renaissance had freely allowed the forms of unreason to come out into the light of day; public outrage gave evil the powers of example and redemption. Gilles de Rais, accused, in the fifteenth century, of having been and of being "a heretic, an apostate, a sorcerer, a sodomite, an invoker of evil spirits, a soothsayer, a slayer of innocents, an idolater, working evil by deviation from the faith," ended by himself admitting to crimes "sufficient to cause the deaths of ten thousand persons" in extrajudiciary confession; he repeated his avowal in Latin before the tribunal; then he asked, of his own accord, that "the said confession should be published in the vulgar tongue and exhibited to each and every one of those present, the majority of whom knew no Latin, the publication and confession to his shame of the said offenses by him committed, in order the more easily to obtain the remission of sins, and the mercy of God for the pardon of the sins by him committed." At the trial, the same confession was required before those assembled: he "was told by the Presiding Judge that he should state his case fully, and the shame that he would gain thereby would serve to lessen the punishment he would suffer hereafter." Until the seventeenth century, evil in all its most violent and most inhuman forms could not be dealt with and punished unless it was brought into the open. The light in which confession was made and punishment executed could alone balance the darkness from which evil issued. In order to pass through all the stages of its fulfillment, evil must necessarily incur public avowal and manifestation before reaching the conclusion which suppresses it.

Confinement, on the contrary, betrays a form of conscience to which the inhuman can suggest only shame. There are aspects of evil that have such a power of contagion, such a force of scandal that any publicity multiplies them infinitely. Only oblivion can suppress them. In a case of poisoning, Pontchartrain orders not a public trial but the secrecy of an asylum: "As the facts of the case concerned a good part of Paris, the King did not believe that so many people should be brought to trial, many of whom had committed crimes unawares, and others only by the ease of doing so; His Majesty so determined the more readily insofar as he is persuaded that there are certain crimes which must absolutely be thrust into oblivion."[1] Beyond the dangers of example, the honor of families and that of religion sufficed to recommend a subject for a house of confinement. Apropos of a priest who was to be sent to Saint-Lazare: "Hence a priest such as this cannot be hidden away with too much care for the honor of religion and that of the priesthood."[2] Even late in the eighteenth century, Malesherbes would defend confinement as a right of families seeking to escape dishonor. "That which is called a base action is placed in the rank of those which public order does not permit us to tolerate. . . . It seems that the honor of a family requires the disappearance from society of the individual who by vile and abject habits shames his relatives." Inversely, liberation is in order when the danger of scandal is past and the honor of families or of the Church can no longer be sullied. The Abbé Bargedé had been confined for a long time; never, despite his requests, had his release been authorized; but now old age and infirmity had made scandal impossible. "And besides, his paralysis persists," writes d'Argenson; "he can neither write nor sign his name; I think that there would be justice and charity in setting him free." All those forms of evil that border on unreason must be thrust into secrecy. Classicism felt a shame in the presence of the inhuman that the Renaissance had never experienced.

Yet there is one exception in this consignment to secrecy: that which is made for madmen.[3] It was doubtless a very old custom of the Middle Ages to display the insane. In certain of the *Narrtürmer* in Germany, barred windows had been installed which permitted those outside to observe the madmen chained within. They thus constituted a spectacle at the city gates. The strange fact is that this custom did not disappear once the doors of the asylums closed, but that on the contrary it then developed, assuming in Paris and London almost an institutional character. As late as 1815, if a report presented in the House of Commons is to be believed, the hospital of Bethlehem exhibited lunatics for a penny, every Sunday. Now the annual revenue from these exhibitions amounted to almost four hundred pounds; which suggests the astonishingly high number of 96,000 visits a year.[4] In France, the excursion to Bicêtre and the display of the insane remained until the Revolution one of the Sunday distractions for the Left Bank bourgeoisie. Mirabeau reports in his *Observations d'un voyageur anglais* that the madmen at Bicêtre were shown "like curious animals, to the first simpleton willing to pay a coin." One went to see the keeper display the madmen the way the trainer at the Fair of Saint-Germain put the monkeys through their tricks.[5] Certain attendants were well known for their ability to make the mad perform dances and acrobatics, with a few flicks of the whip. The only extenuation to be found at the end of the eighteenth century was that the mad were allowed to exhibit the mad, as if it were the responsibility of madness to testify to its own nature. "Let us not slander human nature. The English traveler is right to regard the office of exhibiting madmen as beyond the most hardened humanity. We have already said so. But all dilemmas afford a remedy. It is the madmen themselves who are entrusted in their lucid intervals with displaying their companions, who, in their turn, return the favor. Thus the keepers of these unfortunate creatures enjoy the profits that the spectacle affords, without indulging in a heartlessness to which, no doubt, they could never descend."[6] Here is madness elevated to spectacle above the silence of the asylums, and becoming a public scandal for the general delight. Unreason was hidden in the silence of the houses of confinement, but madness continued to be present on the stage of the world—with more commotion than ever. It would soon reach, under the Empire, a point that had never been attained in the Middle Ages and the Renaissance; the strange Brotherhood of the Blue Ship had once given performances in which madness was mimed; now it was madness itself, madness in flesh and blood, which put on the show. Early in the nineteenth century, Coulmier, the director of Charenton, had organized those famous performances in which madmen sometimes played the roles of actors, sometimes those of watched spectators. "The insane who attended these theatricals were the object of the attention and curiosity of a frivolous, irresponsible, and often vicious public. The bizarre attitudes of these unfortunates and their condition provoked the mocking laughter and the insulting pity of the spectators."[7] Madness became pure spectacle, in a world over which Sade extended his sovereignty and which was offered as a diversion to the good conscience of a reason sure of itself. Until the beginning of the nineteenth century, and to the indignation of Royer-Collard, madmen remained monsters—that is, etymologically, beings or things to be shown.

Confinement hid away unreason, and betrayed the shame it aroused; but it explicitly drew attention to madness, pointed to it. If, in the case of unreason, the chief intention was to avoid scandal, in the case of madness that intention was to organize it. A strange contradiction: the classical age enveloped madness in a total experience of unreason; it re-absorbed its particular forms, which the Middle Ages and the Renaissance had clearly individualized into a general apprehension in which madness consorted indiscriminately with all the forms of unreason. But at the same time it assigned to this same madness a special sign: not that of sickness, but that of glorified scandal. Yet there is nothing in common between this organized exhibition of madness in the eighteenth century and the freedom with which it came to light during the Renaissance. In the Renaissance, madness was present everywhere and mingled with every experience by its images or its dangers. During the classical period, madness was shown, but on the other side of bars; if present, it was at a distance, under the eyes of a reason that no longer felt any relation to it and that would not compromise itself by too close a resemblance. Madness had become a thing to look at: no longer a monster inside oneself, but an animal with strange mechanisms, a bestiality from which man had long since been suppressed. "I can easily conceive of a man without hands, feet, head (for it is only experience which teaches us that the head is more necessary than the feet). But I cannot conceive of man without thought; that would be a stone or a brute."[8]

In his *Report on the Care of the Insane* Desportes describes the cells of Bicêtre as they were at the end of the eighteenth century: "The unfortunate whose entire furniture consisted of this straw pallet, lying with his head, feet, and body pressed against the wall, could not enjoy sleep without being soaked by the water that trickled from that mass of stone." As for the cells of La Salpêtrière, what made "the place more miserable and often more fatal, was that in winter, when the waters of the Seine rose, those cells situated at the level of the sewers became not only more unhealthy, but worse still, a refuge for a swarm of huge rats, which during the night attacked the unfortunates confined there and bit them wherever they could reach them; madwomen have been found with feet, hands, and faces torn by bites which are often dangerous and from which several have died." But these were the dungeons and cells long reserved for the most dangerous and most violent of the insane. If they were calmer, and if no one had anything to fear from them, they were crammed into wards of varying size. One of Samuel Tuke's most active disciples, Godfrey Higgins, had obtained the right, which cost him twenty pounds, to visit the asylum of York as a volunteer inspector. In the course of a visit, he discovered a door that had been carefully concealed and found behind it a room, not eight feet on a side, which thirteen women occupied during the night; by day, they lived in a room scarcely larger.

On the other hand, when the insane were particularly dangerous, they were constrained by a system which was doubtless not of a punitive nature, but simply intended to fix within narrow limits the physical locus of a raging frenzy. Sufferers were generally chained to the walls and to the beds. At Bethlehem, violent madwomen were chained by the ankles to the wall of a long gallery; their only garment was a homespun dress. At another hospital, in Bethnal Green, a woman subject to violent seizures was placed in a pigsty, feet and fists bound; when the crisis had passed she was tied to her bed, covered only by a blanket; when she was allowed to take a few steps, an iron bar was placed between her legs, attached by rings to her ankles and by a short chain to handcuffs. Samuel Tuke, in his *Report on the Condition of the Indigent Insane*, gives the details of a complicated system devised at Bethlehem to control a reputedly dangerous madman: he was attached by a long chain that ran over the wall and thus permitted the attendant to lead him about, to keep him on a leash, so to speak, from outside; around his neck had been placed an iron ring, which was attached by a short chain to another ring; this latter slid the length of a vertical iron bar fastened to the floor and ceiling of the cell. When reforms began to be instituted at Bethlehem, a man was found who had lived in this cell, attached in this fashion, for twelve years.

When practices reach this degree of violent intensity, it becomes clear that they are no longer inspired by the desire to punish nor by the duty to correct. The notion of a "resipiscence" is entirely foreign to this regime. But there was a certain image of animality that haunted the hospitals of the period. Madness borrowed its face from the mask of the beast. Those chained to the cell walls were no longer men whose minds had wandered, but beasts preyed upon by a natural frenzy: as if madness, at its extreme point, freed from that moral unreason in which its most attenuated forms are enclosed, managed to rejoin, by a paroxysm of strength, the immediate violence of animality. This model of animality prevailed in the asylums and gave them their cagelike aspect, their look of the menagerie. Coguel describes La Salpêtrière at the end of the eighteenth century: "Madwomen seized with fits of violence are chained like dogs at their cell doors, and separated from keepers and visitors alike by a long corridor protected by an iron grille; through this grille is passed their food and the straw on which they sleep; by means of rakes, part of the filth that surrounds them is cleaned out." At the hospital of Nantes, the menagerie appears to consist of individual cages for wild beasts. Never had Esquirol seen "such an extravagance of locks, of bolts, of iron bars to shut the doors of the cells. . . . Tiny openings pierced next to the doors were fitted with iron bars and shutters. Quite close to this opening hung a chain fastened to the wall and bearing at its end a cast-iron receptacle, somewhat resembling a wooden shoe, in which food was placed and passed through the bars of these openings." When François-Emmanuel Fodéré arrived at the hospital of Strasbourg in 1814, he found a kind of human stable, constructed with great care and skill: "for troublesome madmen and those who dirtied themselves, a kind of cage, or wooden closet, which could at the most contain one man of middle height, had been devised at the ends of the great wards." These cages had gratings for floors, and did not rest on the ground but were raised about fifteen centimeters. Over these gratings was thrown a little straw "upon which the madman lay, naked or nearly so, took his meals, and deposited his excrement."

This, to be sure, is a whole security system against the violence of the insane and the explosion of their fury. Such outbursts are regarded chiefly as a social danger. But what is most important is that it is conceived in terms of an animal freedom. The negative fact that "the madman is not treated like a human being" has a very positive content: this inhuman indifference actually has an obsessional value: it is rooted in the old fears which since antiquity, and especially since the Middle Ages, have given the animal world its familiar strangeness, its menacing marvels, its entire weight of dumb anxiety. Yet this animal fear which accompanies, with all its imaginary landscape, the perception of madness, no longer has the same meaning it had two or three centuries earlier: animal metamorphosis is no longer the visible sign of infernal powers, nor the result of a diabolic alchemy of unreason. The animal in man no longer has any value as the sign of a Beyond; it has become his madness, without relation to anything but itself: his madness in the state of nature. The animality that rages in madness dispossesses man of what is specifically human in him; not in order to deliver him over to other powers, but simply to establish him at the zero degree of his own nature. For classicism, madness in its ultimate form is man in immediate relation to his animality, without other reference, without any recourse.

The day would come when from an evolutionary perspective this presence of animality in madness would be considered as the sign—indeed, as the very essence—of disease. In the classical period, on the contrary, it manifested the very fact that *the madman was not a sick man.* Animality, in fact, protected the lunatic from whatever might be fragile, precarious, or sickly in man. The animal solidity of madness, and that density it borrows from the blind world of beasts, inured the madman to hunger, heat, cold, pain. It was common knowledge until the end of the eighteenth century that the insane could support the miseries of existence indefinitely. There was no need to protect them; they had no need to be covered or warmed. When, in 1811, Samuel Tuke visited a workhouse in the Southern Counties, he saw cells where the daylight passed through little barred windows that had been cut in the doors. All the women were entirely naked. Now "the temperature was extremely rigorous, and the evening of the day before, the thermometer had indicated a cold of 18 degrees. One of these unfortunate women was lying on a little straw, without covering." This ability of the insane to endure, like animals, the worst inclemencies was still a medical dogma for Pinel; he would always admire "the constancy and the ease with which certain of the insane of both sexes bear the most rigorous and prolonged cold. In the month of Nivôse of the Year III, on certain days when the thermometer indicated 10, 11, and as many as 16 degrees below freezing, a madman in the hospital of Bicêtre could not endure his wool blanket, and remained sitting on the icy floor of his cell. In the morning, one no sooner opened his door than he ran in his shirt into the inner court, taking ice and snow by the fistful, applying it to his breast and letting it melt with a sort of delectation." Madness, insofar as it partook of animal ferocity, preserved man from the dangers of disease; it afforded him an invulnerability, similar to that which nature, in its foresight, had provided for animals. Curiously, the disturbance of his reason restored the madman to the immediate kindness of nature by a return to animality.

This is why, at this extreme point, madness was less than ever linked to medicine; nor could it be linked to the domain of correction. Unchained animality could be mastered only by *discipline* and *brutalizing*. The theme of the animal-madman was effectively realized in the eighteenth century, in occasional attempts to impose a certain pedagogy on the insane. Pinel cites the case of a "very famous monastic establishment, in one of the southern regions of France," where a violent madman would be given "a precise order to change"; if he refused to go to bed or to eat, he "was warned that obstinacy in his deviations would be punished on the next day with ten strokes of the bullwhip." If, on the contrary, he was submissive and docile, he was allowed "to take his meals in the refectory, next to the disciplinarian," but at the least transgression, he was instantly admonished by a "heavy blow of a rod across his fingers." Thus, by the use of a curious dialectic whose movement explains all these "inhuman" practices of confinement, the free animality of madness was tamed only by such discipline whose meaning was not to raise the bestial to the human, but to restore man to what was purely animal within him. Madness discloses a secret of animality which is its own truth, and in which, in some way, it is reabsorbed. Toward the middle of the eighteenth century, a farmer in the north of Scotland had his hour of fame. He was said to possess the art of curing insanity. Pinel notes in passing that this Gregory had the physique of a Hercules: "His method consisted in forcing the insane to perform the most difficult tasks of farming, in using them as beasts of burden, as servants, in reducing them to an ultimate obedience with a barrage of blows at the least act of revolt." In the reduction to animality, madness finds both its truth and its cure; when the madman has become a beast, this presence of the animal in man, a presence which constituted the scandal of madness, is eliminated: not that the animal is silenced, but man himself is abolished. In the human being who has become a beast of burden, the absence of reason follows wisdom and its order: madness is then cured, since it is alienated in something which is no less than its truth.

A moment would come when, from this animality of madness, would be deduced the idea of a mechanistic psychology, and the notion that the forms of madness can be referred to the great structures of animal life. But in the seventeenth and eighteenth centuries, the animality that lends its face to madness in no way stipulates a determinist nature for its phenomena. On the contrary, it locates madness in *an area of unforeseeable freedom* where frenzy is unchained; if determinism can have any effect on it, it is in the form of constraint, punishment, or discipline. Through animality, madness does not join the great laws of nature and of life, but rather the thousand forms of a bestiary. But unlike the one popular in the Middle Ages, which illustrated, in so many symbolic visages, the metamorphoses of evil, this was an abstract bestiary; here evil no longer assumed its fantastic body; here we apprehend only its most extreme form, the truth of the beast which is a truth without content. Evil is freed from all that its wealth of iconographic fauna could do, to preserve only a general power of intimidation: the secret danger of an animality that lies in wait and, all at once, undoes reason in violence and truth in the madman's frenzy. Despite the contemporary effort to constitute a positivist zoology, this obsession with an animality perceived as the natural locus of madness continued to people the hell of the classical age. It was this obsession that created the imagery responsible for all the practices of confinement and the strangest aspects of its savagery.

It has doubtless been essential to Western culture to link, as it has done, its perception of madness to the iconographic forms of the relation of man to beast. From the start, Western culture has not considered it evident that animals participate in the plenitude of nature, in its wisdom and its order: this idea was a late one and long remained on the surface of culture; perhaps it has not yet penetrated very deeply into the subterranean regions of the imagination. In fact, on close examination, it becomes evident that the animal belongs rather to an anti-nature, to a negativity that threatens order and by its frenzy endangers the positive wisdom of nature. The work of Lautréamont bears witness to this. Why should the fact that Western man has lived for two thousand years on his definition as a rational animal necessarily mean that he has recognized the possibility of an order common to reason and to animality? Why should he have necessarily designated, by this definition, the way in which he inserts himself in natural positivity? Independently of what Aristotle really meant, may we not assume that for the West this "rational animal" has long been the measure of the way in which reason's freedom functioned in the locus of unreason, diverging from it until it constituted its opposite term? From the moment philosophy became anthropology, and man sought to recognize himself in a natural plenitude, the animal lost its power of negativity, in order to become, between the determinism of nature and the reason of man, the positive form of an evolution. The formula of the "rational animal" has utterly changed its meaning: the unreason it suggested as the origin of all possible reason has entirely disappeared. Henceforth madness must obey the determinism of man perceived as a natural being in his very animality. In the classical age, if it is true that the scientific and medical analysis of madness, as we shall see below, sought to establish it within this natural mechanism, the real practices that concern the insane bear sufficient witness to the fact that madness was still contained in the anti-natural violence of animality.

In any case, it was this *animality of madness* which confinement glorified, at the same time that it sought to avoid the scandal inherent in the *immorality of the unreasonable*. Which reveals the distance established in the classical age between madness and the other forms of unreason, even if it is true that from a certain point of view they had been identified or assimilated. If a whole range of unreason was reduced to silence, but madness left free to speak the language of its scandal, what lesson could it teach which unreason as a whole was not capable of transmitting? What meaning had the frenzies and all the fury of the insane, which could not be found in the—probably more sensible—remarks of the other internees? In what respect then was madness more particularly significant?

Beginning with the seventeenth century, unreason in the most general sense no longer had much instructive value. That perilous reversibility of reason which was still so close for the Renaissance was to be forgotten, and its scandals were to disappear. The great theme of the madness of the Cross, which belonged so intimately to the Christian experience of the Renaissance, began to disappear in the seventeenth century, despite Jansenism and Pascal. Or rather, it subsisted, but changed and somehow inverted its meaning.

It was no longer a matter of requiring human reason to abandon its pride and its certainties in order to lose itself in the great unreason of sacrifice. When classical Christianity speaks of the madness of the Cross, it is merely to humiliate false reason and add luster to the eternal light of truth; the madness of God-in-man's-image is simply a wisdom not recognized by the men of unreason who live in this world: "Jesus crucified . . . was the scandal of the world and appeared as nothing but ignorance and madness to the eyes of his time." But the fact that the world has become Christian, and that the order of God is revealed through the meanderings of history and the madness of men, now suffices to show that "Christ has become the highest point of our wisdom."[9] The scandal of Christian faith and Christian abasement, whose strength and value as revelation Pascal still preserved, would soon have no more meaning for Christian thought except perhaps to reveal in these scandalized consciences so many blind souls: "Do not permit your Cross, which has subdued the universe for you, to be still the madness and scandal of proud minds." Christian unreason was relegated by Christians themselves into the margins of a reason that had become identical with the wisdom of God incarnate. After Port-Royal, men would have to wait two centuries—until Dostoievsky and Nietzsche—for Christ to regain the glory of his madness, for scandal to recover its power as revelation, for unreason to cease being merely the public shame of reason.

But at the very moment Christian reason rid itself of the madness that had so long been a part of itself, the madman, in his abolished reason, in the fury of his animality, received a singular power as a demonstration: it was as if scandal, driven out of that superhuman region where it related to God and where the Incarnation was manifested, reappeared, in the plenitude of its force and pregnant with a new lesson, in that region where man has a relation to nature and to his animality. The lesson's point of application has shifted to the lower regions of madness. The Cross is no longer to be considered in its scandal; but it must not be forgotten that throughout his human life Christ honored madness, sanctified it as he sanctified infirmity cured, sin forgiven, poverty assured of eternal riches. Saint Vincent de Paul reminds those assigned to tend the mad within the houses of confinement that their "rule in this is Our Lord who chose to be surrounded by lunatics, demoniacs, madmen, the tempted and the possessed." These men ruled by the powers of the inhuman constitute, around those who represent eternal Wisdom, around the Man who incarnates it, a perpetual occasion for glorification: because they glorify, by surrounding it, the wisdom that has been denied them, and at the same time give it a pretext to humiliate itself, to acknowledge that it is granted only by grace. Further: Christ did not merely choose to be surrounded by lunatics; he himself chose to pass in their eyes for a madman, thus experiencing, in his incarnation, all the sufferings of human misfortune. Madness thus became the ultimate form, the final degree of God in man's image, before the fulfillment and deliverance of the Cross: "O my Savior, you were pleased to be a scandal to the Jews, and a madness to the Gentiles; you were pleased to seem out of your senses, as it is reported in the Holy Gospel that it was thought of Our Lord that he had gone mad. *Dicebant quoniam in furorem versus est*. His Apostles sometimes looked upon him as a man in anger, and he seemed such to them, so that they should bear witness that he had borne with all our infirmities and all our states of affliction, and to teach them and us as well to have compassion upon those who fall into these infirmities."[10] Coming into this world, Christ agreed to take upon himself all the signs of the human condition and the very stigmata of fallen nature; from poverty to

death, he followed the long road of the Passion, which was
also the road of the passions, of wisdom forgotten, and of
madness. And because it was one of the forms of the Passion—the ultimate form, in a sense, before death—madness
would now become, for those who suffered it, an object of
respect and compassion.

To respect madness is not to interpret it as the involun-
tary and inevitable accident of disease, but to recognize this
lower limit of human truth, a limit not accidental but essential. As death is the limit of human life in the realm of time,
madness is its limit in the realm of animality, and just as
death had been sanctified by the death of Christ, madness,
in its most bestial nature, had also been sanctified. On
March 29, 1654, Saint Vincent de Paul announced to Jean
Barreau, himself a congreganist, that his brother had just
been confined at Saint-Lazare as a lunatic: "We must
honor Our Lord in the state wherein He was when they
sought to bind Him, saying *quoniam in frenesim versus est*,
in order to sanctify that state in those whom His Divine
Providence has placed there."[11] Madness is the lowest
point of humanity to which God submitted in His incarnation, thereby showing that there was nothing inhuman in
man that could not be redeemed and saved; the ultimate
point of the Fall was glorified by the divine presence: and
it is this lesson which, for the seventeenth century, all madness still taught.

We see why the scandal of madness could be exalted,
while that of the other forms of unreason was concealed
with so much care. The scandal of unreason produced only
the contagious example of transgression and immorality;
the scandal of madness showed men how close to animality
their Fall could bring them; and at the same time how far
divine mercy could extend when it consented to save man.
For Renaissance Christianity, the entire instructive value of

unreason and of its scandals lay in the madness of the Incarnation of God in man. For classicism, the Incarnation is
no longer madness; but what is madness is this incarnation
of man in the beast, which is, as the ultimate point of his
Fall, the most manifest sign of his guilt; and, as the ultimate
object of divine mercy, the symbol of universal forgiveness
and innocence regained. Henceforth, all the lessons of madness and the power of its instruction must be sought in this
obscure region, at the lower confines of humanity, where
man is hinged to nature, where he is both ultimate downfall
and absolute innocence. Does not the Church's solicitude
for the insane during the classical period, as it is symbolized
in Saint Vincent de Paul and his Congregation, or in the
Brothers of Charity, all those religious orders hovering
over madness and showing it to the world—does this not
indicate that the Church found in madness a difficult but an
essential lesson: the guilty innocence of the animal in man?
This is the lesson to be read and understood in its spectacles, in which it exalted in the madman the fury of the
human beast. Paradoxically, this Christian consciousness of
animality prepared the moment when madness would be
treated as a fact of nature; it would then be quickly forgotten what this "nature" meant for classical thought: not
the always accessible domain of an objective analysis, but
that region in which there appears, for man, the always
possible scandal of a madness that is both his ultimate truth
and the form of his abolition.

All these phenomena, these strange practices woven
around madness, these usages which glorify and at the same
time discipline it, reduce it to animality while making it
teach the lesson of the Redemption, put madness in a
strange position with regard to unreason as a whole. In the
houses of confinement, madness cohabits with all the forms

of unreason which envelop it and define its most general truth; and yet madness is isolated, treated in a special manner, manifested in its singularity as if, though belonging to unreason, it nonetheless traversed that domain by a movement peculiar to itself, ceaselessly referring from itself to its most paradoxical extreme.

We have now got in the habit of perceiving in madness a fall into a determinism where all forms of liberty are gradually suppressed; madness shows us nothing more than the natural constants of a determinism, with the sequences of its causes, and the discursive movement of its forms; for madness threatens modern man only with that return to the bleak world of beasts and things, to their fettered freedom. It is not on this horizon of *nature* that the seventeenth and eighteenth centuries recognized madness, but against a background of *Unreason;* madness did not disclose a mechanism, but revealed a liberty raging in the monstrous forms of animality. We no longer understand unreason today, except in its epithetic form: the *Unreasonable,* a sign attached to conduct or speech, and betraying to the layman's eyes the presence of madness and all its pathological train; for us the unreasonable is only one of madness's modes of appearance. On the contrary, unreason, for classicism, had a nominal value; it constituted a kind of substantial function. It was in relation to unreason and to it alone that madness could be understood. Unreason was its support; or let us say that unreason defined the locus of madness's possibility. For classical man, madness was not the natural condition, the human and psychological root of unreason; it was only unreason's empirical form; and the madman, tracing the course of human degradation to the frenzied nadir of animality, disclosed that underlying realm of unreason which threatens man and envelops—at a tremendous distance—all the forms of his natural existence. It was not a question of tending toward a determinism, but of being swallowed up by a darkness. More effectively than any other kind of rationalism, better in any case than our positivism, classical rationalism could watch out for and guard against the subterranean danger of unreason, that threatening space of an absolute freedom.

IV

PASSION AND
DELIRIUM

THE savage danger of madness is related to the danger of
the passions and to their fatal concatenation.

Sauvages had sketched the fundamental role of passion,
citing it as a more constant, more persistent, and somehow
more deserved cause of madness: "The distraction of our
mind is the result of our blind surrender to our desires, our
incapacity to control or to moderate our passions. Whence
these amorous frenzies, these antipathies, these depraved
tastes, this melancholy which is caused by grief, these
transports wrought in us by denial, these excesses in eating,
in drinking, these indispositions, these corporeal vices which
cause madness, the worst of all maladies."[1] But as yet, what
was involved was only passion's moral precedence, its responsibility, in a vague way; the real target of this denunciation was the radical relation of the phenomena of madness
to the very possibility of passion.

Before Descartes, and long after his influence as philosopher and physiologist had diminished, passion continued to be the meeting ground of body and soul; the point where the latter's activity makes contact with the former's passivity, each being a limit imposed upon the other and the locus of their communication.

The medicine of humors sees this unity primarily as a reciprocal interaction: "The passions necessarily cause certain movements in the humors; anger agitates the bile, sadness excites melancholy (black bile), and the movements of the humors are on occasion so violent that they disrupt the entire economy of the body, even causing death; further, the passions augment the quantity of the humors; anger multiplies the bile as sadness increases melancholy. The humors which are customarily agitated by certain passions dispose those in whom they abound to the same passions, and to thinking of the objects which ordinarily excite them; bile disposes to anger and to thinking of those we hate. Melancholy (black bile) disposes to sadness and to thinking of untoward things; well-tempered blood disposes to joy."[2]

The medicine of spirits substitutes for this vague idea of "disposition" the rigor of a physical, mechanical transmission of movements. If the passions are possible only in a being which has a body, and a body not entirely subject to the light of its mind and to the immediate transparence of its will, this is true insofar as, in ourselves and without ourselves, and generally in spite of ourselves, the mind's movements obey a mechanical structure which is that of the movement of spirits. "Before the sight of the object of passion, the animal spirits were spread throughout the entire body in order to preserve all the parts in general; but at the presence of the new object, this entire economy is disrupted. The majority of spirits are impelled into the muscles of the arms, the legs, the face, and all the exterior parts of the body in order to afford it a disposition proper to the prevailing passion and to give it the countenance and movement necessary for the acquisition of the good or the escape from the evil which presents itself."[3] Passion thus disperses the spirits, which are disposed to passion: that is, under the effect of passion and in the presence of its object, the spirits circulate, disperse, and concentrate according to a spatial design which licenses the trace of the object in the brain and its image in the soul, thus forming in the body a kind of geometric figure of passion which is merely its expressive transposition; but which also constitutes passion's essential causal basis, for when all the spirits are grouped around this object of passion, or at least around its image, the mind in its turn can no longer ignore it and will consequently be subject to passion.

One more step, and the entire system becomes a unity in which body and soul communicate immediately in the symbolic values of common qualities. This is what happens in the medicine of solids and fluids, which dominates eighteenth-century practice. Tension and release, hardness and softness, rigidity and relaxation, congestion and dryness—these qualitative states characterize the soul as much as the body, and ultimately refer to a kind of indistinct and composite passional situation, one which imposes itself on the concatenation of ideas, on the course of feelings, on the state of fibers, on the circulation of fluids. The theme of causality here appears as too discursive, the elements it groups too disjunct for its schemas to be applicable. Are the "active passions, such as anger, joy, lust," causes or consequences "of the excessive strength, the excessive tension, and the excessive elasticity of the nervous fibers, and of the excessive activity of the nervous fluid"? Conversely, cannot the "inert passions, such as fear, depression, ennui, lack of appetite, the coldness that accompanies homesickness, bizarre appetites, stupidity, lack of memory" be as readily followed as they are preceded by "weakness of the brain marrow and of the nervous fibers distributed in the organs, by impoverishment and inertia of the fluids"?[4] Indeed, we must no longer try to situate passion in a causal succession, or halfway between the corporeal and the spiritual; passion indicates, at a new, deeper level, that the soul and the body are in a perpetual metaphorical relation in which qualities have no need to be communicated because they are already common to both; and in which phenomena of expression are not causes, quite simply because soul and body are always each other's immediate expression. Passion is no longer exactly at the geometrical center of the body-and-soul complex; it is, a little short of that, at the point where their opposition is not yet given, in that region where both their unity and their distinction are established.

But at this level, passion is no longer simply one of the causes—however powerful—of madness; rather it forms the basis for its very possibility. If it is true that there exists a realm, in the relations of soul and body, where cause and effect, determinism and expression still intersect in a web so dense that they actually form only one and the same movement which cannot be dissociated except after the fact; if it is true that prior to the violence of the body and the vivacity of the soul, prior to the softening of the fibers and the relaxation of the mind, there are qualitative, as yet unshared kinds of *a priori* which subsequently impose the same values on the organic and on the spiritual, then we see that there can be diseases such as madness which are from the start diseases of the body *and* of the soul, maladies in which the affection of the brain is of the same quality, of the same origin, of the same nature, finally, as the affection of the soul.

The possibility of madness is therefore implicit in the very phenomenon of passion.

It is true that long before the eighteenth century, and for a long series of centuries from which we have doubtless not emerged, passion and madness were kept in close relation to one another. But let us allow the classical period its originality. The moralists of the Greco-Latin tradition had found it just that madness be passion's chastisement; and to be more certain that this was the case, they chose to define passion as a temporary and attenuated madness. But classical thought could define a relation between passion and madness which was not on the order of a pious hope, a pedagogic threat, or a moral synthesis; it even broke with the tradition by inverting the terms of the concatenation; it based the chimeras of madness on the nature of passion; it saw that the *determinism of the passions* was nothing but a chance for madness to penetrate the world of reason; and that if the unquestioned union of body and soul manifested man's finitude in passion, it laid this same man open, at the same time, to the infinite movement that destroyed him.

Madness, then, was not merely one of the possibilities afforded by the union of soul and body; it was not just one of the consequences of passion. Instituted by the unity of soul and body, madness turned against that unity and once again put it in question. Madness, made possible by passion, threatened by a movement proper to itself what had made passion itself possible. Madness was one of those unities in which laws were compromised, perverted, distorted—thereby manifesting such unity as evident and established, but also as fragile and already doomed to destruction.

There comes a moment in the course of passion when laws are suspended as though of their own accord, when movement either abruptly stops, without collision or absorption of any kind of active force, or is propagated, the action ceasing only at the climax of the paroxysm. Whytt admits that an intense emotion can provoke madness exactly as impact can provoke movement, for the sole reason that emotion is both impact in the soul and agitation of the nervous fiber: "It is thus that sad narratives or those capable of moving the heart, a horrible and unexpected sight, great grief, rage, terror, and the other passions which make a great impression frequently occasion the most sudden and violent nervous symptoms." But—it is here that madness, strictly speaking, begins—it happens that this movement immediately cancels itself out by its own excess and abruptly provokes an immobility which may reach the point of death itself. As if in the mechanics of madness, repose were not necessarily a quiescent thing but could also be a movement in violent opposition to itself, a movement which under the effect of its own violence abruptly achieves contradiction and the impossibility of continuance. "It is not unheard of that the passions, being very violent, generate a kind of tetanus or catalepsy such that the person then resembles a statue more than a living being. Further, fear, affliction, joy, and shame carried to their excess have more than once been followed by sudden death."[5]

Conversely, it happens that movement, passing from soul to body and from body to soul, propagates itself indefinitely in a locus of anxiety certainly closer to that space where Malebranche placed souls than to that in which Descartes situated bodies. Imperceptible movements, often provoked by a slight external impact, accumulate, are amplified, and end by exploding in violent convulsions. Giovanni Maria Lancisi had already explained that the noble Romans were often subject to the vapors—hysterical attacks, hypochondriacal fits—because in their court life "their minds, continually agitated between fear and hope, never knew a moment's repose." According to many physicians, city life, the life of the court, of the salons, led to madness by this multiplicity of excitations constantly accumulated, prolonged, and echoed without ever being attenuated. But there is in this image, in its more intense forms, and in the events constituting its organic version, a certain force which, increasing, can lead to delirium, as if movement, instead of losing its strength in communicating itself, could involve other forces in its wake, and from them derive an additional vigor. This was how Sauvages explained the origin of madness: a certain impression of fear is linked to the congestion or the pressure of a certain medullary fiber; this fear is limited to an object, as this congestion is strictly localized. In proportion as this fear persists, the soul grants it more attention, increasingly isolating and detaching it from all else. But such isolation reinforces the fear, and the soul, having accorded it too special a condition, gradually tends to attach to it a whole series of more or less remote ideas: "It joins to this simple idea all those which are likely to nourish and augment it. For example, a man who supposes in his sleep that he is being accused of a crime, immediately associates this idea with that of its satellites—judges, executioners, the gibbet." And from being thus burdened with all these new elements, involving them in its course, the idea assumes a kind of additional power which ultimately renders it irresistible even to the most concerted efforts of the will.

Madness, which finds its first possibility in the phenomenon of passion, and in the deployment of that double causality which, starting from passion itself, radiates both toward the body and toward the soul, is at the same time suspension of passion, breach of causality, dissolution of the elements of this unity. Madness participates both in the necessity of passion and in the anarchy of what, released by this very passion, transcends it and ultimately contests all it implies. Madness ends by being a movement of the nerves and muscles so violent that nothing in the course of images, ideas, or wills seems to correspond to it: this is the case of mania when it is suddenly intensified into convulsions, or when it degenerates into continuous frenzy. Conversely, madness can, in the body's repose or inertia, generate and then maintain an agitation of the soul, without pause or pacification, as is the case in melancholia, where external objects do not produce the same impression on the sufferer's mind as on that of a healthy man; "his impressions are weak and he rarely pays attention to them; his mind is almost totally absorbed by the vivacity of certain ideas."[6]

Indeed this dissociation between the external movements of the body and the course of ideas does not mean that the unity of body and soul is necessarily dissolved, nor that each recovers its autonomy in madness. Doubtless the unity is compromised in its rigor and in its totality; but it is fissured, it turns out, along lines which do not abolish it, but divide it into arbitrary sectors. For when melancholia fixes upon an aberrant idea, it is not only the soul which is involved; it is the soul with the brain, the soul with the nerves, their origin and their fibers: a whole segment of the unity of soul and body is thus detached from the aggregate and especially from the organs by which reality is perceived. The same thing occurs in convulsions and agitation: the soul is not excluded from the body, but is swept along so rapidly by it that it cannot retain all its conceptions; it is separated from its memories, its intentions, its firmest ideas, and thus isolated from itself and from all that remains stable in the body, it surrenders itself to the most mobile fibers; nothing in its behavior is henceforth adapted to reality, to truth, or to prudence; though the fibers in their vibration may imitate what is happening in the perceptions, the sufferer cannot tell the difference: "The rapid and chaotic pulsations of the arteries, or whatever other derangement occurs, imprints this same movement on the fibers (as in perception); they will represent as present objects which are not so, as true those which are chimerical."[7]

In madness, the totality of soul and body is parceled out: not according to the elements which constitute that totality metaphysically; but according to figures, images which envelop segments of the body and ideas of the soul in a kind of absurd unity. Fragments which isolate man from himself, but above all from reality; fragments which, by detaching themselves, have formed the unreal unity of a hallucination, and by very virtue of this autonomy impose it upon truth. "Madness is no more than the derangement of the imagination."[8] In other words, beginning with passion, madness is still only an intense movement in the rational unity of soul and body; this is the level of *unreason;* but this intense movement quickly escapes the reason of the mechanism and becomes, in its violences, its stupors, its senseless propagations, an *irrational* movement; and it is then that, escaping truth and its constraints, the Unreal appears.

And thereby we find the suggestion of the third cycle we must now trace: that of chimeras, of hallucinations, and of error—the cycle of non-being.

Let us listen to what is said in these fantastic fragments. Imagination is not madness. Even if in the arbitrariness of hallucination, alienation finds the first access to its vain liberty, madness begins only beyond this point, when the mind binds itself to this arbitrariness and becomes a prisoner of this apparent liberty. At the moment he wakes from a dream, a man can indeed observe: "I am imagining that I am dead": he thereby denounces and measures the arbitrariness of the imagination—he is not mad. He is mad when he posits as an affirmation of his death—when he suggests as having some value as truth—the still-neutral content of the image "I am dead." And just as the consciousness of truth is not carried away by the mere presence of the image, but in the act which limits, confronts, unifies, or dissociates the image, so madness will begin only in the act which gives the value of truth to the image. There is an original innocence of the imagination: "The imagination itself does not err, since it neither denies nor affirms but is fixed to so great a degree on the simple contemplation of an image";[9] and only the mind can turn what is given in the image into abusive truth, in other words, into error, or acknowledged error, that is, into truth: "A drunk man thinks he sees two candles where there is but one; a man who has a strabismus and whose mind is cultivated immediately acknowledges his error and accustoms himself to see but one."[10] Madness is thus beyond imagination, and yet it is profoundly rooted in it; for it consists merely in allowing the image a spontaneous value, total and absolute truth. The act of the reasonable man who, rightly or wrongly, judges an image to be true or false, is beyond this image, transcends and measures it by what is not itself; the act of the madman never oversteps the image presented, but surrenders to its immediacy, and affirms it only insofar is it is enveloped by it: "Many persons, not to say all, succumb to madness only from being too concerned about an object."[11] Inside the image, confiscated by it, and incapable of escaping from it, madness is nonetheless more than imagination, forming an act of undetermined content.

What is this act? An act of faith, an act of affirmation and of negation—a discourse which sustains and at the same time erodes the image, undermines it, distends it in the course of a reasoning, and organizes it around a segment of language. The man who imagines he is made of glass is not mad, for any sleeper can have this image in a dream; but he is mad if, believing he is made of glass, he thereby concludes that he is fragile, that he is in danger of breaking, that he must touch no object which might be too resistant, that he must in fact remain motionless, and so on. Such reasonings are those of a madman; but again we must note that in themselves they are neither absurd nor illogical. On the contrary, they apply correctly the most rigorous figures of logic. And Paul Zacchias has no difficulty finding them, in all their rigor, among the insane. Syllogism, in a man letting himself starve to death: "The dead do not eat; I am dead; hence I do not eat." Induction extended to infinity, in a man suffering from persecution delusions: "A, B, and C are my enemies; all of them are men; therefore all men are my enemies." Enthymeme, in another sufferer: "Most of those who have lived in this house are dead, hence I, who have lived in this house, am dead." The marvelous logic of the mad which seems to mock that of the logicians because it resembles it so exactly, or rather because it is exactly the same, and because at the secret heart of madness, at the core of so many errors, so many absurdities, so many words and gestures without consequence, we discover, finally, the hidden perfection of a language. "From these things," Zacchias concludes, "you truly see how best to discuss the intellect." The ultimate language of madness is that of reason, but the language of reason enveloped in the prestige of the image, limited to the locus of appearance which the image defines. It forms, outside the totality of images and the universality of discourse, an abusive, singular organization whose insistent quality constitutes madness. Madness, then, is not altogether in the image, which of itself is neither true nor false, neither reasonable nor mad; nor is it, further, in the reasoning which is mere form, revealing nothing but the indubitable figures of logic. And yet madness is in one and in the other: in a special version or figure of their relationship.

Let us consider an example borrowed from Diemerbroek. A man was suffering from a profound melancholia. As with all melancholics, his mind was attached to a fixed idea, and this idea was for him the occasion of a constantly renewed sadness. He accused himself of having killed his

son, and in the excess of his remorse, declared that God, for
his punishment, had assigned a demon to tempt him, like
the demon which had tempted the Lord. This demon he
saw, spoke to, heard, and answered. He did not understand
why those around him refused to acknowledge such a presence. Such then is madness: this remorse, this belief, this
hallucination, these speeches; in short, this complex of con-
victions and images which constitutes a delirium. Now
Diemerbroek tries to find out what are the "causes" of this
madness, how it can have originated. And this is what he
learns: this man had taken his son bathing and the boy had
drowned. Hence the father considered himself responsible
for his son's death. We can therefore reconstitute in the
following manner the development of this madness: judging himself guilty, the man decides that homicide is execra-
ble in the sight of God on High; whence it occurs to his
imagination that he is eternally damned; and since he
knows that the chief torment of damnation consists in being delivered into Satan's hands, he tells himself "that a
horrible demon is assigned to him." This demon he does
not as yet see, but since "he does not cease thinking of it,"
and "regards this notion as necessarily true," he imposes on
his brain a certain image of this demon; this image is presented to his soul by the action of the brain and of the
spirits with such insistence that he believes he continually
sees the demon itself."[12]

Hence madness, as analyzed by Diemerbroek, has two
levels; one is manifest to all eyes: an unwarranted melancholia in a man who wrongly accuses himself of having
killed his son; a depraved imagination which pictures de-
mons; a dismantled reason which converses with a phan-
tom. But at a deeper level, we find a rigorous organization
dependent on the faultless armature of a discourse. This
discourse, in its logic, commands the firmest belief in itself,
it advances by judgments and reasonings which connect

together; it is a kind of reason in action. In short, under the chaotic and manifest delirium reigns the order of a secret delirium. In this second delirium, which is, in a sense, pure reason, reason delivered of all the external tinsel of dementia, is located the paradoxical truth of madness. And this in a double sense, since we find here both what makes madness true (irrefutable logic, perfectly organized discourse, faultless connection in the transparency of a virtual language) and what makes it truly madness (its own nature, the special style of all its manifestations, and the internal structure of delirium).

But still more profoundly, this delirious language is the ultimate truth of madness insofar as it is madness's organizing form, the determining principle of all its manifestations, whether of the body or of the soul. For if Diemerbroek's melancholic converses with his demon, it is because the demon's image has been profoundly impressed by the movement of spirits on the still-ductile substance of the brain. But in its turn, this organic figure is merely the other side of a preoccupation which has obsessed the patient's mind; it represents what might be called the sedimentation in the body of an infinitely repeated discourse apropos of the punishment God must reserve for sinners guilty of homicide. The body and the traces it conceals, the soul and the images it perceives, are here no more than stages in the syntax of delirious language.

And lest we be criticized for elaborating this entire analysis around a single observation from a single author (a privileged observation, since it concerns melancholic delirium), we shall also seek confirmation of the fundamental role of delirious discourse in the classical conception of madness in another author, of another period, and apropos of a very different disease. This is a case of "nymphomania" observed by Bienville. The imagination of a young girl, "Julie," had been inflamed by precocious reading and aroused by the remarks of a servant girl "initiated into the secrets of Venus, . . . a virtuous handmaiden in the mother's eyes" but "a dear and voluptuous stewardess of the daughter's pleasures." Yet Julie combats these—to her—new desires with all the impressions she has received in the course of her education; to the seductive language of novels, she opposes the lessons of religion and virtue; and despite the vivacity of her imagination, she does not succumb to disease so long as she possesses "the strength to reason thus with herself: it is neither lawful nor virtuous to obey so shameful a passion."[13] But the wicked remarks, the dangerous readings increase; at every moment, they render more intense the agitation of the weakening fibers; then the fundamental language by which she had hitherto resisted gradually gives way: "Nature alone had *spoken* hitherto; but soon illusion, chimera, and extravagance played their part; at length she acquired the unhappy strength to approve in herself this horrible maxim: nothing is so beautiful nor so sweet as to obey the desires of love." This fundamental discourse opens the gates of madness: the imagination is freed, the appetites continually increase, the fibers reach the final degree of irritation. Delirium, in its lapidary form of a moral principle, leads straight to the convulsions which can endanger life itself.

At the end of this last cycle which had begun with the liberty of the hallucination and which closes now with the rigor of delirious language, we can conclude:

1. *In madness, for the classical age, there exist two forms of delirium.* A special, symptomatic form, proper to some of the diseases of the mind and especially to melancholia; in this sense we can say that there are diseases with or without delirium. In any case, such delirium is always manifest; it forms an integral part of the signs of madness; it is immanent to madness's truth and constitutes only a sector of it. But there exists another delirium which is not always mani-

fest, which is not formulated by the sufferer himself in the course of the disease, but which cannot fail to exist in the eyes of anyone who, seeking to trace the disease from its origins, attempts to formulate its riddle and its truth.

2. *This implicit delirium exists in all the alterations of the mind,* even where we would expect it least. In cases of no more than silent gestures, wordless violence, oddities of conduct, classical thought has no doubt that madness is continually subjacent, relating each of these particular signs to the general essence of madness. James's *Dictionary* expressly urges us to consider as delirious "the sufferers who sin by fault or excess in any of various voluntary actions, in a manner contrary to reason and to propriety; as when they use their hand, for example, to tear out tufts of wool or in an action similar to that which serves to catch flies; or when a patient acts against his custom and without cause, or when he speaks too much or too little against his normal habits; if he abounds in obscene remarks, being, when in health, of measured speech and decent in his discourse, and if he utters words that have no consequence, if he breathes more faintly than he must, or uncovers his private parts in the presence of those who are near him. We also regard as being in a state of delirium those whose minds are affected by some derangement in the organs of sense, or who use them in a fashion not customary to them, as when, for example, a sufferer is deprived of some voluntary action or acts inhabitually."[14]

3. *Thus understood, discourse covers the entire range of madness.* Madness, in the classical sense, does not designate so much a specific change in the mind or in the body, as the existence, under the body's alterations, under the oddity of conduct and conversation, of *a delirious discourse.* The simplest and most general definition we can give of classical madness is indeed *delirium:* "This word is derived from *lira,* a furrow; so that *deliro* actually means to

move out of the furrow, away from the proper path of reason."[15] Hence it is not surprising to find the eighteenth-century nosographers often classifying vertigo as a madness, and more rarely hysterical convulsions; this is because it is often impossible to find in hysterical convulsions the unity of a language, while vertigo affords the delirious affirmation that the world is really "turning around." Such delirium is a necessary and sufficient reason for a disease to be called madness.

4. *Language is the first and last structure of madness*, its constituent form; on language are based all the cycles in which madness articulates its nature. That the essence of madness can be ultimately defined in the simple structure of a discourse does not reduce it to a purely psychological nature, but gives it a hold over the totality of soul and body; such discourse is both the silent language by which the mind speaks to itself in the truth proper to it, and the visible articulation in the movements of the body. Parallelisms, complements, all the forms of immediate communication which we have seen manifested, in madness are suspended between soul and body in this single language and in its powers. The movement of passion which persists until it breaks and turns against itself, the sudden appearance of the image, and the agitations of the body which were its visible concomitants—all this, even as we were trying to reconstruct it, was already secretly animated by this language. If the determinism of passion is transcended and released in the hallucination of the image, if the image, in return, has swept away the whole world of beliefs and desires, it is because the delirious language was already present—a discourse which liberated passion from all its limits, and adhered with all the constraining weight of its affirmation to the image which was liberating itself.

It is in this delirium, which is of both body and soul, of both language and image, of both grammar and physiology, that all the cycles of madness conclude and begin. It is this delirium whose rigorous meaning organized them from the start. It is madness itself, and also, beyond each of its phenomena, its silent transcendence, which constitute the truth of madness.

A last question remains: In the name of what can this fundamental language be regarded as a delirium? Granting that it is the *truth of madness*, what makes it *true madness* and the originating form of insanity? Why should it be in this discourse, whose forms we have seen to be so faithful to the rules of reason, that we find all those signs which will most manifestly declare the very absence of reason?

A central question, but one to which the classical age has not formulated a direct answer. We must approach it obliquely, interrogating the experiences which are to be found in the immediate neighborhood of this essential language of madness: that is, the dream and the delusion.

The quasi-oneiric character of madness is one of the constant themes in the classical period. A theme which doubtless derives from a very old tradition, to which André du Laurens, at the end of the sixteenth century, still testifies; for him melancholia and dreams have the same origin and bear, in relation to truth, the same value. There are "natural dreams" which represent what, during the preceding day, has passed through the senses or the understanding but happens to be modified by the specific temperament of the subject. In the same way, there is a melancholia which has a merely physical origin in the disposition of the sufferer and alters, for his mind, the importance, the value, and so to speak the coloration of real events. But there is also a melancholia which permits the sufferer to predict the future, to speak in an unknown language, to see beings ordinarily invisible; this melancholia originates in a supernatural intervention, the same which brings to the sleeper's mind those dreams which foresee the future, announce events to come, and cause him to see "strange things."

But in fact the seventeenth century preserves this tradition of the resemblance between madness and dreams only to break it all the more completely and to generate new, more essential relations. Relations in which madness and dreams are not only understood in their remote origin or in their imminent value as signs, but are confronted as phenomena, in their development, in their very nature.

Dreams and madness then appeared to be of the same substance. Their mechanism was the same; thus Zacchias could identify in sleepwalking the movements which cause dreams, but which in a waking state can also provoke madness.

In the first moments when one falls asleep, the vapors which rise in the body and ascend to the head are many, turbulent, and dense. They are so dark that they waken no image in the brain; they merely agitate, in their chaotic dance, the nerves and the muscles. The same is true in the frenzied, in maniacs: they suffer few hallucinations, no false beliefs, but an intense agitation which they cannot manage to control. Let us continue the evolution of sleep: after the first period of turbulence, the vapors which rise to the brain are clarified, their movement organized; this is the moment when fantastic dreams are born; one sees miracles, a thousand impossible things. To this stage corresponds that of dementia, in which one is convinced of many things "which are not in real life." Then at last the agitation of the vapors is calmed altogether; the sleeper begins to see things still more clearly; in the transparency of the henceforth limpid vapors, recollections of the day before reappear in accordance with reality; such images are at most transposed, on one point or another—as occurs in melancholics, who recognize all things as they are, "in particular those who are not merely distracted." Between the gradual developments of sleep—with what they contribute at each stage to the quality of the imagination—and the forms of madness, the analogy is constant, because the mechanisms are the same: the same movement of vapors and spirits, the same liberation of images, the same correspondence between the physical qualities of phenomena and the psychological or moral values of sentiments. "To emerge from the insane no differently than from the sleeping."[16]

The important thing, in Zacchias's analysis, is that madness is not associated with dreams in their positive phenomena, but rather to the totality formed by sleep and dreams together: that is, to a complex which includes—besides the image—hallucination, memory, or prediction, the great void of sleep, the night of the senses, and all that negativity which wrests man from the waking state and its apparent truths. Whereas tradition compared the delirium of the madman to the vivacity of the dream images, the classical period identified delirium only with the complex of the image and the night of the mind, against which background it assumed its liberty. And this complex, transposed entire into the clarity of the waking state, constituted madness. This is how we must understand the definitions of madness which insistently recur throughout the classical period. The dream, as a complex figure of image and sleep, is almost always present in that definition. Either in a negative fashion—the notion of the waking state then being the only one that distinguishes madmen from sleepers; or in a positive fashion, delirium being defined as a modality of the dream, with the waking state as the specific difference: "Delirium is the dream of waking persons."[17] The ancients' notion of the dream as a transitory form of madness is inverted; it is no longer the dream which borrows its disturbing powers from alienation—showing thereby how fragile or limited reason is; it is madness which takes its original nature from the dream and reveals in this kinship that it is a liberation of the image in the dark night of reality.

The dream deceives; it leads to confusions; it is illusory. But it is not erroneous. And that is why madness is not exhausted in the waking modality of the dream, and why it overflows into error. It is true that in the dream, the imagination forges "impossible things and miracles," or that it assembles lifelike figures "by an irrational method"; but, Zacchias remarks, "there is no error in these things, and consequently nothing insane." Madness occurs when the images, which are so close to the dream, receive the affirmation or negation that constitutes error. It is in this sense that the *Encyclopédie* proposed its famous definition of madness: to depart from reason "with confidence and in the firm conviction that one is following it—that, it seems to me, is what is called being *mad*." Error is the other element always present with the dream, in the classical definition of insanity. The madman, in the seventeenth and eighteenth centuries, is not so much the victim of an illusion, of a hallucination of his senses, or of a movement of his mind. He is not *abused;* he *deceives himself.* If it is true that on one hand the madman's mind is led on by the oneiric arbitrariness of images, on the other, and at the same time, he imprisons himself in the circle of an erroneous consciousness: "We call madmen," Sauvages was to say, "those who are actually deprived of reason or who persist in some notable error; it is this *constant error* of the soul manifest in its imagination, in its judgments, and in its desires, which constitutes the characteristic of this category."

Madness begins where the relation of man to truth is disturbed and darkened. It is in this relation, at the same time as in the destruction of this relation, that madness assumes its general meaning and its particular forms. Dementia, Zacchias says, using the term here in the most general sense of madness, "lay in this, that the intellect did not distinguish true from false." But this breakdown, if we can understand it only as negation, has positive structures which give it singular forms. According to the different forms of access to the truth, there will be different types of madness. It is in this sense that Chrichton, for example, distinguishes in the order of vesanias, first the class *deliria*, which alter that relation to the truth which takes shape in *perception* ("general delirium of the mental faculties, in which the diseased perceptions are taken for realities"); then the class *hallucinations*, which alter *representation* ("error of the mind in which imaginary objects are taken for realities, or else real objects are falsely represented"); and last, the class *dementias*, which without abolishing or altering the faculties that afford access to truth, weaken them and diminish their powers.

But we can also analyze madness starting with truth itself and with the forms proper to it. It is in this manner that the *Encyclopédie* distinguishes "physical truth" from "moral truth." "Physical truth consists in the accurate relation of our sensations with physical objects"; there will be a form of madness determined by the impossibility of acceding to this form of truth; a kind of madness of the physical world which includes illusions, hallucinations, all perceptual disturbances; "it is a madness to hear choirs of angels, as certain enthusiasts do." "Moral truth," on the other hand, "consists in the exactitude of the relations we discern either between moral objects, or between those objects and ourselves." There will be a form of madness consisting of the loss of these relations; such is the madness of character, of conduct, and of the passions. "Veritable madnesses, then, are all the derangements of our mind, all the illusions of self-love, and all our passions when they are carried to the point of blindness; for blindness is the distinctive characteristic of madness."[18]

Blindness: one of the words which comes closest to the

essence of classical madness. It refers to that night of quasi-sleep which surrounds the images of madness, giving them, in their solitude, an invisible sovereignty; but it refers also to ill-founded beliefs, mistaken judgments, to that whole background of errors inseparable from madness. The fundamental discourse of delirium, in its constitutive powers, thus reveals to what extent, despite analogies of form, despite the rigor of its meaning, it was not a discourse of reason. It spoke, but in the night of blindness; it was more than the loose and disordered text of a dream, since it *deceived* itself; but it was more than an erroneous proposition, since it was plunged into that total *obscurity* which is that of sleep. Delirium, as the principle of madness, is a system of false propositions in the general syntax of the dream.

Madness is precisely at the point of contact between the oneiric and the erroneous; it traverses, in its variations, the surface on which they meet, the surface which both joins and separates them. With error, madness shares non-truth, and arbitrariness in affirmation or negation; from the dream, madness borrows the flow of images and the colorful presence of hallucinations. But while error is merely non-truth, while the dream neither affirms nor judges, madness fills the void of error with images, and links hallucinations by affirmation of the false. In a sense, it is thus plenitude, joining to the figures of night the powers of day, to the forms of fantasy the activity of the waking mind; it links the dark content with the forms of light. But is not such plenitude actually *the culmination of the void?* The presence of images offers no more than night-ringed hallucinations, figures inscribed at the corners of sleep, hence detached from any sensuous reality; however vivid they are, however rigorously established in the body, these images are nothingness, since they represent nothing; as for erroneous judgment, it judges only in appearance: affirming nothing true or real, it does not affirm at all; it is ensnared in the non-being of error.

Joining vision and blindness, image and judgment, hallucination and language, sleep and waking, day and night, madness is ultimately nothing, for it unites in them all that is negative. But the paradox of this *nothing* is to *manifest* itself, to explode in signs, in words, in gestures. Inextricable unity of order and disorder, of the reasonable being of things and this nothingness of madness! For madness, if it is nothing, can manifest itself only by departing from itself, by assuming an appearance in the order of reason and thus becoming the contrary of itself. Which illuminates the paradoxes of the classical experience: madness is always absent, in a perpetual retreat where it is inaccessible, without phenomenal or positive character; and yet it is present and perfectly visible in the singular evidence of the madman. Meaningless disorder as madness is, it reveals, when we examine it, only ordered classifications, rigorous mechanisms in soul and body, language articulated according to a visible logic. All that madness can say of itself is merely reason, though it is itself the negation of reason. In short, *a rational hold over madness is always possible and necessary, to the very degree that madness is non-reason.*

There is only one word which summarizes this experience, *Unreason:* all that, for reason, is closest and most remote, emptiest and most complete; all that presents itself to reason in familiar structures—authorizing a knowledge, and then a science, which seeks to be positive—and all that is constantly in retreat from reason, in the inaccessible domain of nothingness.

And if, now, we try to assign a value, in and of itself, outside its relations with the dream and with error, to classical unreason, we must understand it not as reason diseased, or as reason lost or alienated, but quite simply as *reason dazzled.*

Dazzlement is night in broad daylight, the darkness that rules at the very heart of what is excessive in light's radiance. Dazzled reason opens its eyes upon the sun and sees *nothing,* that is, *does not see;* in dazzlement, the recession of objects toward the depths of night has as an immediate correlative the suppression of vision itself; at the moment when it sees objects disappear into the secret night of light, sight sees itself in the moment of its disappearance.

To say that madness is dazzlement is to say that the madman sees the daylight, the same daylight as the man of reason (both live in the same brightness); but seeing this same daylight, and nothing but this daylight and nothing in it, he sees it as void, as night, as nothing; for him the shadows are the way to perceive daylight. Which means that, seeing the night and the nothingness of the night, he does not see at all. And believing he sees, he admits as realities the hallucinations of his imagination and all the multitudinous population of night. That is why delirium and dazzlement are in a relation which constitutes the essence of madness, exactly as truth and light, in their fundamental relation, constitute classical reason.

In this sense, the Cartesian formula of doubt is certainly the great exorcism of madness. Descartes closes his eyes and plugs up his ears the better to see the true brightness of essential daylight; thus he is secured against the dazzlement of the madman who, opening his eyes, sees only night, and not seeing at all, believes he sees when he imagines. In the uniform lucidity of his closed senses, Descartes has broken with all possible fascination, and if he sees, he is certain of seeing that which he sees. While before the eyes of the madman, drunk on a light which is darkness, rise and multiply images incapable of criticizing themselves (since the madman *sees* them), but irreparably separated from being (since the madman sees *nothing*).

Unreason is in the same relation to reason as dazzlement to the brightness of daylight itself. And this is not a metaphor. We are at the center of the great cosmology which animates all classical culture. The "cosmos" of the Renaissance, so rich in internal communications and symbolisms, entirely dominated by the interacting presence of the stars, has now disappeared, without "nature" having yet assumed its status of universality, without its having received man's lyrical recognition, subjecting him to the rhythm of its seasons. What the classical thinkers retain of the "world," what they already anticipate in "nature," is an extremely abstract law, which nonetheless forms the most vivid and concrete opposition, that of *day and night*. This is no longer the fatal time of the planets, it is not yet the lyrical time of the seasons; it is the universal but absolutely divided time of brightness and darkness. A form which thought entirely masters in a mathematical science—Cartesian physics is a kind of mathesis of light—but which at the same time traces the great tragic caesura in human existence: one that dominates the theatrical time of Racine and the space of Georges de la Tour in the same imperious fashion. The circle of day and night is the law of the classical world: the most reduced but the most demanding of the world's necessities, the most inevitable but the simplest of nature's legalities.

A law which excludes all dialectic and all reconciliation; which establishes, consequently, both the flawless unity of knowledge and the uncompromising division of tragic existence; it rules over a world without twilight, which knows no effusion, nor the attenuated cares of lyricism; everything must be either waking or dream, truth or darkness, the light of being or the nothingness of shadow. Such a law prescribes an inevitable order, a serene division which makes truth possible and confirms it forever.

And yet on either side of this order, two symmetrical, inverse figures bear witness that there are extremities where it can be transgressed, showing at the same time to what degree it is essential not to transgress it. On one side, tragedy. The rule of the theatrical day has a positive content; it forces tragic duration to be poised upon the singular but universal alternation of day and night; the whole of the tragedy must be accomplished in this unity of time, for tragedy is ultimately nothing but the confrontation of two realms, linked to each other by time itself, in the irreconcilable. Every day, in Racine's theater, is overhung by a night, which it brings, so to speak, to light: the night of Troy and its massacres, the night of Nero's desires, Titus's Roman night, Athalie's night. These are the great stretches of night, realms of darkness which haunt the day without yielding an hour, and disappear only in the new night of death. And these fantastic nights, in their turn, are haunted by a light which forms a kind of infernal reflection of the day: the burning of Troy, the torches of the Praetorians, the pale light of the dream. In classical tragedy, day and night are arranged like a pair of mirrors, endlessly reflect each other, and afford that simple couple a sudden profundity which envelops in a single movement all of man's life and his death. In the same fashion, in De la Tour's *Madeleine au miroir*, light and shadow confront each other, divide and at the same time unite a face and its reflection, a skull and its image, a vigil and a silence; and in the *Image Saint-Alexis*, the page holding the torch reveals under the shadow of the vault the man who was his master—a grave and luminous boy encounters all of human misery; a child brings death to light.

On the other side, facing tragedy and its hieratic language, is the confused murmur of madness. Here, too, the great law of the division has been violated; shadow and light mingle in the fury of madness, as in the tragic disorder. But in another mode. In night, the tragic character found a somber truth of day; the night of Troy remained Andromache's truth, as Athalie's night presaged the truth of the already advancing day; night, paradoxically, *revealed*; it was *the profoundest day of being*. The madman, conversely, finds in daylight only the inconsistency of the night's figures; he lets the light be darkened by all the illusions of the dream; his day is only *the most superficial night of appearance*. It is to this degree that tragic man, more than any other, is engaged in being, is the bearer of his truth, since, like Phèdre, he flings in the face of the pitiless sun all the secrets of the night; while the madman is entirely excluded from being. And how could he not be, lending as he does the day's illusory reflection to the night's non-being?

We understand that the tragic hero—in contrast to the baroque character of the preceding period—can never be mad; and that conversely madness cannot bear within itself those values of tragedy, which we have known since Nietzsche and Artaud. In the classical period, the man of tragedy and the man of madness confront each other, without a possible dialogue, without a common language; for the former can utter only the decisive words of being, uniting in a flash the truth of light and the depth of darkness; the latter endlessly drones out the indifferent murmur which cancels out both the day's chatter and the lying dark.

Madness designates the equinox between the vanity of night's hallucinations and the non-being of light's judgments.

And this much, which the archaeology of knowledge has been able to teach us bit by bit, was already offered to us in a simple tragic fulguration, in the last words of *Andromaque*.

As if, at the moment when madness was vanishing from the tragic act, at the moment when tragic man was to separate himself for over two centuries from the man of unreason—as if, at this very moment, an ultimate figuration were demanded of madness. The curtain which falls on the last scene of *Andromaque* also falls on the last of the great tragic incarnations of madness. But in this presence on the threshold of its own disappearance, in this madness incarcerating itself for good, is articulated what it is and will be for the entire classical age. Is it not precisely at the moment of its disappearance that it can best present its truth, its truth of absence, its truth which is that of day at the limits of night? This had to be the *last* scene of the *first* great classical tragedy; or if one prefers, the *first* time in which the classical truth of madness is expressed in a tragic movement which is the *last* of the preclassical theater. A truth, in any case, that is instantaneous, since its appearance can only be its disappearance; the lightning-flash is seen only in the already advancing night.

Orestes, in his frenzy, passes through a triple circle of night: three concentric figurations of dazzlement. Day has just dawned over Pyrrhus's palace; night is still there, edging this light with shadow, and peremptorily indicating its limit. On this morning which is a festival morning, the crime has been committed, and Pyrrhus has closed his eyes on the dawning day: a fragment of shadow cast here on the steps of the altar, on the threshold of brightness and of darkness. The two great cosmic themes of madness are thus present in various forms, as omen, decor, and counterpoint of Orestes' frenzy.[19] It can then begin: in a pitiless clarity which denounces the murder of Pyrrhus and the treachery of Hermione, in that dawn where everything finally explodes in a truth so old and at the same time so young, a first circle of shadow: a dark cloud into which, all around Orestes, the world begins to withdraw; the truth appears in this paradoxical twilight, in this matinal night where the cruelty of truth will be transformed into the fury of hallucination:

> *Mais quelle épaisse nuit, tout à coup, m'environne?*
> (But what thick night suddenly surrounds me?)

It is the empty night of *error;* but against the background of this first obscurity, a brilliance, a false light will appear: that of images. The nightmare rises, not in the bright light of morning, but in a somber scintillation: the light of storm and of murder.

> *Dieux! quels ruisseaux de sang coulent autour de moi!*
> (O Gods! What streams of blood flow around me!)

And then appears the dynasty of the *dream.* In this night the hallucinations are set free; the Erinnyes appear and take over. What makes them precarious also makes them sovereign; they triumph easily in the solitude where they succeed one another; nothing challenges them; images and language intersect, in apostrophes which are invocations, presences affirmed and repulsed, solicited and feared. But all these images converge toward night, toward a second night which is that of punishment, of eternal vengeance, of death within death. The Erinnyes are recalled to that darkness which is their own—their birthplace and their truth, i.e., their own nothingness.

> *Venez-vous m'enlever dans l'éternelle nuit?*
> (Do you come to bear me off into eternal night?)

This is the moment when it is revealed that the images of madness are only dream and error, and if the sufferer who is blinded by them appeals to them, it is only to disappear with them in the annihilation to which they are fated.

A second time, then, we pass through a circle of night. But we are not thereby restored to the daylight reality of the world. We accede, beyond what is manifested in madness, to *delirium*, to that essential and constitutive structure which had secretly sustained madness from the first. This delirium has a name, Hermione; Hermione who no longer reappears as a hallucinatory vision, but as the ultimate truth of madness. It is significant that Hermione intervenes at this very moment of the frenzy: not among the Eumenides, nor ahead of them—to guide them; but behind and separated from them by the night into which they have dragged Orestes and in which they themselves are now scattered. Hermione intervenes as a figure of delirium, as the truth which secretly reigned from the start, and of which the Eumenides were ultimately only the servants. Here we are at the opposite of Greek tragedy, where the Erinnyes were the final destiny and truth which, in the night of time, had awaited the hero; his passion was merely their instrument. Here the Eumenides are merely figures in the service of delirium, the primary and ultimate truth, which was already appearing in passion, and now declares itself in its nakedness. This truth rules alone, thrusting images away:

> *Mais non, retirez-vous, laissez faire Hermione.*
> (But no, begone, let Hermione do her work.)

Hermione, who has always been present from the beginning, Hermione who has always lacerated Orestes, destroying his reason bit by bit, Hermione for whom he has become *"parricide, assassin, sacrilège,"* reveals herself finally as the truth and culmination of his madness. And delirium, in its rigor, no longer has anything to say except to articulate as imminent decision a truth long since commonplace and laughable:

> *Et je lui porte enfin mon coeur à dévorer.*
> (And I bring her at last my heart to devour.)

Days and years ago Orestes had offered up this savage sacrifice. But now he expresses this principle of his madness as an end. For madness cannot go any farther. Having uttered its truth in its essential delirium, it can do no more than collapse in a third night, that night from which there is no return, the night of an incessant devouring. Unreason can appear only for a moment, the instant when language enters silence, when delirium itself is stilled, when the heart is at last devoured.

In the tragedies of the early seventeenth century, madness, too, released drama; but it did so by liberating truth; madness still had access to language, to a renewed language of explanation and of reality reconquered. It could be at most only the penultimate moment of the tragedy. Not the last, as in *Andromaque*, in which no truth is uttered except the truth, in delirium, of a passion which has found with madness the perfection of its fulfillment.

The movement proper to unreason, which classical learning followed and pursued, had already accomplished the whole of its trajectory in the concision of tragic language. After which, silence could reign, and madness disappear in the—always withdrawn—presence of unreason.

What we now know of unreason affords us a better understanding of what confinement was.

This gesture, which banished madness to a neutral and uniform world of exclusion, did not mark a halt in the evolution of medical techniques, nor in the progress of humanitarian ideas. It assumed its precise meaning in this fact: that madness in the classical period ceased to be the sign of another world, and that it became the paradoxical manifestation of non-being. Ultimately, confinement did seek to suppress madness, to eliminate from the social order a figure which did not find its place within it; the essence of confinement was not the exorcism of a danger. Confinement merely manifested what madness, in its essence, was: a manifestation of non-being; and by providing this manifestation, confinement thereby suppressed it, since it restored it to its truth as nothingness. Confinement is the practice which corresponds most exactly to madness experienced as unreason, that is, as the empty negativity of reason; by confinement, madness is acknowledged to be *nothing*. That is, on one hand madness is immediately perceived as difference: whence the forms of spontaneous and collective judgment sought, not from physicians, but from men of good sense, to determine the confinement of a madman; and on the other hand, confinement cannot have any other goal than a correction (that is, the suppression of the difference, or the fulfillment of this nothingness in death); whence those options for death so often to be found in the registers of confinement, written by the attendants, and which are not the sign of confinement's savagery, its inhumanity or perversion, but the strict expression of its meaning: an operation to annihilate nothingness.[20] Confinement sketches, on the surface of phenomena and in a hasty moral synthesis, the secret and distinct structure of madness.

Then did confinement establish its practices in this profound intuition? Was it because madness under the effect of confinement had really vanished from the classical horizon that it was ultimately stigmatized as non-being? Questions whose answers refer to each other in a perfect circularity. It is futile, no doubt, to lose oneself in the endless cycle of these forms of interrogation. Better to let classical culture formulate, in its general structure, the experience it had of madness, an experience which crops up with the same meanings, in the identical order of its inner logic, in both the order of speculation and the order of institutions, in both discourse and decree, in both word and watchword—wherever, in fact, a signifying element can assume for us the value of a language.

V

ASPECTS OF MADNESS

In this chapter we do not wish to write a history of the different notions of psychiatry in the seventeenth and eighteenth centuries, but rather to show the specific faces by which madness was recognized in classical thought. Faces still haunted by mythical figures, but which have often been essential in the organization of our practical knowledge.

I. *Mania and Melancholia*

The notion of melancholia was fixed, in the sixteenth century, between a certain definition by symptoms and an explanatory principle concealed in the very term that designated it. Among the symptoms, we find all the delirious ideas an individual can form about himself: "Some think themselves to be beasts, whose voice and actions they imitate. Some think that they are vessels of glass, and for this reason recoil from passers-by, lest they break; others fear death, which they yet cause most often to themselves. Still others imagine that they are guilty of some crime, so that they tremble with terror when they see another coming toward them, thinking he seeks to take them prisoner and sentence them to death."[1] Delirious themes that remain isolated and do not compromise reason's totality. Thomas Sydenham would even observe that melancholics "are people who, apart from their complaint, are prudent and sensible, and who have an extraordinary penetration and sagacity. Thus Aristotle rightly observed that melancholics have more intelligence than other men."

Now this clear and coherent syndrome was designated by a word that implied an entire causal system, that of melancholia: "I beg you to regard closely the thoughts of melancholics, their words, visions, actions, and you will discover how all their senses are depraved by a melancholic humor spread through their brain."[2] Partial delirium and the action of black bile were juxtaposed in the notion of melancholia, unrelated for the moment beyond a disjunct confrontation of a group of signs by a signifying name. Yet in the eighteenth century a unity would be found, or rather an exchange would be made—the nature of that cold, black humor having become the major coloration of delirium, its positive value in contrast to mania, dementia, and frenzy, its essential principle of cohesion. And while Hermann Boerhaave still defined melancholia as merely "a long, persistent delirium without fever, during which the sufferer is obsessed by only one thought," Dufour, several years later, shifted the weight of his definition to "fear and sadness," which were now supposed to explain the partial character of the delirium: "Hence it is that melancholics love solitude and shun company; this makes them more attached to the object of their delirium or to their dominant passion, whatever it may be, while they seem indifferent to anything else." The concept is fixed not by a new rigor in observation, nor by a discovery in the realm of causes, but by a qualitative transmission proceeding from a cause implied in the designation to a significant perception in the effects.

For a long time—until the beginning of the seventeenth century—the discussion of melancholia remained fixed within the tradition of the four humors and their essential qualities: stable qualities actually inherent in a substance, which alone could be considered as their cause. For Jean Fernel, the melancholic humor, related to earth and to autumn, is a juice "thick in consistency, cold and dry in temperament." But in the first half of the century, a debate began over the origin of melancholia: must one necessarily have a melancholic temperament to be afflicted with melancholia? Is the melancholic humor always cold and dry—is it never warm, or humid? Is it the substance which acts, or the qualities which are transmitted? The results of this long debate may be summarized as follows:

1. The causality of *substances* is increasingly replaced by a movement of *qualities*, which, without any vehicular means, are *immediately* transmitted from body to soul, from humor to ideas, from organs to conduct. Thus, for Duncan's Apologist the best proof that the melancholic juice produces melancholia is that in it one finds the very qualities of the disease: "The melancholic juice possesses to a far greater degree the conditions necessary to produce melancholia than your fiery angers; since by its coldness, it diminishes the quantity of spirits; by its dryness, it renders them capable of preserving for a long time the type of a strong and persistent imagination; and by its blackness, it deprives them of their natural clarity and subtlety."[3]

2. There is, besides this mechanics of qualities, a dynamics that analyzes the strength to be found imprisoned in each. Thus cold and dryness can enter into conflict with the temperament, and this opposition will generate symptoms of melancholia violent in proportion to the struggle:

the strength that prevails and sweeps away all that resists it. Thus women, whose nature is little inclined to melancholy, fall a prey to it all the more seriously: "They are cruelly used and violently disturbed by it, for melancholia being more opposed to their temperament, it removes them further from their natural constitution."[4]

3. But it is sometimes within the quality itself that the conflict is generated. A quality may alter in the course of its development and become the opposite of what it was. Thus when "the entrails are heated, when all simmers within the body . . . and all the juices are consumed," then this conflagration can turn to cold melancholia—producing "almost the same thing caused by the flow of wax in a torch turned upside down. . . . This cooling of the body is the ordinary effect which follows immoderate heat once it has thrown off and exhausted its vigor."[5] There is a kind of dialectic of qualities which, free from any constraint of substance, from any predetermination, makes its way through reversals and contradictions.

4. Finally, qualities may be altered by accidents, circumstances, the conditions of life; so that a being who is dry and cold can become warm and humid, if his way of life inclines him to it; as in the case of women: they "remain in idleness, their bodies tend to perspire less [than those of men], and heat, spirits, and humors remain within."[6]

Thus freed from a confining substantial basis, qualities would be able to play an organizing and integrating role in the notion of melancholia. On the one hand, they would trace, among the symptoms and manifestations, a certain profile of sadness, of blackness, of slowness, of immobility. On the other, they would suggest a causal basis which would no longer be the physiology of a humor, but the pathology of an idea, of a fear, of a terror. The morbid entity was not *defined* from observed signs nor from supposed causes; but somewhere between, and beyond both, it was *perceived* as a certain qualitative coherence, which had its own laws of transmission, of development, and of transformation. It is the secret logic of this quality that controls the development of the idea of melancholia, not medical theory. This is evident as early as Thomas Willis's texts.

At first glance, the coherence of their analyses is vouched for on the level of speculative reflection. Willis's explanation is borrowed whole from animal spirits and their mechanical properties. Melancholia is "a madness without fever or frenzy, accompanied by fear and sadness." To the extent that it is delirium—that is, an essential break with truth—its origin resides in a disordered movement of the spirits and in a defective state of the brain; but can that fear, that anxiety which makes melancholics "sad and punctilious," be explained by movements alone? Might there be a mechanism of fear and a circulation of spirits that is peculiar to sadness? This is obvious to Descartes; it is no longer so for Willis. Melancholia cannot be treated like a paralysis, an apoplexy, a vertigo, or a convulsion. In fact, it cannot even be analyzed as a simple dementia, although melancholic delirium supposes a similar disorder in the movement of spirits; disturbances in the mechanism easily explain delirium—that error common to all madness, dementia or melancholia—but not the *quality* peculiar to delirium, the coloration of sadness and fear which makes its landscape so unique. One must penetrate the secret of predispositions. After all, it is these essential qualities, hidden in the very grain of the subtle matter, that explain the paradoxical movements of the spirits.

In melancholia, the spirits are swept by an agitation, but a feeble agitation, without power or violence: a sort of impotent jostling which does not follow marked paths, nor open roads (*aperta opercula*), but traverses the cerebral matter by endlessly creating new pores; yet the spirits do not wander far upon the paths they trace; very soon their agitation languishes, their strength fails, and the movement stops: "they do not reach far."[7] Thus such disturbance, common to all delirium, can produce on the surface of the body neither those violent movements nor those cries that may be observed in mania and frenzy; melancholia never reaches violence; it is madness at the limits of its powerlessness. This paradox is the result of the secret alterations of the spirits. Usually they have the quasi-immediate rapidity and the absolute transparence of luminous rays; but in melancholia, they are charged with darkness; they become "obscure, opaque, shadowy"; and the images of things which they bear to the brain and to the mind are veiled with "shadow and with shades." They become heavy and closer to a dark chemical vapor than to pure light. A chemical vapor that would be of an acid nature, rather than sulfurous or alcoholic: for in acid vapors the particles are mobile, and even incapable of rest, but their activity is weak, without effect; when they are distilled, nothing remains in the alembic but an insipid phlegm. Do not acid vapors have the very properties of melancholia, whereas alcoholic vapors, always ready to burst into flame, suggest frenzy; and sulfurous vapors, agitated by a violent and continuous movement, indicate mania? If, then, one were to seek "the formal reason and the causes" of melancholia, one would consider the vapors that rise from the blood to the brain and that have degenerated into an acid and corrosive vapor. In appearance, it is a melancholia of the spirits, a chemistry of the humors that oriented Willis's analysis; but in fact, the principal clue is afforded by the immediate qualities of melancholic suffering: an impotent disorder, and then that shadow over the mind, along with that acid bitterness which corrodes thought and feeling alike. The chemistry of acids is not the explanation of the symptoms; it is a qualitative option: a phenomenology of melancholic experience.

Some seventy years later, animal spirits lost their scientific prestige. Now it was from the body's liquid and solid elements that the secret of disease was sought. The *Medical Dictionary* which Robert James published in England in 1743 proposes, under *Mania*, a comparative etiology of that disease and of melancholia: "It is evident that the brain is the seat . . . of all diseases of this nature. . . . It is there that the Creator has fixed, although in a manner which is inconceivable, the lodging of the soul, the mind, genius, imagination, memory, and all sensations. . . . All these noble functions will be changed, depraved, diminished, and totally destroyed, if the blood and the humors corrupted in quality and quantity are no longer carried to the brain in a uniform and temperate manner, but instead circulate there with violence and impetuosity, or move about slowly, with difficulty or with languor." It is this languishing flow, these choked vessels, this heavy, clogged blood that the heart labors to distribute throughout the organism, and which has difficulty penetrating into the very fine arterioles of the brain, where the circulation ought to be very rapid in order to maintain the movement of thought—it is all this distressing obstruction which explains melancholia. Heaviness, encumbrance—here again the primitive qualities guide analysis. The explanation becomes a transfer to the organism of qualities perceived in the condition, the conduct, the words of the sick person. We move from qualitative apprehension to supposed explanation. But it is this apprehension that continues to prevail and always wins out over theoretical coherence. Anne-Charles Lorry juxtaposes the two main forms of medical explanation—by solids and by fluids—and ultimately causes them to intersect, thus distinguishing two kinds of melancholia. The one whose origin is in solids is nervous melancholia: a particularly strong sensation agitates the fibers which receive it; as a result, tension increases in the other fibers, which become more rigid and at the same time susceptible to further vibration. But should the sensation become even stronger, then the tension increases to such a degree in the other fibers that they become incapable of vibrating; the state of rigidity is such that the flow of blood is stopped and the animal spirits immobilized. Melancholia has set in. In the other form of disease, the "liquid form," the humors are impregnated with black bile; they become thicker; clogged with these humors, the blood thickens and stagnates in the meninges until it compresses the principal organs of the nervous system. Then we find again the rigidity of the fibers, but in this case it is no more than a consequence of a humoral phenomenon. Lorry distinguishes two melancholias: actually it is the same group of qualities, affording melancholia its real unity, that he employs successively in two explanatory systems. Only the theoretical edifice has been doubled. The qualitative basis in experience remains the same.

A symbolic unity formed by the languor of the fluids, by the darkening of the animal spirits and the shadowy twilight they spread over the images of things, by the viscosity of the blood that laboriously trickles through the vessels, by the thickening of vapors that have become blackish, deleterious, and acrid, by visceral functions that have become slow and somehow slimy—this unity, more a product of sensibility than of thought or theory, gives melancholia its characteristic stamp.

It is this undertaking, more than faithful observation, which reorganizes melancholia's symptoms and mode of appearance. The theme of a partial delirium increasingly disappears as a major symptom of melancholics in favor of qualitative data like sadness, bitterness, a preference for solitude, immobility. At the end of the eighteenth century, all forms of madness without delirium, but characterized by inertia, by despair, by a sort of dull stupor, would be readily classified as melancholia.[8] And as early as James's

Dictionary, an apoplectic melancholia is discussed, in which the sufferers "refuse to rise from their beds . . . ; once on their feet, they will not walk unless they are forced by their friends or attendants; they in no way avoid others, but they seem to pay no attention to what is said to them; they make no answer." If, in this case, immobility and silence prevail and determine the diagnosis of melancholia, there are cases in which one observes only bitterness, languor, and a preference for isolation; their very agitation must not deceive the observer nor authorize a hasty diagnosis of mania; these patients are definitely suffering from melancholia, for "they avoid company, prefer solitary places, and wander without knowing where they are going; they have a yellowish color, a dry tongue as in a person suffering from great thirst, and their eyes are dry, hollow, never moistened with tears; their entire body is dry and burning hot, their face dark, and expressing only horror and sadness."[9]

The analyses of mania and their evolution during the classical period obey the same principles of coherence.

Willis opposes mania to melancholia. The mind of the melancholic is entirely occupied by reflection, so that his imagination remains at leisure and in repose; the maniac's imagination, on the contrary, is occupied by a perpetual flux of impetuous thoughts. While the melancholic's mind is fixed on a single object, imposing unreasonable proportions upon it, but upon it alone, mania deforms all concepts and ideas; either they lose their congruence, or their representative value is falsified; in any case, the totality of thought is disturbed in its essential relation to truth. Melancholia, finally, is always accompanied by sadness and fear; on the contrary, in the maniac we find audacity and fury. Whether it is a question of mania or melancholia, the cause of the disease is always in the movement of the animal spirits. But this movement is quite particular in mania: it is continuous, violent, always capable of piercing new pores in the cerebral matter, and it creates, as the material basis of incoherent thoughts, explosive gestures, continuous words which betray mania. Is not such pernicious mobility that of an infernal water, sulfurous liquid, those *aquae stygiae, ex nitro, vitriolo, antimonio, arsenico, et similibus exstillatae:* its particles are in perpetual movement; they are capable of provoking new pores and new channels in any substance; and they have strength enough to spread themselves far, exactly as the maniacal spirits are capable of spreading agitation through all the parts of the body. An infernal water gathers in the secrecy of its movements all the images in which mania takes its concrete form. It constitutes, in an indissociable way, both its chemical myth and its dynamic truth.

In the course of the eighteenth century, the image, with all its mechanical and metaphysical implications, of animal spirits in the channels of the nerves, was frequently replaced by the image, more strictly physical but of an even more symbolic value, of a tension to which nerves, vessels, and the entire system of organic fibers were subject. Mania was thus a tension of the fibers carried to its paroxysm, the maniac a sort of instrument whose strings, by the effect of an exaggerated traction, began to vibrate at the remotest and faintest stimulus. Maniacal delirium consisted of a continual vibration of the sensibility. Through this image, the differences from melancholia became precise and were organized into a rigorous antithesis: the melancholic can no longer enter into a resonance with the external world, because his fibers are relaxed or because they have been immobilized by too great a tension (we see how the mechanics of tension explains melancholic immobility as well as maniacal agitation): only a few fibers vibrate in the melancholic, those which correspond to the precise point of his delirium. On the contrary, the maniac vibrates to any and every stimulus; his delirium is universal; stimuli do not vanish into the density of his immobility, as in the melancholic's case; when his organism returns them, they have been multiplied, as if the maniac had accumulated a supplementary energy in the tension of his fibers. It is this very fact, moreover, that makes the maniac, in his turn, insensible, not with the somnolent insensibility of the melancholic, but with an insensibility taut with interior vibrations; this is doubtless why maniacs "fear neither heat nor cold, tear off their clothes, sleep naked in the dead of winter without feeling the cold." It is also why they substitute for the real world, which nonetheless continues to solicit them, the unreal and chimerical world of their delirium: "The essential symptoms of mania result from the fact that objects do not present themselves to the sufferers as they are in reality."[10] The delirium of maniacs is not determined by a particular error of judgment; it constitutes a defect in the transmission of sense impressions to the brain, a flaw in communication. In the psychology of madness, the old idea of truth as "the conformity of thought to things" is transposed in the metaphor of a resonance, a kind of musical fidelity of the fibers to the sensations which make them vibrate.

This theme of manic tension develops, beyond a medicine of solids, into intuitions that are still more qualitative. The rigidity of fibers in a maniac always belongs to a dry landscape; mania is regularly accompanied by a wasting of the humors, and by a general aridity in the entire organism. The essence of mania is desertic, sandy. Théophile Bonet, in his *Sepulchretum anatomicum*, declares that the brains of maniacs, insofar as he had been able to observe them, always seemed to be in a state of dryness, of hardness, and of friability. Later, Albrecht von Haller also found that the maniac's brain was hard, dry, and brittle. Menuret repeats an observation of Forestier's that clearly shows how an excessive loss of a humor, by drying out the vessels and fibers, may provoke a state of mania; this was the case of a young man who "having married his wife in the summertime, became maniacal as a result of the excessive intercourse he had with her."

What some imagined or supposed, what others saw in a quasi-perception, Dufour proved, numbered, named. During an autopsy, he removed part of the medullary substance from the brain of a subject who had died in a state of mania; he cut out "a cube six lines in each direction" the weight of which was 3 j.g. III, while the same volume taken from an ordinary brain weighed 3 j.g. V: "this inequality in weight, which seems at first of little consequence, is no longer so slight if we consider the fact that the specific difference between the total mass of the brain of a madman and that of a normal man is around 7 *gros* less in the adult, in whom the brain's entire mass ordinarily weighs three *livres*." Mania's dessication and lightness show even on the scale.

Were not this internal dryness and this heat further proved by the ease with which maniacs endured great cold? It was an established fact that they had been seen walking naked in the snow, that there was no need to warm them when they were confined in the asylum, that they could even be cured by cold. Since Jean-Baptiste van Helmont, the immersion of maniacs in ice water had been widely practiced, and Menuret states that he knew a maniac who, having escaped from the prison where he was kept, "walked several leagues in a violent rain without a hat and almost without clothing, and who by this means recovered perfect health." Montchau, who cured a maniac by "pouring ice water upon him, from as high above as possible," was not astonished by so favorable a result; to explain it he united all the themes of organic calefaction that had succeeded and intersected each other since the seventeenth century: "One need not be surprised that ice water produces such a prompt and perfect cure precisely when boiling blood, furious bile, and mutinous liquors carried disturbance and irritation everywhere"; by the impression of coldness, "the vessels contracted more violently and freed themselves of the liquors that crammed them; the irritation of the solid parts caused by the extreme heat of the liquors they contained ceased, and when the nerves relaxed, the course of the spirits that had proceeded irregularly from one side to the other was re-established in its natural state."

The world of melancholia was humid, heavy, and cold; that of mania was parched, dry, compounded of violence and fragility; a world which heat—unfelt but everywhere manifested—made arid, friable, and always ready to relax under the effect of a moist coolness. In the development of all these qualitative simplifications, mania attained both its full scope and its unity. It has doubtless remained what it was at the beginning of the seventeenth century, "fury without fever," but beyond these two characteristics, which were still only *descriptive*, there developed a *perceptual* theme which was the real organizer of the clinical picture. Once the explanatory myths disappeared, and humors, spirits, solids, fluids no longer had any currency, there would remain only the schema of coherent qualities which would no longer even be named, and what this dynamics of heat and movement slowly formed into a constellation characteristic of mania would now be observed as a natural complex, as an immediate truth of psychological observation. What had been perceived as heat, imagined as agitation of spirits, conceived as fibrous tension, would henceforth be recognized in the neutralized transparency of psychological notions: exaggerated vivacity of internal impressions, rapidity in the association of ideas, inattention to the external world. De la Rive's description already has this limpidity: "External objects do not produce upon the mind of a sufferer the same impression as upon the mind of a healthy man; these impressions are weak, and the sufferer rarely heeds them; his mind is almost entirely absorbed by the action of the ideas produced by the deranged state of his brain. These ideas have such a degree of vivacity that the sufferer believes they represent real objects, and judges accordingly." But we must not forget that this psychological structure of mania, as it appeared and was stabilized at the end of the eighteenth century, is only the superficial sketch of an entire profound organization, which itself would capsize and which had developed according to the half-perceptual, half-iconographic laws of a qualitative world.

No doubt this entire universe of heat and cold, of humidity and dryness, reminded medical thought, about to accede to positivism, of the circumstances of its own origin. But this blazon of images was not simply reminiscence; it was also an undertaking. In order to form the practical experience of mania or melancholia, this gravitation, against a background of images, of qualities attracted to each other by a whole system of sensuous and affective affinities was essential. If mania, if melancholia henceforth assumed the aspects our science knows them by, it is not because in the course of centuries we have learned to "open our eyes" to real symptoms; it is not because we have purified our perception to the point of transparency; it is because in the experience of madness, these concepts were organized around certain qualitative themes that lent them their unity, gave them their significant coherence, made them finally perceptible. We have passed from a simple notional description (fury without fever, delirious *idée fixe*) to a qualitative realm, apparently less organized, simpler, less precisely limited, but which alone was able to constitute recognizable, palpable units *really present* in the total experience of madness. The field of observation of these diseases was partitioned into landscapes that obscurely gave them their style and their structure. On the one hand, a sodden, almost diluvian world, where man remained deaf, blind, and numb to all that was not his one terror: a world simplified in the extreme, and immoderately enlarged in a single one of its details. On the other, a parched and desertic world, a panic world where all was flight, disorder, instantaneous gesture. It was the rigor of these themes in their cosmic form—not the approximations of an observing caution—which organized the experience (already almost our own experience) of mania and melancholia.

It is Willis, with his spirit of observation, the purity of his medical perception, whom we honor as the "discoverer" of the mania-melancholia alternation. Certainly Willis's methods are of great interest, chiefly in this particular: the transition from one affection to the other is seen not as a phenomenon of observation for which it was then a matter of discovering the explanation, but rather as the consequence of a profound natural affinity which was of the order of their secret nature. Willis does not cite a single case of alternation which he had occasion to observe; what he first discovered was an internal relation which engendered strange metamorphoses: "After melancholia, we must consider mania, with which it has so many affinities that these complaints often change into one another": it happens, in fact, that the melancholic predisposition, if aggravated, becomes frenzy; frenzy, on the contrary, when it decreases and loses its force, finally grows calm and turns to melancholic diathesis. A rigorous empiricism would see two related diseases here, or even two successive symptoms of the same disease. However, Willis does not pose the problem in terms of symptoms nor in terms of disease; he merely seeks the link connecting two states in the dynamics of animal spirits. In the melancholic, we remember, the spirits were somber and dim; they cast their shadows over the images of things and formed a kind of dark tide; in the maniac, on the contrary, the spirits seethed in a perpetual ferment; they were carried by an irregular movement, constantly repeated; a movement that eroded and consumed, and even without fever, sent out its heat. Between mania and melancholia, the affinity is evident: not the affinity of symptoms linked in experience, but the affinity—more powerful and so much more evident in the landscapes of the imagination—that unites in the same fire both smoke and flame. "If we can say that in melancholia, the brain and the animal spirits are obscured by smoke and a dense vapor, mania seems to ignite a kind of conflagration hitherto muffled by them." The flame in its rapid movement dissipates the smoke; but the smoke, when it falls back, smothers the flame and extinguishes its brightness. The combination of mania and melancholy is not, for Willis, a disease; it is a secret fire in which flame and smoke are in conflict; it is the vehicle of that light and that shadow.

Virtually all of the physicians of the eighteenth century acknowledged the proximity of mania and melancholia. Several, however, refused to call them two manifestations of the same disease. Many observed a succession without perceiving a symptomatic unity. Sydenham prefers to divide the domain of mania itself: on one hand, ordinary mania—due to "an overexcited and too rapid blood"; on the other, a mania which, as a general rule, "degenerates into stupidity." The latter "results from the weakness of the blood which too long a fermentation has deprived of its most spirituous parts." Even more often, it is acknowledged that the succession of mania and melancholia is a phenomenon either of metamorphosis or of remote causality. For Joseph Lieutaud, a melancholia that lasts a long time and whose delirium is exacerbated loses its traditional symptoms and assumes a strange resemblance to mania: "the last stage of melancholia has many affinities with mania." But the status of this analogy is not elaborated. For Dufour, the link is even looser: it is a remote causal connection, melancholia being able to provoke mania, as well as "worms in the frontal sinuses, or dilated or varicose vessels." Without the support of an image, no observation succeeded in transforming the evidence of succession into a symptomatic structure that was both precise and essential.

Of course the image of flame and smoke disappeared in Willis's successors; but it was still by images that the work of organization was accomplished—images increasingly functional, more firmly fixed in the great physiological themes of circulation and heating, increasingly remote from the cosmic figures Willis had borrowed them from. For Boerhaave and his commentator Gerard van Swieten, mania formed quite naturally the highest degree of melancholia—not only following a frequent metamorphosis, but as the result of a necessary dynamic sequence: the cerebral liquid, which stagnates in the melancholic, becomes agitated after a certain time, for the black bile that fills the viscera becomes by its very immobility "bitterer and more malignant"; there then form in it more acid and subtler elements which, carried to the brain by the blood, provoke the maniac's great agitation. Mania is thus distinguished from melancholia only by a difference of degree: it is its natural consequence, it results from the same causes, and is ordinarily treated by the same remedies. For Friedrich Hoffmann, the unity of mania and melancholia is a natural effect of the laws of movement and shock; but what is pure mechanics on the level of principles becomes dialectics in the development of life and of disease. Melancholia, in effect, is characterized by immobility; in other words, the thickened blood congests the brain where it accumulates; where it ought to circulate, it tends to stop, immobilized by its heaviness. But if this heaviness retards movement, it also makes the shock more violent at the moment it occurs; the brain, the vessels by which it is traversed, its very substance, more violently jarred, tend to resist more, therefore to harden, and by this hardening the thickened blood is sent back more energetically; its movement increases and it is soon caught up in that agitation which is mania. We have thus passed quite naturally from the image of an immobile congestion to images of dryness, of hardness, of rapid movement, and this by a sequence in which the principles of classical mechanics are at every moment influenced, deflected, distorted by a fidelity to iconographic themes which are the true organizers of this functional unity.

Subsequently other images will be added, but will no longer play a constitutive role; they will function only as so many interpretive variations upon the theme of a previously acquired unity. Witness for example the explanation Spengler proposed for the alternation between mania and melancholia, borrowing its principle from the electric battery. First there is a concentration of nervous power and of its fluid in a certain region of the system; only this sector is agitated, all the rest is in a state of sleep: this is the melancholic phase. But when it reaches a certain degree of intensity, this local charge suddenly expands into the entire system, which it agitates violently for a certain time, until its discharge is complete: this is the manic episode. At this level of elaboration, the image is too complex and too complete, it is borrowed from a model too remote to have an organizing role in the perception of a pathological unity. It is, on the contrary, suggested by that perception, which itself is based on unifying, though much more elementary, images.

It is these images which are secretly present in the text of James's *Dictionary*, one of the first in which the manic-depressive cycle is given as an observed phenomenon, as a unity easily perceived by an unprejudiced scrutiny. "It is absolutely necessary to reduce melancholia and mania to a single species of disease, and consequently to consider them in one and the same glance, for we find from our experiments and our day-to-day observations that one and the other have the same origin and the same cause. . . . The most exact observations and our daily experience confirm the fact, for we see that melancholics, especially those in whom the disposition is inveterate, easily become maniacal, and when the mania ceases, the melancholia begins again, in such a way that there is a passage and return from one to the other after certain periods of time."[11] What was constituted, in the seventeenth and eighteenth centuries, under the influence of images, was therefore a perceptual structure, and not a conceptual system or even a group of symptoms. The proof of this is that, just as in a perception, qualitative transitions could occur without affecting the integrity of the figure. Thus William Cullen would discover in mania, as in melancholia, "a principal object of delirium"—and, inversely, would attribute melancholia to "a drier and firmer tissue of the brain's medullary substance."

The essential thing is that the enterprise did not proceed from observation to the construction of explanatory images; that on the contrary, the images assured the initial role of synthesis, that their organizing force made possible a structure of perception, in which at last the symptoms could attain their significant value and be organized as the visible presence of the truth.

II. *Hysteria and Hypochondria*

Two problems arise where these are concerned.

1. To what degree is it legitimate to treat them as mental diseases, or at least as forms of madness?

2. Are we entitled to treat them together, as if they constituted a virtual couple, similar to that formed quite early by mania and melancholia?

A glance at the classifications is enough to convince us; hypochondria does not always appear beside dementia and mania; hysteria is very rarely found there. Felix Plater mentioned neither one among the lesions of the senses; and at the end of the classical period, Cullen still catalogued them in another category than that of the vesanias: hypochondria among the "adynamias, or diseases which consist of a weakness or a loss of movement in the vital or animal functions"; hysteria among "the spasmodic affections of the natural functions."

Moreover, in nosographic charts one rarely finds these two diseases grouped in a logical proximity, or even combined in the form of an opposition. Sauvages classifies hypochondria among the hallucinations—"hallucinations that concern only the health"—hysteria among the forms of convulsion. Linnaeus employs the same distinctions. Are they not both faithful to the teaching of Willis, who had studied hysteria in his book *De morbis convulsivis* and hypochondria in the section of *De anima brutorum* which dealt with diseases of the head, giving it the name of *passio colica?* Here it is certainly a question of two quite different diseases: in one case, the overheated spirits are subject to a reciprocal pressure which may give the impression that they are exploding—provoking those irregular or preternatural movements whose insane aspect constitutes hysterical convulsions. On the contrary, in *passio colica*, the spirits are irritated because of a matter that is hostile and inappropriate to them (*infesta et improportionnata*); they then provoke disturbances, irritations, *corrugationes* in the sensitive fibers. Willis therefore advises us not to be surprised by certain analogies of symptoms: certainly, we have seen convulsions produce pains as if the violent movement of hysteria could provoke the sufferings of hypochondria. But the resemblances are deceptive. "The substance is not the same, but a little different."

But beneath these fixed distinctions of the nosographers, a slow labor was being performed which tended increasingly to identify hysteria and hypochondria, as two forms of one and the same disease. In 1725 Richard Blackmore published a *Treatise of the Spleen and Vapours, or Hypochondriacal and Hysterical Affections;* in it the two illnesses were defined as two varieties of a single affection—either a "morbific constitution of the spirits" or a "disposition to leave their reservoirs and to consume themselves." For Whytt, in the middle of the eighteenth century, the identification was complete; the system of symptoms is henceforth identical: "An extraordinary sensation of cold and heat, of pains in several parts of the body; syncopes and vaporous convulsions; catalepsy and tetanus; gas in the stomach and intestines; an insatiable appetite for food; vomiting of black matter; a sudden and abundant flow of clear, pale urine; marasma or nervous atrophy; nervous cough; palpitations of the heart; variations in the pulse; periodic headaches; vertigo and dizzy spells; diminution and failure of eyesight; depression, despair, melancholia or even madness; nightmares or incubi."

Moreover, during the classical period hysteria and hypochondria slowly joined the domain of mental diseases. Richard Mead could still write apropos of hypochondria: "It is an illness of the whole body." And we must restore its true value to Willis's text on hysteria: "Among the diseases of women, hysterical affection is of such bad repute that like the *semi-damnati* it must bear the faults of numerous other affections; if a disease of unknown nature and hidden origin appears in a woman in such a manner that its cause escapes us, and that the therapeutic course is uncertain, we immediately blame the bad influence of the uterus, which, for the most part, is not responsible, and when we are dealing with an inhabitual symptom, we declare that there is a trace of hysteria hidden beneath it all, and what has so often been the subterfuge of so much ignorance we take as the object of our treatment and our remedies." With all due regard to the traditional commentators on this text, which is inevitably cited in any study on hysteria, it does not mean that Willis suspected the absence of an organic basis in symptoms of hysterical affection. He merely says, and in an explicit way, that the idea of hysteria is a catchall for the fantasies, not of the person who is or believes himself ill, but of the ignorant doctor who pretends to know why. Nor does the fact that hysteria is classified by Willis among diseases of the head indicate that he considered it a disorder of the mind; but only that he attributed its origin to a change in the nature, the origin, and the initial course of the animal spirits.

However, at the end of the eighteenth century, hypochondria and hysteria figured, almost without dispute, on the escutcheon of mental disease. In 1755 Alberti published at Halle his dissertation *De morbis imaginariis hypochondriacorum;* and Lieutaud, while defining hypochondria by its spasms, recognized that "the mind is affected as much as and perhaps more than the body; hence the term hypochondriac has become almost an offensive name avoided by physicians who would please." As for hysteria, Joseph Raulin no longer ascribes to it any organic reality, at least in his basic definition, establishing it from the start in a pathology of the imagination: "This disease in which women invent, exaggerate, and repeat all the various absurdities of which a disordered imagination is capable, has sometimes become epidemic and contagious."

There were thus two essential lines of development, during the classical period, for hysteria and hypochondria. One united them to form a common concept which was that of a "disease of the nerves"; the other shifted their meaning and their traditional pathological basis—sufficiently indicated by their names—and tended to integrate them gradually into the domain of diseases of the mind, beside mania and melancholia. But this integration was not achieved, as in the case of mania and melancholia, on the level of primitive qualities, perceived and imagined in their iconographic values. We are dealing here with an entirely different type of integration.

The physicians of the classical period certainly tried to discover the qualities peculiar to hysteria and hypochondria. But they never reached the point of perceiving that particular coherence, that qualitative cohesion which gave mania and melancholia their unique contour. All qualities were contradictorily invoked, each annulling the others, leaving untouched the problem of what was the ultimate nature of these two diseases.

Often hysteria was perceived as the effect of an internal heat that spread throughout the entire body, an effervescence, an ebullition ceaselessly manifested in convulsions and spasms. Was this heat not related to the amorous ardor with which hysteria was so often linked, in girls looking for husbands and in young widows who had lost theirs? Hysteria was ardent, by nature; its symptoms referred more easily to an image than to an illness; that image was drawn by Jacques Ferrand, at the beginning of the seventeenth century, in all its material precision. In his *Maladie d'amour ou mélancholie érotique*, he declared that women were more often distracted by love than men; but with what art they could dissimulate it! "In which their mien is similar to alembics featly resting upon cylinders, without one's being able to see the fire from without, yet if one looks beneath the alembic, and places one's hand upon a woman's heart, one will find in both places a fiery furnace." An admirable image, in its symbolic weight, its affective overtones, and the referential play of its imagery. Long after Ferrand, one finds the qualifying theme of humid heat used to characterize the secret distillations of hysteria and of hypochondria; but the image yielded to a more abstract motif. Already in Nicolas Chesneau, the flame of the feminine alembic had grown quite colorless: "I say that the hysterical affection is not a simple one, but that we understand by this name several diseases caused by a malign vapor which arises in some way or other, is corrupted, and undergoes an extraordinary effervescence." For others, on the contrary, the heat rising from the hypochondriac regions is completely dry: hypochondriacal melancholia is a "hot, dry" illness, caused by "humors of the like quality." But some perceived no heat in either hysteria or hypochondria: the quality peculiar to these maladies was on the contrary languor, inertia, and a cold humidity like that of the stagnant humors: "I think that these affections [hypochondriacal and hysterical], when they last for some time, come from the fibers of the brain and the nerves when they are slack and therefore feeble, without action or elasticity; as a consequence of which the nervous fluid is impoverished and without force."[12] There is probably no text that bears better witness to the qualitative instability of hysteria than George Cheyne's book *The English Malady:* according to Cheyne, the disease maintains its unity only in an abstract manner; its symptoms are dispersed into different qualitative regions and attributed to mechanisms that belong to each of these regions in its own right. All symptoms of spasm, cramp, and convulsion derive from a pathology of heat symbolized by "harmful, bitter, or acrimonious vapors." On the contrary, all psychological or organic signs of weakness—"depression, syncopes, inactivity of the mind, lethargic torpor, melancholia, and sadness"—manifest a condition of fibers which have become too humid or too weak, doubtless under the effect of cold, viscous, thick humors that obstruct the glands and the vessels, serous and sanguine alike. As for paralyses, they signify both a chilling and an immobilization of the fibers, "an interruption of vibrations," frozen so to speak in the general inertia of solids.

It was as difficult for the phenomena of hysteria and hypochondria to find a place within the compass of qualities as it was easy for mania and melancholia to be established there.

The medicine of movement was just as indecisive in dealing with them, its analyses just as unstable. It was quite clear, at least to any perception that did not reject its own images, that mania was related to an excessive mobility; melancholia, on the contrary, to a diminution of movement. For hysteria and for hypochondria as well, the choice was a difficult one. Georg Ernst Stahl opts instead for an increasing heaviness of the blood, which becomes so abundant and so thick that it is no longer capable of circulating regularly through the portal vein; it has a tendency to stagnate, to collect there, and the crisis is a result "of the effort it makes to effect an issue either by the higher or the lower parts." For Boerhaave, on the contrary, and for Van Swieten, hysterical movement is due to an excessive mobility of all the fluids, which become so volatile, so inconsistent, that they are agitated by the least movement: "In weak constitutions," Van Swieten explains, "the blood is dissolved; it barely coagulates, the serum is thus without consistency, without quality; the lymph resembles the se-

rum, as do the other fluids which the latter provides. . . .
In this way, it becomes probable that the so-called immaterial hysterical affection and hypochondriacal disease derive from the dispositions of the particular state of the fibers." It is to this sensibility, this mobility, that we must attribute the sufferings, the spasms, the singular pains so readily suffered by "young girls of pale complexion, and individuals too much given to study and meditation." Hysteria is indiscriminately mobile or immobile, fluid or dense, given to unstable vibrations or clogged by stagnant humors. No one has managed to discover the actual nature of its movements.

We receive the same impression in the realm of chemical analogies: for Lange, hysteria is a product of fermentation, quite precisely of the fermentation "of salts, sent into different parts of the body," with "the humors that are located there." For others, it is of an alkaline nature. Michael Ettmüller, on the contrary, considers that diseases of this kind belong to a chain of acid reactions, "the immediate cause being the acid rawness of the stomach; the chyle being acid, the quality of the blood is corrupted; it no longer furnishes spirits; the lymph is acid, the bile without strength; the nervous system suffers irritation, the digestive leaven, spoiled, is less volatile and too acid." Viridet undertakes to reconstitute, apropos of "vapors which we experience," a dialectic of alkalis and acids whose movements and violent collisions, in the brain and the nerves, provoke the signs of hysteria and hypochondria. Certain particularly volatile animal spirits are alkaline salts that move with great speed and transform themselves into vapors when they become too tenuous; but there are other vapors that are volatilized acids; the ether gives these latter enough movement to carry them to the brain and the nerves where, "encountering the alkalis, they cause infinite ills."

Strange, the qualitative instability of these hysterical and hypochondriacal illnesses; strange, the confusion of their dynamic properties and the secret nature of their chemistry! To the very degree that the diagnosis of mania and melancholia seemed simple in the context of qualities, so the decipherment of these illnesses seemed hesitant. No doubt, this imaginary landscape of qualities which was decisive for the constitution of the melancholia-mania couple remained secondary in the history of hysteria and hypochondria, where it probably played no more than the role of continually shifted scenery. The progress of hysteria did not lead, as did that of mania, through the world's obscure qualities reflected in a medical imagery. The space in which it assumed its dimensions was of another kind: that of the body, in the coherence of its organic values and its moral values.

It is customary to credit Charles le Pois and Willis with liberating hysteria from the old myths of uterine displacement. Jean Liébault, translating or rather adapting Marinello's book to seventeenth-century standards, still accepted, despite some restrictions, the idea of a spontaneous movement of the womb; if it shifted position "it was to be more at ease; not that this was done out of prudence, behest, or animal stimulus, but to preserve health and to experience the enjoyment of something delectable." No doubt, it was no longer deemed possible for the womb to change place or to course through the body somersaulting as it went, for it was "strictly attached" by its neck, by ligaments, by vessels, and finally by the tunic of the peritoneum; yet it could change position: "And so the womb, though it be so strictly attached to the parts we have described that it may not change place, yet often changes position, and makes curious and so to speak petulant movements in the woman's body. These movements are various: to wit, ascending, descending, convulsive, vagrant, prolapsed. The womb rises to the liver, spleen, diaphragm, stomach, breast, heart, lung, gullet, and head." The physicians of the classical period were almost unanimous in refusing to accept such an explanation.

At the beginning of the seventeenth century, Le Pois could write, speaking of hysterical convulsions: "Of all these one source is the father, and this not through sympathy but through idiopathy." More precisely, their origin is in an accumulation of fluids toward the posterior part of the skull: "Just as a river results from the confluence of a quantity of smaller vessels which join to form it, so the sinuses that are on the surface of the brain and terminate in the posterior part of the head amass the liquid because of the head's inclined position. The heat of the parts then causes the liquid to warm and affect the origin of the nerves." Willis, in his turn, makes a minute critique of the uterine explanation: it is especially from affections of the brain and the nervous system "that all the derangements and irregularities which obtain in the movement of the blood during this illness derive." And yet all these analyses did not thereby abolish the idea of an essential link between hysteria and the womb. But the link is differently conceived: it is no longer regarded as the trajectory of a real displacement through the body, but as a sort of secret propagation through the pathways of the organism and through functional proximities. We cannot say that the seat of the disease had become the brain, nor that Willis had made possible a psychological analysis of hysteria. But the brain now played the part of a relay station and the distributor of a disease whose origin was visceral: the womb occasioned it along with all the other viscera. Until the end of the eighteenth century, until Pinel, the uterus and the womb remained present in the pathology of hysteria, but as the result of a privileged diffusion by the humors and nerves, and not by a special prestige of their nature.

Stahl justifies the parallelism of hysteria and hypochondria by a curious comparison of menstrual flow and hemorrhoids. He explains, in his analysis of spasmodic movements, that the hysterical affection is a violent pain, "accompanied by tension and compression, which makes itself principally felt below the hypochondriac regions." It is called a hypochondriacal disease when it attacks men "in whom nature makes an effort to be rid of excess blood by vomiting or hemorrhoids"; it is called a hysterical affection when it attacks women "the course of whose periods is not as it should be. However, there is no essential difference between these two affections." Hoffman's opinion is quite similar, in spite of many theoretical differences. The *cause* of hysteria is in the womb—loosening and weakening—but the seat of the disease is to be sought, as in the case of hypochondria, in the stomach and the intestines; the blood and the vital humors begin to stagnate "in the membranous and nervous tunics of the intestines"; gastric disturbances result, which spread thence throughout the whole body. At the very center of the organism, the stomach serves as a relay station and diffuses the maladies that come from the interior and subterranean cavities of the body: "It is not to be doubted that the spasmodic affections experienced by hypochondriacs and hysterics have their seat in the nervous parts, and especially in the membranes of the stomach and the intestines, from which they are communicated by the intercostal nerve to the head, to the chest, to the kidneys, to the liver, and to all the principal organs of the body."

The role Hoffmann assigns to the intestines, the stomach, and the intercostal nerve is indicative of the manner in which the problem was presented in the classical period. It was not so much a question of escaping the old localization in the uterus, but of discovering the principle and the pathways of a diverse, polymorphous disease dispersed throughout the entire body. A disease was to be accounted for that could attack the head as well as the legs, express itself in a paralysis or in frenzied movements, that could bring on catalepsy or insomnia: in short, a disease that traversed corporeal space so rapidly and so ingeniously that it was virtually present throughout the entire body.

It is futile to insist on the change of medical horizons that occurred from Marinello to Hoffmann. Nothing subsists of that famous mobility ascribed to the uterus, which had constantly figured in the Hippocratic tradition. Nothing, except perhaps a certain theme which appeared more clearly now that it was no longer confined to a single medical theory, but persisted unchanged through the succession of speculative concepts and explanatory schemas. This was the theme of a dynamic upheaval of corporeal space, of a tide of the lower powers, which, too long constrained and, as it were, congested, began to seethe and ultimately spread their disorder—with or without the brain's mediation— through the entire body. This theme remained almost stationary until the beginning of the eighteenth century, despite the complete reorganization of physiological concepts. And strangely enough, it was during the eighteenth century, when no theoretical or experimental innovation in pathology had occurred, that the theme was suddenly modified, changed direction—that a dynamics of corporeal space was replaced by a morality of sensibility. It was then, and only then, that the ideas of hysteria and hypochondria were to *veer*, and definitively enter the world of madness.

We must try now to reconstitute the evolution of the theme, in each of its three stages:

1. a dynamics of organic and moral penetration;
2. a physiology of corporeal continuity;
3. an ethic of nervous sensibility.

If corporeal space is perceived as a solid and continuous whole, the disordered movement of hysteria and of hypochondria could result only from an element whose extreme tenuousness and incessant mobility permitted it to penetrate into the place occupied by the solids themselves. As Nathaniel Highmore put it, the animal spirits, "because of their igneous tenuity, can penetrate even the densest, the most compact bodies . . . , and because of their activity, can penetrate the entire microcosm in a single instant." The spirits, if their mobility increased, if penetration occurred, chaotically and in an untimely manner, in all the parts of the body to which they were unsuited, provoked a thousand diverse signs of disturbance. Hysteria, for Highmore as for Willis, his adversary, and for Sydenham as well, was the disease of a body indiscriminately penetrable to all the efforts of the spirits, so that the internal order of organs gave way to the incoherent space of masses passively subject to the chaotic movement of the spirits. These latter "move impetuously and in excessive quantity upon such or such a part, there causing spasms or even pain . . . and disturbing the function of the organs, both those which they abandon and those toward which they move, neither being able to avoid serious damage from this unequal distribution of spirits, which is entirely contrary to the laws of animal economy."[13] The hysterical body was thus given over to that disorder of the spirits which, outside of all organic laws and any functional necessity, could successively seize upon all the available spaces of the body.

The effects varied according to the regions affected, and the disease, undifferentiated in the pure source of its movement, assumed various configurations depending on the spaces it traversed and the surfaces where it appeared: "Having accumulated in the stomach, they rush in a host and with impetuosity upon the muscles of the larynx and the pharynx, producing spasms throughout the entire area they traverse, and causing in the stomach a swelling which resembles a large ball." A little higher, the hysterical affection, "seizing upon the colon and upon the region which is below the heart cavity, causes there an insupportable pain which resembles the iliac affection." Should it rise still higher, the disease attacks "the vital parts and causes so violent a palpitation of the heart that the sick person does not doubt that his attendants must be able to hear the sound his heart makes as it beats against his ribs." Finally, if it attacks "the exterior part of the head, between the cranium and the pericranium, and there remains fixed in a single spot, it causes an extreme pain that is accompanied by violent fits of vomiting."[14] Each part of the body determines in its own right and by its own nature the form of the symptom produced. Hysteria thus appears as the most real and the most deceptive of diseases; real because it is based upon a movement of the animal spirits; illusory as well, because it generates symptoms that seem provoked by a disorder inherent in the organs, whereas they are only the formation, at the level of these organs, of a central or rather general disorder; it is the derangement of internal mobility that assumes the appearance, on the body's surface, of a local symptom. Actually suffering from the disordered and excessive movement of spirits, the organ imitates its own illness; starting from a defect in the movement within internal space, it imitates a disorder that strictly belongs to itself; in this manner, hysteria "imitates almost all the maladies to which human flesh is subject, for in whatever part of the body it lodges, it immediately produces the symptoms that are proper to that part, and if the physician does not have great wisdom and experience, he will easily be deceived and will attribute to an illness essential and proper to such and such a part, symptoms that are entirely the result of hysterical affection":[15] stratagems of a disease that, traversing corporeal space in the homogenous form of movement, manifests itself in specific aspects; but the type, here, is not essence; it is a ruse of the body.

The more easily penetrable the internal space becomes, the more frequent is hysteria and the more various its aspects; but if the body is firm and resistant, if internal space is dense, organized, and solidly heterogeneous in its different regions, the symptoms of hysteria are rare and its effects will remain simple. Is this not exactly what separates female hysteria from the male variety, or, if you will, hysteria from hypochondria? Neither symptoms, in fact, nor even causes form the principle of separation between the diseases, but only the spatial solidarity of the body, and so to speak the density of the interior landscape: "Beyond what we may call the exterior man, who is composed of parts which are visible to the senses, there is an interior man formed of a system of animal spirits, a man who can be seen only with the eyes of the mind. This latter man, closely joined and so to speak united with the corporeal constitution, is more or less deranged from his state to the degree that the principles which form the machine have a natural firmness. That is why this disease attacks women more than men, because they have a more delicate, less firm constitution, because they lead a softer life, and because they are accustomed to the luxuries and commodities of life and not to suffering." And already, in the lines of this text, this spatial density yields one of its meanings: it is also a *moral* density; the resistance of the organs to the disordered penetration of the spirits is perhaps one and the same thing as that strength of soul which keeps the thoughts and the desires in order. This internal space which has become permeable and porous is perhaps only the laxity of the heart. Which explains why so few women are hysterical when they are accustomed to a hard and laborious life, yet strongly incline to become so when they lead a soft, idle, luxurious, and lax existence; or if some sorrow manages to conquer their resolution: "When women consult me about some complaint whose nature I cannot determine, I ask if

the malady from which they are suffering attacks them
only when they have some sorrow . . . : if they admit as
much, I am fully assured that their complaint is an hysterical affection."[16]

Thus we have a new formulation of the old moral intuition that from the time of Hippocrates and Plato had made
the womb a living and perpetually mobile animal, and distributed the spatial ordering of its movements; this intuition
perceived in hysteria the incoercible agitation of desires in
those who had neither the possibility of satisfying them nor
the strength to master them; the image of the female organ
rising to the breast and to the head gave a mythical expression to an upheaval in the great Platonic tripartition and in
the hierarchy that was intended to assure its immobility.
For Sydenham, for the disciples of Descartes, the moral
intuition is identical; but the spatial landscape in which it is
expressed has changed; Plato's vertical and hieratic order is
replaced by a volume which is traversed by incessant motion whose disorder is no longer a revolution of the depths
to the heights but a lawless whirlwind in a chaotic space.
This "interior body" which Sydenham tried to penetrate
with "the eyes of the mind" was not the objective body
available to the dull gaze of a neutralized observation; it
was the site where a certain manner of imagining the body
and of deciphering its internal movements combined with a
certain manner of investing it with moral values. The
development is completed, the work done on the level of
this *ethical perception*. In this perception the ever pliant
images of medical theory are inflected and altered; in it,
too, the great moral themes are formulated and gradually
alter their initial aspect.

This penetrable body must, however, be a continuous
body. The dispersion of the disease through the organs is
only the reverse of a movement of propagation which per-

mits it to pass from one to another and to affect them all in succession. If the body of the hypochondriac or the hysteric is a porous body, separated from itself, distended by the invasion of disease, this invasion can be effected only by means of a certain spatial continuity. The body in which the disease circulates must have other properties than the body in which the sufferer's dispersed symptoms appear.

The problem haunted eighteenth-century medicine, and was to make hypochondria and hysteria diseases of the "nervous type"; that is, *idiopathic* diseases of the general agency of all the *sympathies*.

The nervous fiber is endowed with remarkable properties, which permit it to integrate the most heterogeneous elements. Is it not astonishing that, responsible for transmitting the most diverse impressions, the nerves should be of the same nature everywhere, and in every organ? "The nerve whose expansion at the back of the eye makes it possible to receive the impression of so subtle a matter as light; the nerve which, in the organ of hearing, becomes sensitive to the vibrations of sonorous bodies, differs no whit in nature from those which serve the grosser sensations such as touch, taste, and odor." This identity of nature, in different functions, assures the possibility of communication between the most distant organs, and those most dissimilar physiologically: "This homogeneity in the nerves of the animal, combined with the numerous communications that all maintain with each other . . . establishes among the organs a harmony that often makes one or several parts participate in the affections of those which are injured."[17] But what is still more admirable, a nervous fiber can transmit simultaneously the stimulus of a voluntary movement and the impression left on the organ by the senses. Simon-André Tissot conceived this double function of one and the same fiber as the combination of an *undulatory* movement for voluntary stimulus ("this is the movement of a fluid enclosed in a malleable container, in a bladder, for example, that when I press it would eject liquid through a tube") and a *corpuscular* movement for sensation ("this is the movement of a succession of ivory balls"). Thus sensation and movement can be produced at the same time in the same nerve: any tension and any relaxation in the fiber will alter both movements and sensations, as we can observe in all nervous diseases.

And yet, despite all these unifying virtues of the nervous system, is it certain that we can explain, by the real network of its fibers, the cohesion of such diverse disorders as those which characterize hysteria or hypochondria? How conceive the liaison among the signs that from one part of the body to the other betray the presence of a nervous affection? How explain, and by tracing what line of connection, that in certain "delicate and highly sensitive" women a heady perfume or the too vivid description of a tragic event or even the sight of a combat produces such an impression that they "fall into syncopes or suffer convulsions"? One seeks in vain: no precise liaison of the nerves; no path proceeding from the original cause; but only a remote, indirect action which is rather on the order of a physiological solidarity. This is because the different parts of the body possess a "very determined faculty, which is either general and extends throughout the entire system of animal economy, or particular and influences certain parts principally." This very distinct property of both "the faculty of feeling and that of moving" which permits the organs to communicate with each other and to suffer together, to react to a stimulus, however distant—is sympathy. As a matter of fact, Whytt succeeded neither in isolating sympathy in the ensemble of the nervous system, nor in defining it in relation to sensibility and to movement. Sympathy exists in the organs only insofar as it is received there through the intermediary of the nerves; it is the more marked in proportion to their mobility, and at the same time it is one of the forms of sensibility: "All sympathy, all consensus presupposes sentiment and consequently can exist only by the mediation of the nerves, which are the only instruments by which sensation operates."[18] But the nervous system is no longer invoked here to explain the exact transmission of a movement or a sensation, but to justify, in its totality and its mass, the body's sensibility with regard to its own phenomena, and its own echo across the volumes of its organic space.

Diseases of the nerves are essentially disorders of sympathy; they presuppose a state of general vigilance in the nervous system which makes each organ susceptible of entering into sympathy with any other: "In such a state of sensibility of the nervous system, the passions of the soul, violations of diet, sudden alternation of heat and cold or of heaviness and humidity of the atmosphere, will very readily produce morbific symptoms; so that with such a constitution, one will not enjoy steady or constant health, but generally suffer a continual succession of more or less severe pains." Doubtless this exaggerated sensibility is compensated by zones of insensibility, of sleep, as it were; in a general way, hysterical sufferers are those in whom this internal sensibility is the most exquisite, hypochondriacs possessing it, on the contrary, in a relatively blunted form. And of course women belong to the first category: is not the womb, with the brain, the organ that maintains most sympathy with the whole organism? It suffices to cite "the vomiting that generally accompanies the inflammation of the womb; the nausea, the disordered appetite that follow conception; the constriction of the diaphragm and of the muscles of the abdomen during childbirth; the headache, the heat and the pains in the back, the intestinal colic suffered when the time of the menstrual flow approaches." The entire female body is riddled by obscure but strangely direct paths of sympathy; it is always in an immediate complicity with itself, to the point of forming a kind of absolutely privileged site for the sympathies; from one extremity of its organic space to the other, it encloses a perpetual possibility of hysteria. The sympathetic sensibility of her organism, radiating through her entire body, condemns woman to those diseases of the nerves that are called vapors. "The women whose systems have generally more mobility than those of men are more subject to nervous diseases, which are also more serious in them."[19] And Whytt assures us he has witnessed that "the pain of a toothache caused convulsions in a young girl whose nerves were weak, and an unconsciousness lasting several hours and returning when the pain became more acute."

Diseases of the nerves are diseases of corporeal continuity. A body too close to itself, too intimate in each of its parts, an organic space which is, in a sense, strangely constricted: this is what the theme common to hysteria and hypochondria has now become; the *rapprochement* of the body with itself assumes, for some, the aspect of a precise—all too precise—image: such is the celebrated "shriveling of the nervous system" described by Pomme. Such images mask the problem, but do not suppress it, and do not keep the enterprise from continuing.

Is this sympathy, basically, a property hidden in each organ—that "sentiment" which Cheyne spoke of—or a real propagation through an intermediary element? And is the pathological proximity which characterizes these nervous diseases an exasperation of this sentiment, or a greater mobility of this interstitial body?

It is a curious but doubtless characteristic phenomenon of medical thought in the eighteenth century, in the period when physiologists tried to define most precisely the functions and the role of the nervous system (sensibility and irritability; sensation and movement), that physicians used these ideas indiscriminately in the undifferentiated unity of pathological perception, articulating them according to a schema entirely different from that proposed by physiology.

Sensibility and movement are not distinguished. Tissot explains that the child has more sensibility than anyone else because in him everything is lighter and more mobile; irritability, in the sense in which Haller understood a property of the nervous fiber, is identified with irritation, understood as the pathological state of an organ aroused by a prolonged stimulus. It would thus be acknowledged that nervous diseases were states of irritation combined with an excessive mobility of the fibers.

"On occasion one sees persons for whom the smallest moving cause occasions much more movement than it produces in healthy persons; they cannot sustain the slightest alien impression. The faintest sound, the weakest light affords them extraordinary symptoms."[20] By this deliberately preserved ambiguity in the notion of irritation, medicine at the end of the eighteenth century could in effect show the continuity between disposition (irritability) and the pathological event (irritation); but it could also maintain both the theme of a disorder proper to an organ which suffers, but in a fashion all its own, a general attack (it is the sensibility particular to the organ which assures this nonetheless discontinuous communication), and the idea of a propagation in the organism of a single disorder that can attack it in each of its parts (it is the mobility of the fiber which is responsible for this continuity, despite the diverse forms it assumes in the organs).

But if the notion of "irritated fiber" certainly plays this role of concerted confusion, it also permits a decisive distinction in pathology. On one hand, nervous sufferers are the most irritable, that is, have the most sensibility: tenuousness of fiber, delicacy of organism; but they also have an easily impressionable soul, an unquiet heart, too strong a sympathy for what happens around them. This sort of universal resonance—simultaneously sensation and mobility—constitutes the first determination of the illness. Women who have "frail fibers," who are easily carried away, in their idleness, by the lively movements of their imagination, are more often attacked by nervous diseases than men who are "more robust, drier, hardened by work." But this excess of irritation has this peculiarity: that in its vivacity it attenuates, and sometimes ends by extinguishing, the sensations of the soul; as if the sensibility of the nervous organ itself overcharged the soul's capacity to feel, and appropriated for its own advantage the multiplicity of sensations aroused by its extreme mobility; the nervous system "is in such a state of irritation and reaction that it is then incapable of transmitting to the soul what it is experiencing; all its figures are disordered; it can no longer interpret them."[21] Thus appears the idea of a sensibility which is not sensation, and of an inverse relation between that delicacy which derives as much from the soul as from the body, and a certain numbness of the sensations that prevents nervous shocks from reaching the soul. The hysteric's unconsciousness is only the reverse of his sensibility. It is this relation, which the notion of sympathy could not define, which was contributed by the concept of irritability, though so little elaborated and still so confused in the thinking of pathologists.

But by this very fact, the moral significance of "nervous complaints" was profoundly altered. Insofar as diseases of the nerves had been associated with the organic movements of the lower parts of the body (even by the many and confused paths of sympathy), they were located within a certain ethic of desire: they represented the revenge of a crude body; it had been as the result of an excessive violence that one became ill. From now on one fell ill from too much feeling; one suffered from an excessive solidarity with all the beings around one. One was no longer compelled by one's secret nature; one was the victim of everything which, on the surface of the world, solicited the body and the soul.

And as a result, one was both more innocent and more guilty. More innocent, because one was swept by the total irritation of the nervous system into an unconsciousness great in proportion to one's disease. But more guilty, much more guilty, because everything to which one was attached in the world, the life one had led, the affections one had had, the passions and the imaginations one had cultivated too complacently—all combined in the irritation of the nerves, finding there both their natural effect and their moral punishment. All life was finally judged by this degree of irritation: abuse of things that were not natural, the sedentary life of cities, novel reading, theatergoing, immoderate thirst for knowledge, "too fierce a passion for the sex, or that other criminal habit, as morally reprehensible as it is physically harmful."[22] The innocence of the nervous sufferer, who no longer even feels the irritation of his nerves, is at bottom only the just punishment of a deeper guilt: the guilt which makes him prefer the world to nature: "Terrible state! . . . This is the torment of all effeminate souls whom inaction has plunged into dangerous sensuality, and who, to rid themselves of the labors imposed by nature, have embraced all the phantoms of opinion. . . . Thus the rich are punished for the deplorable use of their fortune."[23]

We stand here on the threshold of the nineteenth century, where the irritability of the fibers will enjoy physiological and pathological fortunes. What it leaves for the moment, in the domain of nervous diseases, is nonetheless something very important.

This is, on the one hand, the complete identification of

hysteria and hypochondria as mental diseases. By the capital distinction between sensibility and sensation, they enter into that domain of unreason which we have seen was characterized by the essential moment of error and dream, that is, of blindness. As long as vapors were convulsions or strange sympathetic communications through the body, even when they led to fainting and loss of consciousness, they were not madness. But once the mind becomes blind through the very excess of sensibility—then madness appears.

But on the other hand, such an identification gives madness a new content of guilt, of moral sanction, of just punishment which was not at all a part of the classical experience. It burdens unreason with all these new values: instead of making blindness the condition of possibility for all the manifestations of madness, it describes blindness, the blindness of madness, as *the psychological effect of a moral fault*. And thereby compromises what had been essential in the experience of unreason. What had been blindness would become unconsciousness, what had been error would become fault, and everything in madness that designated the paradoxical manifestation of non-being would become the natural punishment of a moral evil. In short, that whole vertical hierarchy which constituted the structure of classical madness, from the cycle of material causes to the transcendence of delirium, would now collapse and spread over the surface of a domain which psychology and morality would soon occupy together and contest with each other.

The "scientific psychiatry" of the nineteenth century became possible.

It was in these "diseases of the nerves" and in these "hysterias," which would soon provoke its irony, that this psychiatry took its origin.

VI

DOCTORS AND
PATIENTS

THE therapeutics of madness did not function in the hospital, whose chief concern was to sever or to "correct." And yet in the non-hospital domain, treatment continued to develop throughout the classical period: long cures for madness were elaborated whose aim was not so much to care for the soul as to cure the entire individual, his nervous fiber as well as the course of his imagination. The madman's body was regarded as the visible and solid presence of his disease: whence those physical cures whose meaning was borrowed from a moral perception and a moral therapeutics of the body.

1. *Consolidation.* There exists in madness, even in its most agitated forms, an element of weakness. If in madness the spirits are subjected to irregular movements, it is because they have not enough strength or weight to follow the gravity of their natural course; if spasms and convul-

sions so often occur in nervous illnesses, it is because the fiber is too mobile, or too irritable, or too sensitive to vibrations; in any case, it lacks robustness. Beneath the apparent violence of madness, which sometimes seems to multiply the strength of maniacs to considerable proportions, there is always a secret weakness, an essential lack of resistance; the madman's frenzies, in fact, are only a passive violence. What is wanted, then, is a cure that will give the spirits or the fibers a vigor, but a calm vigor, a strength no disorder can mobilize, since from the start it will be subject to the course of natural law. More than the image of vivacity and vigor, it is one of robustness that prevails, enveloping the theme in a new resistance, a young elasticity, but subjugated and already domesticated. A force must be found within nature to reinforce nature itself.

The ideal remedy would "take the part" of the spirits, and "help them conquer the cause that ferments them." To take the part of the spirits would be to struggle against the vain agitation to which they are subject in spite of themselves; it would also permit them to escape from all the chemical ebullition that heats and troubles them; finally it would give them enough solidity to resist the vapors that try to suffocate them, to make them inert, and to carry them off in their whirlwind. Against the vapors, the spirits are reinforced "by the most stinking odors"; disagreeable sensation vivifies the spirits, which in a sense rebel and vigorously flock to the place where the assault must be repelled; to this effect "asafetida, oil of amber, burnt leather and feathers will be used—that is, whatever can provide the soul with strong and disagreeable feelings." Against fermentation, theriac must be given, "anti-epileptic spirits of Charras," or best of all, the famous Queen of Hungary water;[1] acidity disappears and the spirits regain their true influence. Finally, to restore their true mobility, Lange recommends that the spirits be subjected to sensations and movements that are both agreeable, measured, and regular: "When the animal spirits are dispersed and disunited, remedies are necessary which calm their movement and return them to their natural situation, such things as give the soul a sweet and moderate feeling of pleasure: agreeable odors, walks in delightful spots, the sight of persons who are in the habit of providing diversion, and Music." This firm gentleness, a proper gravity, ultimately a vivacity intended only to protect the body—all these are means to consolidate, within the organism, the fragile elements connecting body and soul.

But there is probably no better fortifying procedure than the use of the substance which is both the most solid and the most docile, the most resistant but the most pliable in the hands of the man who knows how to forge it to his purposes: iron. Iron unites, in its privileged nature, all those qualities that quickly become contradictory when they are isolated. Nothing resists better, nothing can better obey; it is a gift of nature, but it is also at the disposal of all of man's techniques. How could man help nature and lend it an abundance of strength by a surer means—that is, one closer to nature and more obedient to man—than by the application of iron? The old example of Dioscorides is always cited, who gave to the inertia of water the vigorous virtues foreign to it by plunging into it a bar of red-hot iron. The ardor of fire, the calm mobility of water, the rigor of a metal treated until it had become supple—all these elements, united, conferred upon water powers of reinforcent, of vivification, of consolidation, which it could transmit to the organism. But iron is efficacious even aside from any preparation; Sydenham recommends it in its simplest form, by the direct absorption of iron filings. Whytt instances a man who, in order to cure himself of a weakness of the stomach nerves involving a permanent state of hypochondria, took 230 grains of iron every day. This was because to all its virtues, iron added the remarkable property of transmitting itself directly, without intermediary or transformation. What it communicated was not its substance but its strength; paradoxically, though itself so resistant, it immediately dissolved in the organism, depositing there only its qualities, without rust or waste. It is evident here that an imagery of wonder-working iron governs discursive thought and prevails over observation itself. If experiments were made, it was not to reveal a positive sequence of effects, but to emphasize this immediate communication of qualities. Wright fed a dog Mars salts; he observed that an hour later the chyle, if mixed with tincture of nut gall, did not display that purple color it invariably assumed if the iron had been absorbed. This must have been because the iron, without mixing with the digestion, without passing into the blood, without penetrating the organism substantially, fortified the membranes and fibers directly. More than an observed effect, the consolidation of the spirits and the nerves appears rather as an operative metaphor which implies a transfer of strength without any discursive dynamics. Strength is supplied by contact, exclusive of any exchange or substance, any communication of movements.

2. *Purification.* Clogging of the viscera, ebullition of false ideas, fermentation of vapors, violence, corruption of liquids and spirits—madness elicits an entire series of therapeutics, each of which can be attached to the identical operation of purification.

The ideal was a sort of total purification: the simplest but also the most impossible of cures. It would consist of substituting for the melancholic's overcharged, thick blood, encumbered with bitter humors, a light, clear blood whose new movement would dissipate the delirium. In 1662 Moritz Hoffman suggested blood transfusion as a remedy for melancholia. Some years later, the idea had attained sufficient currency for the Philosophical Society of London to plan a series of experiments upon the subjects confined in Bedlam; Allen, the doctor entrusted with the enterprise, refused. But Jean-Baptiste Denis tried it upon one of his patients stricken with amorous melancholia; he drew off ten ounces of blood, which he replaced with a slightly smaller quantity taken from the femoral artery of a calf; the following day he began again, but this time the operation involved only a few ounces. The patient became calm; the following day his mind cleared; he was soon entirely cured; "all the professors of the Academy of Surgeons attested it." The technique, however, was quickly abandoned, despite a few later attempts.

The preferred medications were those that forestalled corruption. We know "as a result of more than three thousand years of experience that Myrrh and Aloes preserve corpses."[2] Are not these deteriorations of bodies of the same nature as those that accompany the diseases of the humors? Then nothing would be more recommendable against the vapors than products like myrrh or aloes, and especially the famous elixir of Paracelsus. But more must be attempted than to forestall corruptions; they must be destroyed. Whence the therapeutics that attack deterioration itself, and seek either to deflect the corrupt substances or to dissolve the corrupting ones: techniques of deflection and techniques of detersion.

To the first belong all the strictly physical methods that seek to create wounds or sores on the surface of the body, both centers of infection that relieve the organism, and centers of evacuation into the outside world. Thus Fallowes explains the beneficial mechanism of his *oleum cephalicum;* in madness, "black vapors clog the very fine vessels through which the animal spirits must pass"; the blood is thus deprived of direction; it encumbers the veins of the brain where it stagnates, unless it is agitated by a confused movement "that distracts the ideas." *Oleum cephalicum* has the advantage of provoking "little pustules on the head"; they are anointed with oil to keep them from drying out and so that "the black vapors lodged in the brain" may continue to escape. But burning and cauterizing the body at any point produces the same effect. It was even supposed that diseases of the skin such as scabies, eczema, or smallpox could put an end to a fit of madness; the corruption then left the viscera and the brain, to spread on the surface of the body, where it was released externally. By the end of the century, it became customary to inoculate scabies in the most resistant cases of mania. In his *Instructions* of 1785, addressed to the directors of hospitals, François Doublet recommends that if bleedings, purges, baths, and showers do not cure mania, the use of "cauters, setons, superficial abscesses, inoculation of scabies" will.

But the principal task is to dissolve the fermentations which, having formed in the body, give rise to madness. To accomplish this, the chief agent is bitters. Bitterness has all the harsh virtues of sea water; it purifies by wearing away, it works its corrosion on everything useless, unhealthy, and impure that the disease may have deposited in the body and the soul. Bitter and active, coffee is useful for "fat persons whose thickened humors circulate with difficulty"; it dries without burning—for it is the property of such substances to dissipate superfluous humidity without dangerous heat; there is in coffee, as it were, fire without flame, a purifying power that does not calcine; coffee reduces impurities: "those who take it feel by long experience that it restores the stomach, consumes its superfluous humidity, dissipates wind, dissolves the phlegm of the bowels, where it performs a mild abstersion, and what is most considerable, prevents the fumes from rising to the head and consequently reduces the aches and pains customarily suffered there; finally, it affords strength, vigor, and cleanliness to the animal spirits, without leaving any great impression of heat, even upon the most inured persons who are accustomed to use it."[3] Bitter, but tonic also, is the quinine Whytt freely prescribes to persons "whose nervous system is very delicate"; it is efficacious against "weakness, discouragement, and depression"; two years of a cure consisting only of a tincture of quinine, "occasionally discontinued for a month at most," were sufficient to cure a woman suffering from a nervous complaint. For delicate persons, quinine must be associated with "a bitterness pleasant to the taste"; but if the organism is able to withstand stronger attacks, vitriol, mixed with quinine, cannot be too strongly recommended. Twenty or thirty drops of elixir of vitriol are sovereign.

Quite naturally, soaps and soap products inevitably enjoy privileged effects in this purificatory enterprise. "Soap dissolves almost anything that is concrete."[4] Tissot believes that soap can be consumed directly, and that it will calm many nervous ailments; but more often it is sufficient to consume, first thing in the morning, by themselves or with bread, "soapy fruits"—that is, cherries, strawberries, currants, figs, oranges, grapes, ripe pears, and "other fruits of this nature." But there are cases where the difficulty is so serious, the obstruction so irreducible, that no soap can conquer it. Soluble tartar is then recommended. Muzzell was the first to have the idea of prescribing tartar for "madness and melancholia," and published several triumphant observations on the subject. Whytt confirms them, and shows at the same time that tartar functions as a detersive, since it is especially efficacious against obstructive illnesses: "Insofar as I have observed it, soluble tartar is more useful in maniac or melancholic affections produced by harmful humors amassed in the primary canals, than for those produced by a flaw in the brain." Among the dissolvants, Raulin also cites honey, chimney soot, Oriental saffron, wood lice, powdered lobster claw, and bezoar.

Halfway between these internal methods of dissolution and the external techniques of deflection, we find a series of practices of which the most frequent are applications of vinegar. As an acid, vinegar dissolves obstructions, destroys foreign bodies as they are fermenting. But in external application, it can serve as a revulsive, and draw harmful humors and liquids to the surface. It is curious but quite characteristic of the therapeutic thinking of this period that no contradiction was admitted between these two modes of action. Given what it is by *nature*—detersive and revulsive—vinegar would act in any situation according to this double determination, even though one of these two modes of action can no longer be analyzed in a rational and discursive fashion. It functions, then, directly, without intermediary, through the simple contact of two natural elements. Hence it is recommended to rub the head, shaved if possible, with vinegar. The *Gazette de médecine* cites the case of an empiric who managed to cure "a quantity of madmen by a very swift and very simple means. Here is his secret. After he has purged them above and below, he has them soak their head and hands in vinegar, and leaves them in this situation until they fall asleep, or rather until they wake up, and most of them are cured upon waking. He also applies to the patient's shaved head chopped leaves of Dipsacus, or fuller's weed."

3. *Immersion.* Here two themes intersect: the theme of ablution, with all that relates it to the rites of purity and rebirth; and the much more physiological theme of impregnation or immersion, which modifies the essential qualities of liquids and solids. Despite their different origin, and the gap between their levels of conceptual elaboration, they form, up to the end of the eighteenth century, a unity

coherent enough so that their opposition is not experienced as such. The idea of nature, with its ambiguities, serves as their element of cohesion. Water, the simple and primitive liquid, belongs to all that is purest in nature; all the dubious modifications man has been able to add to nature's essential kindness cannot change the beneficence of water; when civilization, life in society, the imaginary desires aroused by novel reading and theatergoing provoke nervous ailments, the return to water's limpidity assumes the meaning of a ritual of purification; in that transparent coolness, one is reborn to one's first innocence. But at the same time, the water naturally inherent in the composition of all bodies restores each to its own equilibrium; water serves as a universal physiological regulator. All these themes were expressed by Tissot, a disciple of Rousseau, whose imagination was as moral as it was medical: "Nature has prescribed water as the unique beverage of all nations; she gave it the power to dissolve all sorts of nourishment; it is agreeable to the palate; choose therefore a good cold water, fresh and light; it fortifies and cleans the bowels; the Greeks and Romans regarded it as a universal remedy."

The practice of immersion reaches far back into the history of madness; the baths taken at Epidaurus alone would bear witness to this; and cold applications of all kinds must have been current throughout antiquity, since Soranus of Ephesus, if we are to believe Caelius Aurelianus, already protested against their abuse. In the Middle Ages, the traditional treatment of a maniac was to plunge him several times into water "until he had lost his strength and forgotten his fury." Franciscus Sylvius recommends immersions in cases of melancholia or frenzy. And the story, accepted in the eighteenth century, of Van Helmont's sudden discovery of the usefulness of hydrotherapy, was actually a reinterpretation. According to Menuret, this invention, supposedly dating from the middle of the seventeenth century, was the fortunate result of chance: a heavily chained madman was being transported on an open wagon; he managed, however, to free himself from his chains and jumped into a lake, tried to swim, fainted; when he was rescued, everyone thought he was dead, but he quickly recovered his spirits, which were abruptly restored to their natural order, and he "lived a long time without experiencing any further attack of madness." This anecdote supposedly enlightened Van Helmont, who began to plunge the insane indiscriminately into the sea or into fresh water; "the only care that must be taken, is to plunge the sufferers into the water suddenly and unawares, and to keep them there for a long time. One need have no fear for their lives."

The truth of the story is of little importance; one thing is certain, which it conveys in the form of an anecdote: from the end of the seventeenth century, the water cure takes or regains its place as a major therapeutics of madness. When Doublet published his *Instructions* shortly before the Revolution, he prescribed, for the four major pathological forms he recognized (frenzy, mania, melancholia, imbecility), the regular use of baths, adding the use of cold showers for the first two. And at this period, Cheyne had already long since recommended that "all those who need to fortify their temperament" install baths in their house, and use them every two, three, or four days; or "if they have not the means, to bathe in some manner either in a lake or in running water, whenever they have occasion."

The advantages of water are evident, to a medicine dominated by the concern to equilibrate liquids and solids. For if water has powers of impregnation, which place it first among the humectants, it has, insofar as it can receive supplementary qualities like cold and heat, the virtues of constriction, of cooling or of heating, and it can even have those effects of consolidation attributed to substances like iron. In fact, the interplay of qualities is very labile, in the fluid substance of water; just as it penetrates easily into the web of all the tissues, it may be easily impregnated by all the qualitative influences to which it is subjected. Paradoxically, its universal use in the eighteenth century was not the result of a general recognition of its effect and mode of action, but of the ease with which the most contradictory forms and modalities could be attributed to its action. It is the locus of all possible therapeutic themes, forming an inexhaustible reservoir of operative metaphors. In this fluid element occurs the universal exchange of qualities.

Of course, cold water cools. Otherwise would it be used in frenzy and mania—diseases of heat, in which the spirits boil, solids stretch, liquids seethe to the point of evaporation, leaving the brains of these sufferers "dry and fragile," as anatomy can daily testify? Reasonably enough, Barthélemy-Camille Boissieu cites cold water among the essential means of cooling cures; as a bath, it comes first among the "antiphlogistics" which tear from the body the excessive igneous particles found there; as a drink, it is a "procrastinative dilution" which diminishes the resistance of fluids to the actions of solids, and thus indirectly lowers the general heat of the body.

But it can just as well be said that cold water heats and hot water cools. It is precisely this thesis which Darut defends. Cold baths attack the blood that is at the periphery of the body and "drive it more vigorously toward the heart." But the heart being the seat of natural heat, there the blood is heated, especially because "the heart, which struggles alone against the other parts, makes new efforts to drive out the blood and to overcome the resistance of the capillaries. Whence a great intensity of circulation, the division of the blood, the fluidity of the humors, the destruction of the encumbrances, the augmentation of the forces of natural heat, of the appetite of the digestive forces, of the activity of the body and the mind." The paradox of the hot bath is symmetrical: it draws the blood to the periphery, as well as the humors, perspiration, and all liquids, useful or harmful. Thus the vital centers are relieved; the heart now must function slowly; and the organism is thereby cooled. Is not this fact confirmed by "those syncopes, those lipothymias, that weakness, that lack of vigor" which accompany the too constant use of hot baths?

Further still: so rich is water's polyvalence, so great its aptitude for submitting to the qualities it bears, that it even manages to lose its efficacity as a liquid, and to act as a desiccant. Water can conjure away humidity. It revives the old principle "like to like," but in another sense, and by the intermediary of an entire visible mechanism. For some, it is cold water that dries, heat on the contrary preserving water's humidity. Heat, in fact, dilates the pores of the organism, distends its membranes, and permits humidity to impregnate them by a secondary effect. Heat clears the way for liquids. It is precisely for this reason that all the hot drinks the seventeenth century used and abused risk becoming harmful: relaxation, general humidity, softness of the entire organism—this is what threatens those who consume too many such infusions. And since these are the distinctive traits of the female body, as opposed to virile dryness and solidity, the abuse of hot drinks risks leading to a general feminization of the human race: "Most men are censured, not without reason, for having degenerated in contracting the softness, the habits, and the inclinations of women; there is lacking only a resemblance in bodily constitution. Excessive use of humectants immediately accelerates the metamorphosis and makes the two sexes almost as alike in the physical as in the moral realm. Woe to the human race, if this prejudice extends its reign to the common people; there will be no more plowmen, artisans, soldiers, for they will soon be robbed of the strength and vigor necessary to their profession."[5] In cold water, it is the cold that vanquishes all the powers of humidity, for by tightening the tissues, it closes them to all possibility of impregnation: "Do we not see how much the vessels, the tissues of our flesh tighten when we wash in cold water or when we are numbed with cold?"[6] Cold baths thus have the paradoxical property of consolidating the organism, of guaranteeing it against the softness of humidity, of "giving tone to the parts," as Hoffmann said, "and augmenting the systaltic power of the heart and the vessels."

But in other qualitative intuitions, the relationship is reversed; here it is heat that dries up water's humectant properties, while cold ceaselessly preserves and renews them. Against diseases of the nerves due to "a shriveling of the nervous system" and "the dryness of the membranes," Pomme does not recommend hot baths—which abet the heat that reigns in the body—but tepid or cold baths that can permeate the tissues of the organism and restore their suppleness. Is this not the method spontaneously practiced in America? And are not its effects, its very mechanism visible to the naked eye in the development of the cure, since at the most acute point of the crisis, the sufferers float in the water of the bath—to such an extent has internal heat rarified the air and the liquids of their bodies; yet if they remain a long time in the bath water, "three, four, or even six hours a day," then relaxation takes place, the water gradually impregnates the membranes and the fibers, the body becomes heavy and sinks naturally to the bottom.

At the end of the eighteenth century, the powers of water wane in the very excess of its qualitative versatility: cold, it can heat; hot, it can cool; instead of humidifying, it is even capable of solidifying, of petrifying by cold, or of sustaining a fire with its own heat. In it, all the values of beneficence and maleficence indiscriminately combine. It is endowed with all possible complicities. In medical thought, it forms a therapeutic theme which can be used and manipulated unconditionally, and whose effect can be understood in the most diverse physiologies and pathologies. It has so many values, so many different modes of action, that it can confirm anything, cancel anything. No doubt it was this very polyvalence, with all the disputes it generated, that finally neutralized water. By Pinel's day, water was still used, but it had again become entirely limpid, its qualitative overtones had been eliminated, and its mode of action could no longer be anything but mechanical.

Showers, hitherto less used than baths and drinks, now become the favored technique. And paradoxically, water regains, beyond all the physiological variations of the preceding epoch, its simple function of purification. The only quality attributed to it is violence, an irresistible flow washing away all the impurities that form madness; by its own curative power, it reduces the individual to his simplest possible expression, to his merest and purest form of existence, thus affording him a second birth; it is a matter, Pinel explains, "of destroying even the smallest traces of the extravagant ideas of the insane, which can be done only by obliterating, so to speak, these ideas in a state close to that of death." Whence the famous techniques used in asylums like Charenton at the end of the eighteenth and the beginning of the nineteenth century: the shower proper—"the insane man, fastened to an armchair, was placed beneath a reservoir filled with cold water which poured directly upon his head through a large pipe"; and surprise baths—"the sufferer came down the corridors to the ground floor, and arrived in a square vaulted room, in which a pool had been constructed; he was pushed over backwards and into the water."[7] Such violence promised the rebirth of a baptism.

4. *Regulation of Movement.* If it is true that madness is the irregular agitation of the spirits, the disordered movement of fibers and ideas, it is also obstruction of the body

and the soul, stagnation of the humors, immobilization of the fibers in their rigidity, fixation of ideas and attention on a theme that gradually prevails over all others. It is then a matter of restoring to the mind and to the spirits, to the body and to the soul, the mobility which gives them life. This mobility, however, must be measured and controlled; it must not become a vain agitation of the fibers which no longer obey the stimuli of the exterior world. The animating idea of this therapeutic theme is the restitution of a movement that corresponds to the prudent mobility of the exterior world. Since madness can be dumb immobility, obstinate fixation as well as disorder and agitation, the cure consists in reviving in the sufferer a movement that will be both regular and real, in the sense that it will obey the rules of the world's movements.

Physicians of the period evoke the firm belief of the ancients, who attributed salutary effects to various forms of walking and running: simple walking, which both limbers and strengthens the body; running at an ever increasing speed, which better distributes the juices and humors throughout the body, at the same time that it diminishes the weight of the organs; running fully dressed, which heats and loosens the tissues, softens too rigid fibers. Sydenham especially recommends horseback riding in cases of melancholia and hypochondria: "But the best thing I have yet found to fortify and animate the blood and the spirits, is to ride almost every day, and in this manner to make rather long excursions in the fresh air. This exercise, by the extraordinary jolting it causes the lungs and especially the viscera of the lower stomach, rids the blood of the excremental humors that reside there, gives resilience to the fibers, re-establishes the functions of the organs, reanimates natural heat, evacuates degenerate juices by perspiration or other means, or else re-establishes them in their previous state, dissipates obstructions, opens all passages, and finally, through the continual movement it causes the blood, renews it, so to speak, and accords it an extraordinary vigor."[8] The rolling of the sea, the most regular, the most natural movement in the world, and the one most in accord with cosmic order—that same movement which De Lancre once considered so dangerous for the human heart, offering as it did so many hazardous temptations, improbable and always unfulfilled dreams, constitutive of the image, in fact, of infinite evil—was considered by the eighteenth century as a powerful regulator of organic mobility. In it, the very rhythm of nature spoke. Gilchrist wrote an entire treatise "on the use of sea voyages in Medicine"; Whytt found the remedy difficult to apply to those subject to melancholia; it is "difficult to convince such patients to undertake a long sea voyage; but a case must be cited of hypochondriacal vapors that immediately disappeared in a young man who was constrained to travel in a ship for four or five weeks."

Travel has the additional interest of acting directly upon the flow of ideas, or at least by a more direct means, since it passes only through the sensations. The variety of the landscape dissipates the melancholic's obstinacy: a remedy in use since antiquity, but which the eighteenth century prescribed with a new insistence, and whose forms it varied, from real travel to the imaginary voyages of literature and the theater. Antoine le Camus prescribes "in order to relax the brain" in all cases of vaporous affections: "walks, journeys, rides, exercise in the fresh air, dancing, spectacles, diverting reading, occupations that can cause the obsessive idea to be forgotten." The country, by the gentleness and variety of its landscapes, wins melancholics from their single obsession "by taking them away from the places that might revive the memory of their sufferings."

But inversely, the agitation of mania can be corrected by the good effects of a regular movement. This is no longer a restoring of motion but a regulation of agitation, momentarily stopping its course, fixing the attention. Travel is efficacious not by its incessant breaks in continuity, but by the novelty of the objects it affords, by the curiosity to which it gives birth. It should permit the external distraction of a mind which has escaped all control, and has escaped from itself in the vibration of its interior movement. "If one can discover objects or persons who may be able to distract the attention from the pursuit of deranged ideas and who may be able to fix it somewhat upon others, they must be presented often to maniacs; and it is for this reason that advantages may often be obtained from travel, which interrupts the sequence of former ideas and offers objects that fix the attention."[9]

Utilized for the changes it affords in melancholia, or for the regularity it imposes upon mania, the therapeutics of movement conceals the idea of a seizure by the world of the alienated mind. It is both a "falling in step" and a conversion, since movement prescribes its rhythm, but constitutes, by its novelty or variety, a constant appeal to the mind to leave itself and return to the world. If it is true that the techniques of immersion always concealed the ethical, almost religious memories of ablution, of a second birth, in these cures by movement we can also recognize a symmetrical moral theme, but one that is the converse of the first: to return to the world, to entrust oneself to its wisdom by returning to one's place in the general order of things, thus forgetting madness, which is the moment of pure subjectivity. We see how even in empiricism, the means of cure encounter the great organizing structures of the experience of madness in the classical period. Being both error and sin, madness is simultaneously impurity and solitude; it is withdrawn from the world, and from truth; but it is by that very fact imprisoned in evil. Its double nothingness is to be the visible form of that non-being which is *evil*, and to utter, in the void and in the sensational appearances of its delirium, the non-being of *error*. It is totally *pure*, since it is nothing if not the evanescent point of a subjectivity from which all presence of the truth has been removed; and totally *impure*, since this nothingness is the non-being of evil. The technique of cure, down to its physical symbols most highly charged with iconographic intensity—consolidation and return to movement on the one hand, purification and immersion on the other—is secretly organized around these two fundamental themes: the subject must be restored to his initial purity, and must be wrested from his pure subjectivity in order to be initiated into the world; the non-being that alienates him from himself must be annihilated, and he must be restored to the plenitude of the exterior world, to the solid truth of being.

The techniques were to subsist longer than their meaning. When, outside the experience of unreason, madness had received a purely psychological and moral status, when the relations of error and fault by which classicism defined madness were crammed into the single notion of guilt, the techniques still remained, but with a much more restricted significance; all that was sought was a mechanical effect, or a moral punishment. It was in this manner that the methods of regulating movement degenerated into the famous "rotatory machine" whose mechanism and efficacity were demonstrated by Mason Cox at the beginning of the nineteenth century:[10] a perpendicular pillar is attached to both floor and ceiling; the sufferer is attached to a chair or a bed hung from a horizontal arm moving around the pillar; by means of a "not very complicated system of gears" the machine is set for "the degree of speed desired." Cox cites one of his own observations; it concerns a man whom melancholia had thrown into a kind of stupor: "His complexion was dark and leaden, his eyes yellow, his looks constantly fixed upon the ground, his limbs motionless, his tongue dry and paralyzed, and his pulse slow." This sufferer was placed upon the rotatory machine, which was set at an increasingly rapid movement. The effect surpassed expectation; the sufferer became excessively disturbed: melancholic rigidity gave way to manic agitation. But this first effect passed, and the invalid relapsed into his initial state. The rhythm was then changed; the machine was made to turn very rapidly, but it was stopped at regular intervals, and in a very abrupt manner. The melancholia was driven out, without the rotation having had time to release the manic agitation. This "centrifugation" of melancholia is very characteristic of the new use of the old therapeutic themes. Movement no longer aimed at restoring the invalid to the truth of the exterior world, but only at producing a series of internal effects, purely mechanical and purely psychological. It was no longer the presence of the truth that determined the cure, but a functional norm. In this reinterpretation of the old method, the organism was no longer related to anything but itself and its own nature, while in the initial version, what was to be restored was its relation with the world, its essential link with being and with truth: if we add that the rotatory machine was soon used as a threat and a punishment, we see the impoverishment of the meanings which had richly sustained the therapeutic methods throughout the entire classical period. Medicine was now content to regulate and to punish, with means which had once served to exorcise sin, to dissipate error in the restoration of madness to the world's obvious truth.

In 1771, Bienville wrote apropos of *Nymphomania* that there were times when it could be cured "merely by treating the imagination; but there were none or almost none when physical remedies alone could effect a radical cure." And a little later, Beauchesne: "One would undertake in vain to cure a man suffering from madness, if one tried to succeed by physical means alone. . . . Material remedies can never enjoy a complete success without that succor which a strong and healthy mind affords a weak and sick one."

Such texts do not discover the necessity of a psychological treatment; rather they mark the end of an era: the era when the difference between physical medicaments and moral treatments was not yet accepted as obvious by medical thought. The unity of the symbols begins to break down, and the techniques lose their total significance. They are no longer credited with more than a local efficacity—on the body or on the soul. The cure again changes direction; it is no longer determined by the meaningful unity of the disease, organized around its major qualities; but, segment by segment, must address itself to the various elements that compose the disease; the cure will consist of a series of partial destructions, in which psychological attack and physical intervention are juxtaposed, complement each other, but never interpenetrate.

In fact, what to us seems already the outline of a psychological cure was no such thing to the classical physicians who applied it. Since the Renaissance, music had regained all those therapeutic virtues antiquity had attributed to it. Its effects were especially remarkable upon madness. Johann Schenck cured a man "fallen into a profound melancholia" by having him attend "concerts of musical instruments that particularly pleased him"; Wilhelm Albrecht also cured a delirious patient, after having tried all other remedies in vain, by prescribing the performance, during one of his attacks, of "a little song which awakened the sufferer, pleased him, excited him to laugh, and dispelled the paroxysm forever." Even cases of frenzy were cited as having been cured by music. Now, such observations were never meant to suggest psychological interpretations. If music cured, it was by acting upon the entire human being, by penetrating the body as directly, as efficaciously as it did the soul: did not Diemerbroek know of people stricken with the plague who had been cured by music? Doubtless most people no longer believed, as Giambattista della Porta still did, that music, in the material reality of its sounds, afforded the body the secret virtues hidden in the very substance of the instruments; no longer believed, as he did, that lymphatics were cured by "a lively air played on a holly flute," or that melancholics were soothed by "a soft air played on a hellebore flute," or that it was necessary to use "a flute made of larkspur or iris stems to cure impotent and frigid men." But if music no longer transmitted the virtues sealed in substances, it was efficacious upon the body because of the qualities it imposed upon it. It even constituted the most rigorous of all the mechanisms of quality, since at its origin it was nothing but movement, whereas once it had reached the ear it immediately became qualitative effect. Music's therapeutic value occurred because this transformation was undone in the body, quality there re-decomposed into movements, the pleasure of sensation became what it had always been: regular vibrations and equilibrium of tensions. Man, as unity of soul and body, followed the cycle of harmony in a reverse direction, redescending from the harmonious to the harmonic. In him, music was decomposed, but health restored. But there was another avenue, still more direct and more efficacious: by taking it, man no longer played the negative role of anti-instrument; he reacted as if he himself were the instrument: "If one were to consider the human body as merely an assemblage of more or less taut fibers, ignoring their sensibility, their life, their movement, one would easily conceive that music must produce the same effect on the fibers as it does on the strings of similar instruments;"[11] an effect of resonance which has no need to follow the long and complex paths of auditory sensation. The nervous system vibrates with the music that fills the air; the fibers are like so many "deaf dancers" whose movement keeps time to a music they do not hear. And this time, it is within the body itself, from the nervous fiber to the soul, that the music is recomposed, the harmonic structure of consonance restoring the harmonious functioning of the passions.

The very use of passion in the therapeutics of madness must not be understood as a form of psychological medication. To employ passion against dementia is merely to attack the unity of soul and body at its most rigorous point, to utilize an event in the double system of its effects, and in the immediate correspondence of their meaning. To cure madness by passion implies that one accepts the reciprocal symbolism of soul and body. Fear, in the eighteenth century, was regarded as one of the passions most advisable to arouse in madmen. It was considered the natural complement of the constraints imposed upon maniacs and lunatics; a sort of discipline was even imagined which would immediately accompany and compensate every attack of anger in a maniac by a reaction of fear: "It is by force that the furies of a maniac are overcome; it is by opposing fear to anger that anger may be mastered. If the terror of punishment and public shame are associated in the mind during attacks of anger, one will not appear without the other; the poison and the antidote are inseparable."[12] But fear is efficacious not only at the level of the effects of the disease; it is the disease itself that fear attacks and suppresses. It has, in fact, the property of petrifying the operations of the nervous system, somehow congealing its too mobile fibers, controlling all their disordered movements; "fear being a passion that diminishes the excitation of the brain, it can consequently calm its excesses, and especially the irascible excitation of maniacs."[13]

If the fear-anger antithesis is efficacious against manic irritation, it can be used inversely against the unmotivated fears of melancholics, hypochondriacs, and all those who have a lymphatic temperament. Tissot, reviving the traditional idea that anger is a discharge of bile, considers that it is useful for dissolving the phlegms amassed in the stomach and in the blood. By subjecting the nervous fibers to a stronger tension, anger gives them more vigor, thus restoring their lost elasticity and permitting fear to disappear. The cure by passion is based on a constant metaphor of qualities and movements; it always implies that they are immediately transferable in their own modality from the body to the soul, and vice versa. It must be used, says Scheidenmantel in the treatise he devotes to this form of cure, "when the cure necessitates in the body changes identical to those which this passion produces." And it is in this sense that it can be the universal substitute for all other physical therapeutics; it is only another way to produce the same sequence of effects. Between a cure by the passions and a cure by the prescriptions of the pharmacopoeia, there is no difference in nature; but only a diversity in the mode of access to those mechanisms which are common to the body and to the soul. "The passions must be utilized, if the sufferer cannot be led by reason to do what is necessary for the restoration of his health."

It is thus not possible to use as a valid or at least meaningful distinction for the classical period the difference—immediately apparent to us—between physical medications and psychological or moral medications. The difference only begins to exist in all its profundity the day when fear is no longer used as a method for arresting movement, but as a punishment; when joy does not signify organic expansion, but reward; when anger is nothing more than a response to concerted humiliation; in short, when the nineteenth century, by inventing its famous "moral methods," has brought madness and its cure into the domain of guilt. The distinction between the physical and the moral becomes a practical concept in the medicine of the mind only when the problematics of madness shifts to an interrogation of the subject responsible. The purely moral space, which is then defined, gives the exact measurements of that psychological inwardness where modern man seeks both his depth and his truth. Physical therapeutics tends to become, in the first half of the nineteenth century, a cure devised by an innocent determinism, and moral treatment a cure wrought by a culpable freedom. Psychology, as a means of curing, is henceforth organized around punishment. Before seeking to relieve, it inflicts suffering within the rigor of a moral necessity. "Do not employ consolations, they are useless; have no recourse to reasoning, it does not persuade; do not be sad with melancholics, your sadness sustains theirs; do not assume an air of gaiety with them, they are only hurt by it. What is required is great *sang-froid*, and when necessary, severity. Let your reason be their rule of conduct. A single string still vibrates in them, that of pain; have courage enough to pluck it."[14]

The heterogeneity of the physical and the moral in medical thought is not a result of Descartes's definition of substances; a century and a half of post-Cartesian medicine did not succeed in assimilating that separation on the level of problems and methods, nor in understanding the distinction of substances as an opposition of organic to psychological. Cartesian or anti-Cartesian, classical medicine never introduced Descartes's metaphysical dualism into anthropology. And when the separation did occur, it was not by a renewed loyalty to the *Meditations*, but by a new privilege accorded to transgression. Only the use of punishment distinguished, in treating the mad, the medications of the body from those of the soul. A purely psychological medicine was made possible only when madness was alienated in guilt.

Of this, however, a whole aspect of medical practice during the classical period might stand as a long denial. The psychological element, in its purity, seems to have its place among the techniques. How else explain the importance attached to exhortation, to persuasion, to reasoning, to that whole dialogue in which the classical physician engages with his patient, independently of the cure by bodily remedies? How explain that Sauvages can write, in agreement with all his contemporaries: "One must be a philosopher to be able to cure the diseases of the soul. For as the origin of these diseases is nothing more than a violent desire for a thing which the sufferer envisages as a good, it is part of the physician's duty to prove to him by solid reasons that what he desires so ardently is an apparent good but a real evil, in order to make him renounce his error."

In fact this approach to madness is neither more nor less psychological than any of those we have already discussed. Language, the formulations of truth or morality, are in direct contact with the body; and it is Bienville again, in his treatise on *Nymphomania*, who shows how the adoption or the rejection of an ethical principle can directly modify the course of organic processes. However, there is a difference in nature between those techniques which consist in modifying the qualities common to body and soul, and those which consist in treating madness by discourse. In the first case, the technique is one of metaphors, at the level of a disease that is a deterioration of nature; in the second, the technique is one of language, at the level of a madness perceived as reason's debate with itself. The technique, in this last form, functions in a domain where madness is "treated" —in all the senses of the word—in terms of truth and error. In short, there always existed, throughout the classical period, a juxtaposition of two technical universes in the therapeutics of madness. One, which is based on an implicit mechanics of qualities, and which addresses madness as essentially *passion*—that is, a certain compound (movement-quality) belonging to both body and soul; the other, which is based on the discursive movement of reason reasoning with itself, and which addresses madness as error, as double inanity of language and image, as *delirium*. The structural cycle of passion and of delirium which constitutes the classical experience of madness reappears here in the world of techniques—but in a syncopated form. Its unity is expressed only distantly. What is immediately visible, in capital letters, is the duality, almost the opposition, in the medicine of madness, of the methods of suppressing the disease, and of the forms of treating unreason. These latter can be reduced to three essential configurations.

1. *Awakening.* Since delirium is the dream of waking persons, those who are delirious must be torn from this quasi-sleep, recalled from their waking dream and its images to an authentic awakening, where the dream disappears before the images of perception. Descartes sought this absolute awakening, which dismisses one by one all the forms of illusion, at the beginning of his *Meditations*, and found it, paradoxically, in the very awareness of the dream, in the consciousness of deluded consciousness. But in madmen, it is medicine which must effect the awakening, transforming the solitude of Cartesian courage into an authoritarian intervention, by the man awake and certain of his wakefulness, into the illusion of the man who sleeps waking: a short cut that dogmatically reduces Descartes's long road. What Descartes discovers at the end of his resolution and in the *doubling* of a consciousness that never separates from itself and does not split, medicine imposes from outside, and in the dissociation of doctor and patient. The physician, in relation to the madman, reproduces the mo-

ment of the Cogito in relation to the time of the dream, of illusion, and of madness. A completely exterior Cogito, alien to cogitation itself, and which can be imposed upon it only in the form of an invasion.

This structure of invasion by wakefulness is one of the most constant forms among the therapeutics of madness. It often assumes the simplest aspects, simultaneously those most highly charged with images and those most credited with immediate powers. It is asserted that a gun discharged near her cured a young girl of convulsions contracted as the result of severe grief. Without going so far as this icon-ographic representation of the methods of awakening, sud-den and strong emotions achieve the same result. It is in this spirit that Boerhaave performed his famous cure of con-vulsives at Haarlem. In the city hospital, an epidemic of convulsions had broken out. Antispasmodics, administered in strong doses, did no good. Boerhaave ordered "that stoves filled with burning coals be brought, and that iron hooks of a certain form be heated in them; thereupon, he said in a loud voice that since all the means hitherto em-ployed in attempting to cure the convulsions had been use-less, he knew of only one other remedy, which was to burn to the bone, with red-hot irons, a certain spot on the arm of any person, male or female, who suffered an attack of a convulsive illness."[15]

Slower, but also more certain of the truth it confronts, is the awakening that proceeds from wisdom itself and from its insistent, imperative progress through the landscapes of madness. From this wisdom, in its various forms, Willis sought the cure of the various madnesses. For imbeciles, a pedagogical wisdom; an "attentive and devoted master must educate them completely"; they must be taught, little by little and very slowly, what children are taught in school. For melancholics, a wisdom that takes as its model the most rigorous and most evident forms of truth: what is imaginary in their delirium will disappear in the light of an incontestable truth; this is why "mathematical and chemical" studies are strongly recommended. For the others, the wisdom of a well-ordered life will reduce their delirium; there is no need to impose upon them any other truth than that of their everyday life; remaining in their homes, "they must continue to manage their affairs, direct their families, order and cultivate their estates, their gardens, their orchards, their fields." It is, on the contrary, the exactitude of a social order, imposed from without and, if necessary, by force, that can gradually restore the minds of maniacs to the light of truth: "For this, the insane person, placed in a special house, will be treated, either by the doctor or by trained assistants, in such a way that he may be always maintained in his duty, in his appearance and habits, by warnings, by remonstrances, and by punishments immediately inflicted."[16]

Little by little during the classical period, this authoritarian awakening of madness would lose its original meaning and limit itself to being no more than recollection of moral law, return to the good, fidelity to the law. What Willis still intended as a reintroduction to truth would no longer be entirely understood by Sauvages, who speaks of lucidity in the recognition of the good: "Thus, one can recall to reason those whom false principles of moral philosophy have caused to lose their own, as long as they are willing to examine with us what is truly good, and what things are to be preferred to others." Already it is no longer as awakener that the physician is to function, but as moralist. Against madness, Tissot considers that "a pure conscience, without reproach, is an excellent preservative." And soon comes Pinel, for whom the awakening to truth no longer has a meaning in the cure, but only obedience and blind submission: "A fundamental principle for the cure of mania in a great number of cases is to resort first of all to an energetic repression, and to proceed subsequently to methods of benevolence."

2. *Theatrical Representation.* In appearance at least, this is a technique rigorously opposed to that of *awakening*. There, delirium, in all its immediate vivacity, was confronted by the patient work of reason. Either in the form of a slow pedagogy, or the form of an authoritarian invasion, reason was imposed, as if by the weight of its own being. The non-being of madness, the inanity of error, was forced to yield, finally, to this pressure of the truth. Here, the therapeutic operation functions entirely in the space of the imagination; we are dealing with a complicity of the unreal with itself; the imagination must play its own game, voluntarily propose new images, espouse delirium for delirium's sake, and without opposition or confrontation, without even a visible dialectic, must, paradoxically, cure. Health must lay siege to madness and conquer it in the very nothingness in which the disease is imprisoned. When the imagination "is sick, it can be cured only by the effect of a healthy and active imagination. . . . It is all one whether the invalid's imagination is cured by fear, by a strong and painful impression upon the senses, or by an illusion."[17] Illusion can cure the illusory—while reason alone can free from the unreasonable. What then is this dark power of the imaginary?

Insofar as it is of the essence of the image to be taken for reality, it is reciprocally characteristic of reality that it can mime the image, pretend to the same substance, the same significance. Without a break, without a jolt, perception can continue the dream, fill in its gaps, confirm what is precarious about it, and lead it to its fulfillment. If illusion can appear as true as perception, perception in its turn can become the visible, unchallengeable truth of illusion. Such is the first step of the cure by "theatrical representation": to integrate the unreality of the image into perceived truth, without the latter seeming to contradict or even contest the former. Thus Zacatus Lusitanus describes the cure of a melancholic who believed himself damned while still on earth because of the enormity of the sins he had committed. In the impossibility of convincing him by reasonable arguments that he could be saved, his physicians accepted his delirium and caused an "angel" dressed in white, with a sword in its hand, to appear to him, and after a severe exhortation this delusive vision announced that his sins had been remitted.

From this very example, we see the next step: *representation* within the *image* is not enough; it is also necessary to *continue* the delirious *discourse*. For in the patient's insane words there is a voice that speaks; it obeys its own grammar, it articulates a meaning. Grammar and meaning must be maintained in such a way that the representation of the hallucination in reality does not seem like the transition from one register to another, like a translation into a new language, with an altered meaning. The same language must continue to make itself understood, merely bringing a new deductive element to the rigor of its discourse. Yet this element is not indifferent; the problem is not to pursue the delirium, but by continuing it to bring it to an end. It must be led to a state of paroxysm and crisis in which, without any addition of a foreign element, it is confronted by itself and forced to argue against the demands of its own truth. The real and perceptual discourse that prolongs the delirious language of the images must therefore, without escaping the latter's laws, without departing from its sovereignty, exercise a positive function in relation to it; it tightens that language around its essential element; if it represents it at the risk of confirming it, it is in order to dramatize it. The case is cited of a sufferer who thought that he was dead, and was really dying from not eating; "a group of people who had made themselves pale and were dressed like the dead, entered his room, set up a table, brought food, and began to eat and drink before the bed. The starving 'dead man' looked at them; they were astonished that he stayed in bed; they persuaded him that dead people eat at least as much as living ones. He readily accommodated himself to this idea."[18] It is within a continuous discourse that the elements of delirium, coming into contradiction, bring on the crisis. A crisis which is, in a very ambiguous manner, both medical and theatrical; a whole tradition of Western medicine dating from Hippocrates here intersects, suddenly and for only a few years, with one of the major forms of theatrical experience. Before us appears the great theme of a crisis that confronts the madman with his own meaning, reason with unreason, man's lucid ruse with the blindness of the lunatic—a crisis which marks the point at which illusion, turned back upon itself, will open to the dazzlement of truth.

This opening is imminent in the crisis; in fact it is this opening, with its immediate proximity, that constitutes the essential element of the crisis. But the opening does not result from the crisis itself. In order for the crisis to be medical and not simply dramatic, in order for it to be not an annihilation of the man, but simply a suppression of the disease; in short, in order for the dramatic representation of the delirium to have an effect of comic purification, a ruse must be introduced at a given moment. A ruse, or at least an element which surreptitiously alters the autonomous operation of the delirium, and which, ceaselessly confirming it, does not bind it to its own truth without at the same time linking it to the necessity for its own suppression. The simplest example of this method is the ruse employed with delirious patients who imagine they perceive within their bodies an object or an extraordinary animal: "When an invalid believes that he has a living animal shut up within his body, one must pretend to have withdrawn it; if it is in the stomach, one may, by means of a powerful purge, produce this effect, throwing such an animal into the basin without the patient's noticing."[19] The theatrical device represents the object of the delirium but cannot do so without externalizing it, and if it gives the invalid a perceptual confirmation of his illusion, it does so only while ridding him of it by force. The artificial reconstitution of delirium constitutes the real distance in which the sufferer recovers his liberty.

But sometimes, there is even no need of this "distancing." It is within the quasi-perception of the delirium that there is established, by means of a ruse, a perceptual element, silent at first, but whose gradual affirmation will come to contest the entire system. It is in himself and in the perception which confirms his delirium that the sufferer perceives the liberating reality. Trallion reports how a physician dissipated the delirium of a melancholic who imagined he had no head, but only a kind of void in its place; the physician, entering into the delirium, agreed at the sufferer's request to fill up this space, and placed upon his head a great ball of lead. Soon the discomfort that resulted from the painful weight convinced the invalid that he had a head. Ultimately the ruse and its function of comic reduction can be assured, with the complicity of the physician but without any other direct intervention on his part, by the spontaneous reaction of the sufferer's organism. In the case cited above of the melancholic who was really dying because he would not eat, believing himself already dead, the theatrical representation of a dead men's banquet incited him to eat; this nourishment restored him, "the consumption of food made him quieter," and the organic disorder thus disappearing, the delirium which was indissociably cause and effect disappeared forthwith. Thus the real death that would have resulted from the imaginary death was avoided by reality, by the mere representation of unreal death. The exchange of non-being with itself is carried out in this ingenious play: the non-being of delirium is turned against the being of the illness, and suppresses it by the simple fact that it is driven out of the delirium by dramatic representation. The fulfillment of delirium's non-being in being is able to suppress it as non-being itself; and this by the pure mechanism of its internal contradiction—a mechanism that is both a play on words and a play of illusion, games of language and of the image; the delirium, in effect, is suppressed as non-being since it becomes a perceived form of being; but since the being of delirium is entirely in its non-being, it is suppressed as delirium. And its confirmation in theatrical fantasy restores it to a truth which, by holding it captive in reality, drives it out of reality itself, and makes it disappear in the non-delirious discourse of reason.

3. *The Return to the Immediate.* Since madness is illusion, the cure of madness, if it is true that such a cure can be effected by theater, can also and still more directly be effected by the suppression of theater. To entrust madness and its empty world directly to the plenitude of a nature which does not deceive because its immediacy does not acknowledge non-being, is to deliver madness both to its own truth (since madness, as a disease, is after all only a natural being), and to its closest contradiction (since delirium, as appearance without content, is the very contrary of the often secret and invisible wealth of nature). This contradiction thus appears as the reason of unreason, in a double sense: it withholds unreason's causes, and at the same time conceals the principle of its suppression. It must be noted, however, that these themes are not contemporary with the classical period for its entire duration. Although they are organized around the same experience of unreason, they follow after the themes of theatrical representation; and their appearance marks the moment when the debate on being and illusion begins to yield to a problematics of na-

ture. Games of theatrical illusion lose their meaning, and the artificial techniques of iconographic representation are replaced by the simple and confident act of a natural reduction. And this in an ambiguous direction, since it is as much a question of reduction *by* nature as of a reduction *to* nature.

The return to the immediate is the therapeutics *par excellence*, because it is the rigorous refusal of therapeutics: it cures insofar as it is a disregard of all cures. It is in man's passivity with regard to himself, in the silence he imposes on his art and his artifices, that nature engages in an activity which is exactly reciprocal to renunciation. For, to consider it more closely, this passivity of man is real activity; when man entrusts himself to medicine, he escapes the law of labor that nature itself imposes on him; he sinks into the world of artifice, and of anti-nature, of which his madness is only one of the manifestations; it is by ignoring this disease and resuming his place in the activity of natural beings that man in an apparent passivity (which is in fact only an industrious fidelity) succeeds in being cured. Thus Bernadin de Saint-Pierre explains how he cured himself of a "strange disease," in which, "like Oedipus, he saw two suns." Medicine had offered him its succor, and had informed him that "the seat of his disease was in the nerves." In vain he applied the most highly prized medicaments; he soon noticed that the physicians themselves were killed by their own remedies: "It was to Jean-Jacques Rousseau that I owed my return to health. I had read, in his immortal writings, among other natural truths, that man is made to work, not to meditate. Until that time I had exercised my soul and rested my body; I changed my ways; I exercised my body and rested my soul. I gave up most books; I turned my eyes to the works of nature, which addressed all my senses in a language that neither time nor nations can corrupt. My history and my newspapers were the plants of the field and forest; it was not my thoughts that struggled to them, as in the system of men, but their thoughts that came to me in a thousand agreeable shapes."[20]

Despite the formulations of it which certain disciples of Rousseau managed to propose, this return to the immediate was neither absolute nor simple. For madness, even if it is provoked or sustained by what is most artificial in society, appears, in its violent forms, as the savage expression of the most primitive human desires. Madness in the classical period, as we have seen, is rooted in the threats of bestiality— a bestiality completely dominated by predatory and murderous instincts. To entrust madness to nature would be, by an uncontrolled reversal, to abandon it to that fury of anti-nature. The cure of madness thus supposes a return to what is immediate, not in relation to desire, but in relation to the imagination—a return that dismisses from man's life and pleasures everything that is artificial, unreal, imaginary. The therapeutics, by the reflective plunge into the immediate, secretly supposes the mediation of a wisdom which distinguishes, in nature, between what derives from violence and what derives from truth. This is the whole difference between the *Savage* and the *Laborer.* "Savages . . . lead the life of a carnivorous animal rather than that of a reasonable being"; the life of the Laborer, on the other hand, "is in fact happier than that of the man of the world." On the savage's side, immediate desire, without discipline, without constraint, without real morality; on the laborer's side, pleasure without mediation, in other words, without vain stimulus, without provocation or imaginary achievement. What, in nature and its immediate virtues, cures madness is pleasure—but a pleasure that on one hand makes desire vain without even having to repress it, since it offers a plenitude of satisfaction in advance, and on the other makes imagination absurd, since it spontaneously contributes the happy presence of reality. "Pleasures enter into the eternal order of things; they exist invariably; certain conditions are necessary to form them . . . ; these conditions are not arbitrary; nature has formed them; imagination cannot create, and the man most devoted to pleasures can increase them only by renouncing all those which do not bear this stamp of nature."[21] The immediate world of the laborer is thus a world suffused with wisdom and measure, which cures madness insofar as it renders desire useless, along with the movements of passion desire gives rise to, and also insofar as it reduces along with the imaginary all the possibilities of delirium. What Tissot understands by "pleasure" is this immediate curative agent, liberated from both passion and language: that is, from the two great forms of human experience that give birth to unreason.

And perhaps nature, as the concrete form of the immediate, has an even more fundamental power in the suppression of madness. For it has the power of freeing man from his freedom. In nature—that nature, at least, which is measured by the double exclusion of the violence of desire and the unreality of hallucination—man is doubtless liberated from social constraints (those which force him "to calculate and draw up the balance sheet of his imaginary pleasures which bear that name but are none") and from the uncontrollable movement of the passions. But by that very fact, he is gently and as it were internally bound by a system of natural obligations. The pressures of the healthiest needs, the rhythm of the days and the seasons, the calm necessity to feed and shelter oneself, constrain the disorder of madmen to a regular observance. The excessively remote inventions of the imagination are dismissed, along with the excessively urgent disguises of desire. In the gentleness of a pleasure that does not constrain, man is linked to the wisdom of nature, and this fidelity in the form of freedom dissipates the unreason which juxtaposes in its paradox the extreme determinism of passion and the extreme fantasy of the image. Thus one begins to dream, in these mingled landscapes of ethics and medicine, of a liberation from madness: a liberation that must not be understood in its origin as the discovery, by philanthropy, of the humanity of madmen, but as a desire to open madness to the gentle constraints of nature.

The old village of Gheel which, from the end of the Middle Ages, still bore witness to the now forgotten relation between the confinement of madmen and the exclusion of lepers, also received in the last years of the eighteenth century a sudden reinterpretation. What had once marked, here, the entire violent, pathetic separation of the world of madmen from the world of men, now conveyed the idyllic values of a rediscovered unity of unreason and nature. This village had once signified that madmen were confined, and that therefore the man of reason was protected from them; now it manifested that the madman was liberated, and that, in this liberty which put him on a level with the laws of nature, he was reconciled with the man of reason. At Gheel, according to Jouy's description of it, "four-fifths of the inhabitants are mad, but mad in the full sense of the word, and they enjoy without restraint the same freedom as the other citizens. . . . Healthful food, pure air, all the devices of liberty: such is the regimen prescribed for them, and to which the greatest number, by the end of a year, owe their cure." Without anything in the institutions having as yet really changed, the meaning of exclusion and of confinement begins to alter: it slowly assumes positive values, and the neutral, empty, nocturnal space in which unreason was formerly restored to its nothingness begins to be peopled by a nature to which madness, liberated, is obliged to submit. Confinement, as the separation of reason from unreason, is not suppressed; but at the very heart of its intention, the space it occupies reveals natural powers, more constraining for madness, more likely to subjugate it in its essence, than the whole of the old limiting and repressive system. Madness must be liberated from that system so that, in the space of confinement, now endowed with a positive efficacity, it will be free to slough off its savage freedom, and to welcome the demands of nature that are for it both truth and law. Insofar as it is law, nature constrains the violence of desire; insofar as it is truth, it reduces anti-nature, and all the hallucinations of the imaginary.

Here is how Pinel describes that nature, speaking of the hospital of Saragossa: there has been established here "a sort of counterpoise to the mind's extravagances by the attraction and the charm inspired by the cultivation of the fields, by the natural instinct that leads man to sow the earth and thus to satisfy his needs by the fruit of his labors. From morning on, you can see them . . . leaving gaily for the various parts of a vast enclosure that belongs to the hospital, sharing with a sort of emulation the tasks appropriate to the seasons, cultivating wheat, vegetables, concerned in turn with the harvest, with trellises, with the vintage, with olive picking, and finding in the evening, in their solitary asylum, calm and quiet sleep. The most constant experience has indicated, in this hospital, that this is the surest and most efficacious way to restore man to reason."[22] Beneath the conventional images, the rigor of a meaning is easily perceived. The return to the immediate is effective against unreason only insofar as the immediate is controlled—and divided against itself; an immediate in which violence is isolated from truth, savagery separated from liberty, in which nature can no longer recognize itself in the fantastic figures of anti-nature. In short, an immediate in which nature is mediatized by morality. In a space so arranged, madness will never again be able to speak the language of unreason, with all that in it transcends the natural phenomena of disease. It will be entirely enclosed in a pathology. A transformation which later periods have received as a positive acquisition, the accession, if not of a truth, at least of what would make the recognition of truth possible; but which in the eyes of history must appear as what it was: that is, the reduction of the classical experience of unreason to a strictly moral perception of madness, which would secretly serve as a nucleus for all the concepts that the nineteenth century would subsequently vindicate as scientific, positive, and experimental.

This metamorphosis, which occurred in the second half of the eighteenth century, was initiated in the techniques of cure. But it very quickly appeared more generally, winning over the minds of reformers, guiding the great reorganization of the experience of madness in the last years of the century. Very soon Pinel could write: "How necessary it is, in order to forestall hypochondria, melancholia, or mania, to follow the immutable laws of morality!"

In the classical period, it is futile to try to distinguish physical therapeutics from psychological medications, for the simple reason that psychology did not exist. When the consumption of bitters was prescribed, for example, it was not a question of physical treatment, since it was the soul as well as the body that was to be scoured; when the simple life of a laborer was prescribed for a melancholic, when the comedy of his delirium was acted out before him, this was not a psychological intervention, since the movement of the spirits in the nerves, the density of the humors were principally involved. But in the first case, we are dealing with an art of *the transformation of qualities*, a technique in which the essence of madness is taken as nature, and as disease; in the second, we are dealing with an art of discourse, and of *the restitution of truth*, in which madness is significant as unreason.

When, in the years that followed, this great experience of unreason, whose unity is characteristic of the classical period, was dissociated, when madness, entirely confined within a moral intuition, was nothing more than disease, then the distinction we have just established assumed another meaning; what had belonged to disease pertained to the organic, and what had belonged to unreason, to the transcendence of its discourse, was relegated to the psychological. And it is precisely here that psychology was born —not as the truth of madness, but as a sign that madness was now detached from its truth which was unreason and that it was henceforth nothing but a phenomenon adrift, *insignificant* upon the undefined surface of nature. An enigma without any truth except that which could reduce it.

This is why we must do justice to Freud. Between Freud's *Five Case Histories* and Janet's scrupulous investigations of *Psychological Healing*, there is more than the density of a *discovery;* there is the sovereign violence of a *return*. Janet enumerated the elements of a division, drew up his inventory, annexed here and there, perhaps conquered. Freud went back to madness at the level of its *language,* reconstituted one of the essential elements of an experience reduced to silence by positivism; he did not make a major addition to the list of psychological treatments for madness; he restored, in medical thought, the possibility of a dialogue with unreason. Let us not be surprised that the most "psychological" of medications has so quickly encountered its converse and its organic confirmations. It is not psychology that is involved in psychoanalysis: but precisely an experience of unreason that it has been psychology's meaning, in the modern world, to mask.

VII

THE GREAT FEAR

"ONE afternoon, I was there, looking a great deal, speaking rarely, listening as little as I could, when I was accosted by one of the most bizarre persons in this country, where God has not let them lack. He was a mixture of loftiness, baseness, good sense, and unreason."

In doubt's confrontation with its major dangers, Descartes realized that he could not be mad—though he was to acknowledge for a long time to come that all the powers of unreason kept vigil around his thought; but as a philosopher, resolutely undertaking to doubt, he could not be "one of these insane ones." Rameau's Nephew, though, knew quite well—and among his fleeting certainties, this was the most obstinate—that he was mad. "Before beginning, he heaved a profound sigh and raised his hands to his forehead; then he regained his calm demeanor and said to me: you know I am ignorant, mad, impertinent, and lazy."[1]

The eighteenth century could not exactly understand the meaning expressed in *Le Neveu de Rameau*. Yet something had happened, just when the text was written, which promised a decisive change. A curious thing: the unreason that had been relegated to the distance of confinement reappeared, fraught with new dangers and as if endowed with a new power of interrogation. Yet what the eighteenth century first noticed about it was not the secret interrogation, but only the social effects: the torn clothing, the arrogance in rags, the tolerated insolence whose disturbing powers were silenced by an amused indulgence. The eighteenth century might not have recognized itself in Rameau's Nephew, but it was entirely present in the *I* who served him as interlocutor and as a type of "exhibitor," amused yet reticent, and with a secret anxiety: for this was the first time since the Great Confinement that the madman had become a social individual; it was the first time that anyone had entered into conversation with him, and that, once again, he was questioned. Unreason reappeared as a classification, which is not much; but it nonetheless reappeared, and slowly recovered its place in the familiarity of the social landscape. It was there some ten years before the Revolution, when Mercier found it without more astonishment than: "Go into another café; a man whispers to you in a calm and confident tone: 'You cannot imagine, Monsieur, the Government's ingratitude toward me, and its blindness to its own interests! For thirty years I have neglected my own affairs; I have shut myself up in my study, meditating, dreaming, calculating; I have devised a project to pay all the State's debts; another to enrich the King and assure him an income of 400 million; another to destroy England forever, whose very name affronts me. . . . When, utterly devoted to these vast operations that demand all the application of genius, I was distracted by domestic problems, some nagging creditors kept me in prison for three years. . . . But, Monsieur, you see how patriotism is valued—I die unknown and a martyr for my country.' "[2] At a distance, such persons form a circle around Rameau's Nephew; they do not have his dimensions; it is only in the search for the picturesque that they can pass for his epigones.

And yet they are a little more than a social profile, a caricatural silhouette. There is something inside them that concerns and touches the unreason of the eighteenth century. Their chatter, their anxiety, that vague delirium and that ultimate anguish they experience commonly enough—and in real existences which can still be traced. As with the libertine, the debauchee, or the ruffian of the end of the seventeenth century, it is difficult to say whether they are mad, sick, or criminal. Mercier himself does not quite know what status to give them: "Thus there are in Paris some very good people, economists and anti-economists, who have warm hearts, eager for the public good; but unfortunately they have *cracked heads;* that is, they are short-sighted, they do not know what century they are in, nor what men they are dealing with; more unbearable than idiots, because with pennies and false lights they start from an impossible principle and reason falsely therefrom." They really existed, these schemers with "cracked heads," adding a muffled accompaniment of unreason to the reason of the philosophers, and around those plans for reform, those constitutions, those projects; the rationality of the Enlightenment found in them a sort of darkened mirror, an inoffensive caricature. But is it not essential that in a movement of amused indulgence, a personage of unreason is allowed back into daylight, at the very moment he was believed to be most profoundly hidden in the space of confinement? As if classical reason once again admitted a proximity, a relation, a quasi-resemblance between itself and the images of unreason. As if, at the moment of its triumph, reason revived and permitted to drift on the margins of order a character whose mask it had fashioned in derision—a sort of double in which it both recognized and revoked itself.

Yet fear and anxiety were not far off: in the reaction of confinement, they reappeared, doubled. People were once afraid, people were still afraid, of being confined; at the end of the eighteenth century, Sade was still haunted by fear of what he called "the black men" who lay in wait to put him away. But now the estate of confinement acquired its own powers; it became in its turn the birthplace of evil, and could henceforth spread that evil by itself, instituting another reign of terror.

Suddenly, in a few years in the middle of the eighteenth century, a fear arose—a fear formulated in medical terms but animated, basically, by a moral myth. People were in dread of a mysterious disease that spread, it was said, from the houses of confinement and would soon threaten the cities. They spoke of prison fevers; they evoked the wagons of criminals, men in chains who passed through the cities, leaving disease in their wake; scurvy was thought to cause contagions; it was said that the air, tainted by disease, would corrupt the residential quarters. And the great image of medieval horror reappeared, giving birth, in the metaphors of dread, to a second panic. The house of confinement was no longer only the lazar house at the city's edge; it was leprosy itself confronting the town: "A terrible ulcer upon the body politic, an ulcer that is wide, deep, and draining, one that cannot be imagined except by looking full upon it. Even the air of the place, which can be smelled four hundred yards away—everything suggests that one is approaching a place of violence, an asylum of degradation and infortune."[3] Many of these centers of confinement were built in the very places where the lepers had once been kept; it was as if, across the centuries, the new tenants had received the contagion. They revived the blazon and the meaning that had been borne in those places: "Too great a leper for the capital! The name of Bicêtre is a word no one can pronounce without an inexpressible feeling of repugnance, of horror and contempt. . . . It has become the receptacle for all the most monstrous and vile things to be found in society."[4]

The evil which men had attempted to exclude by confinement reappeared, to the horror of the public, in a fantastic guise. There appeared, ramifying in every direction, the themes of an evil, both physical and moral, that enveloped in this very ambiguity the mingled powers of corrosion and horror. There prevailed, then, a sort of undifferentiated image of "rottenness" that had to do with the corruption of morals as well as with the decomposition of the flesh, and upon which were based both the repugnance and the pity felt for the confined. First the evil began to ferment in the closed spaces of confinement. It had all the virtues attributed to acid in eighteenth-century chemistry: its fine particles, sharp as needles, penetrated bodies and hearts as easily as if they were passive and friable alkaline particles. The mixture boiled immediately, releasing harmful vapors and corrosive liquids: "These wards are a dreadful place where all crimes together ferment and spread around them, as by fermentation, a contagious atmosphere which those who live there breathe and which seems to become attached to them."[5] These burning vapors then rise, spread through the air, and finally fall upon the neighborhood, impregnating bodies and contaminating souls. Thus the idea of a contagion of evil-as-rottenness is articulated in images. The palpable agent of this epidemic is air, that air which is called "tainted," the term obscurely suggesting that it is not in conformity with the purity of its nature, and that it acts as the communicating element of the taint. It is sufficient to remember the value, both moral and medical, ascribed at about the same period to country air (bodily health, spiritual vigor), to realize the whole complex of contrary meanings conveyed by the corrupted air of hospitals, prisons, houses of confinement. By this atmosphere laden with maleficent vapors, entire cities were threatened, whose inhabitants would be slowly impregnated with rottenness and taint.

And these are not only reflections halfway between morality and medicine. We must doubtless take into account an entire literary development, a whole emotional, perhaps political exploitation of vague fears. But in certain cities there were movements of panic as real, as easy to date, as the great crises of horror that wracked the Middle Ages from time to time. In 1780 an epidemic spread through Paris: its origin was attributed to the infection of the Hôpital Général; there was even talk of burning the buildings of Bicêtre. The police lieutenant, faced with the frenzy of the population, sent a commission of inquiry which included, together with several staff doctors, the Dean of the Faculté and the physician of the Hôpital Général. According to their findings, Bicêtre was subject to a "putrid fever" which was linked to the bad quality of the air. As for the original source of the disease, the report denied that it lay in the internees and the infection they might spread; it must be attributed quite simply to the bad weather that made the disease endemic in the capital; the symptoms that were to be observed at the Hôpital Général were "in accordance with the nature of the season and exactly the same as the illnesses observed in Paris at the same period." The population had to be reassured and Bicêtre cleared of its guilt: "The rumors that have begun to spread concerning a contagious illness at Bicêtre that is capable of infecting the capital are without foundation." Evidently the report did not check the rumors completely, since some time later the physician of the Hôpital Général issued another in which he made the same statement; he was forced to acknowledge the poor sanitary conditions of Bicêtre, but "matters have not, for all that, reached the cruel extremity of converting the refuge of these unfortunates into another source of inevitable evils much more lamentable than those which require a remedy as prompt as it is efficacious."

The circle was closed: all those forms of unreason which had replaced leprosy in the geography of evil, and which had been banished into the remotest social distance, now became a visible leprosy and offered their running sores to the promiscuity of men. Unreason was once more present; but marked now by an imaginary stigma of disease, which added its powers of terror.

Thus it is in the realm of the fantastic and not within the rigor of medical thought that unreason joins illness and draws closer to it. Long before the problem of discovering to what degree the unreasonable is pathological was formulated, there had formed, in the space of confinement and by an alchemy peculiar to it, a mélange combining the dread of unreason and the old specters of disease. From a great distance, the old confusions about leprosy functioned once again; and it is the vigor of these fantastic themes which was the first agent of synthesis between the world of unreason and the medical universe. They first communicated through the hallucinations of fear, combining the infernal mixtures of "corruption" and "taint." It is important, perhaps decisive for the place madness was to occupy in modern culture, that *homo medicus* was not called into the world of confinement as an *arbiter*, to divide what was crime from what was madness, what was evil from what was illness, but rather as a *guardian*, to protect others from the vague danger that exuded through the walls of confinement. It is easy to suppose that a free and generous sympathy awakened interest in the fate of the confined, and that a more diligent and informed medical attention could recognize disease where previously the authorities had indiscriminately punished transgressions. As it happened, the atmosphere was not one of such benevolent neutrality. If a doctor was summoned, if he was asked to observe, it was because people were afraid—afraid of the strange chemistry that seethed behind the walls of confinement, afraid of the powers forming there that threatened to propagate. The doctor came, once the conversion of images was effected, the disease having already assumed the ambiguous aspects of fermentation, of corruption, of tainted exhalations, of decomposed flesh. What is traditionally called "progress" toward madness's attaining a medical status was in fact made possible only by a strange regression. In the inextricable mixture of moral and physical contagions,[6] and by virtue of that symbolism of Impurity so familiar to the eighteenth century, very early images rose again to the surface of human memory. And it was as a result of this reactivation of images, more than by an improvement of knowledge, that unreason was eventually confronted by medical thought. Paradoxically, in the return to that fantastic life which mingles with the contemporary images of illness, positivism would gain a hold over unreason, or rather would discover a new reason for protecting itself against it.

The question, for the moment, was not to suppress the houses of confinement, but to neutralize them as potential causes of a new evil. The problem was to organize them while purifying them. The great reform movement that developed in the second half of the eighteenth century originated in the effort to reduce contamination by destroying impurities and vapors, abating fermentations, preventing evil and disease from tainting the air and spreading their contagion in the atmosphere of the cities. The hospital, the house of correction, all the places of confinement, were to be more completely isolated, surrounded by a purer air: this period produced a whole literature concerning the airing of hospitals, which tentatively approaches the medical problem of contagion, but aims more specifically at themes of moral communication. In 1776 a decree of the Council of State appointed a commission to determine "the degree of amelioration of which the various hospitals in France are in need." Viel was instructed to rebuild the wards of La Salpêtrière. The ideal was an asylum which, while preserving its essential functions, would be so organized that the evil could vegetate there without ever spreading; an asylum where unreason would be entirely contained and offered as a spectacle, without threatening the spectators; where it would have all the powers of example and none of the risks of contagion. In short, an asylum restored to its truth as a cage. It is this "sterilized" confinement, if we may employ an anachronistic term, that was still, in 1789, the dream of the Abbé Desmonceaux, in a little work dedicated to *National Benevolence;* he planned to create a pedagogical instrument—a spectacle conclusively proving the drawbacks of immorality: "these guarded asylums . . . are retreats as useful as they are necessary. . . . The sight of these shadowy places and the guilty creatures they contain is well calculated to preserve from the same acts of just reprobation the deviations of a too licentious youth; it is thus prudent of mothers and fathers to familiarize their children at an early age with these horrible and detestable places, where shame and turpitude fetter crime, where man, corrupted in his essence, often loses forever the rights he had acquired in society."

Such are the dreams by which morality, in complicity with medicine, tried to defend itself against the dangers contained but insufficiently restricted by confinement. These same dangers, at the same time, fascinated men's imaginations and their desires. Morality dreams of exorcising them, but there is something in man which makes him dream of experiencing them, or at least of approaching them and releasing their hallucinations. The horror that now surrounded the fortresses of confinement also exercised an irresistible attraction. Such nights were peopled with inaccessible pleasures; such corrupt and ravaged faces became masks of voluptuousness; against these dark landscapes appeared forms—pains and delights—which echoed Hieronymus Bosch and his delirious gardens. The secrets that escaped from the château in the *One Hundred and Twenty Days of Sodom* have been murmured ever since: "There, the most infamous excesses are committed upon the very person of the prisoner; we hear of certain vices practiced frequently, notoriously, and even publicly in the common room of the prison, vices which the propriety of modern times does not permit us to name. We are told that numerous prisoners, *simillimi feminis mores stuprati et constupratores;* that they return from this obscure, forbidden place covered over with their own and others' debaucheries, lost to all shame and ready to commit all sorts of crimes."[7] And La Rochefoucauld–Liancourt in his turn evoked those figures of Old Women and Young Women in the correction wards of La Salpêtrière, who from generation to generation communicate the same secrets and the same pleasures: "The correction ward is the place of greatest punishment for the House, containing when we visited it forty-seven girls, most of them very young, more thoughtless than guilty. . . . And always this confusion of ages, this shocking mixture of frivolous girls with hardened women who can teach them only the art of the most unbridled corruption." For a long time these visions would prowl insistently through the nights of the eighteenth century. For a moment they would be picked out by the pitiless light of Sade's work and placed by it in the rigorous geometry of Desire. They would be taken up again and wrapped in the murky light of Goya's *Madhouse,* or the twilight that surrounds the Quinta del Sordo. How closely the faces of the *Disparates* resemble them! A whole imaginary landscape reappears, conveyed by the Great Fear confinement now inspires.

What the classical period had confined was not only an abstract unreason which mingled madmen and libertines, invalids, and criminals, but also an enormous reservoir of the fantastic, a dormant world of monsters supposedly engulfed in the darkness of Hieronymus Bosch which had once spewed them forth. One might say that the fortresses of confinement added to their social role of segregation and purification a quite opposite cultural function. Even as they separated reason from unreason on society's surface, they preserved in depth the images where they mingled and exchanged properties. The fortresses of confinement functioned as a great, long silent memory; they maintained in the shadows an iconographic power that men might have thought was exorcised; created by the new classical order, they preserved, against it and against time, forbidden figures that could thus be transmitted intact from the sixteenth to the nineteenth century. In this abolished time, the Brocken joined Dulle Griet in the same imaginary landscape, and Noirceuil, the great legend of the Maréchal de Rais. Confinement allowed, indeed called for, this resistance of imagery.

But the images liberated at the end of the eighteenth century were not identical at all points with those the seventeenth century had tried to eliminate. Something had happened, in the darkness, which detached them from that secret world where the Renaissance, after the Middle Ages, had found them; they had lodged in the hearts, in the desires, in the imaginations of men; and instead of manifesting to sight the abrupt presence of the insane, they seethed as the strange contradiction of human appetites: the complicity of desire and murder, of cruelty and the longing to suffer, of sovereignty and slavery, of insult and humiliation. The great cosmic conflict whose peripities had been revealed by the Insane in the fifteenth and sixteenth centuries, shifted until it became, at the end of the classical period, a dialectic lacking the heart's mediation. Sadism is not a name finally given to a practice as old as Eros; it is a massive cultural fact which appeared precisely at the end of the eighteenth century, and which constitutes one of the greatest conversions of Western imagination: unreason transformed into delirium of the heart, madness of desire, the insane dialogue of love and death in the limitless presumption of appetite. Sadism appears at the very moment that unreason, confined for over a century and reduced to silence, reappears, no longer as an image of the world, no longer as a *figura*, but as language and desire. And it is no accident that sadism, as an individual phenomenon bearing the name of a man, was born of confinement and, within confinement, that Sade's entire *oeuvre* is dominated by the images of the Fortress, the Cell, the Cellar, the Convent, the inaccessible Island which thus form, as it were, the natural habitat of unreason. It is no accident, either, that all the fantastic literature of madness and horror, which is contemporary with Sade's *oeuvre*, takes place, preferentially, in the strongholds of confinement. And this whole sudden conversion of Western memory at the end of the eighteenth century, with its possibility of rediscovering—deformed and endowed with a new meaning—figures familiar at the end of the Middle Ages: was this conversion not authorized by the survival and the reawakening of the fantastic in the very places where unreason had been reduced to silence?

In the classical period, the awareness of madness and the awareness of unreason had not separated from one another. The experience of unreason that had guided all the practices of confinement so enveloped the awareness of madness that it very nearly permitted it to disappear, sweeping it along a road of regression where it was close to losing its most specific elements.

But in the anxiety of the second half of the eighteenth century, the fear of madness grew at the same time as the dread of unreason: and thereby the two forms of obsession, leaning upon each other, continued to reinforce each other. And at the very moment we note the liberation of the iconographic powers that accompany unreason, we hear on all sides complaints about the ravages of madness. Already we are familiar with the concern generated by "nervous diseases," and the awareness that man becomes more delicate in proportion as he perfects himself. As the century advanced, the concern became more pressing, the warnings more solemn. Already Raulin had observed that "since the birth of medicine . . . these illnesses have multiplied, have become more dangerous, more complicated, more problematical and difficult to cure." By Tissot's time, this general impression became a firm belief, a sort of medical dogma: nervous diseases "were formerly much less frequent than they are nowadays; and this for two reasons: one, that men were in general more robust, and less frequently ill; there were fewer diseases of any kind; the other, that the causes which produce nervous diseases in especial have multiplied in a greater proportion, in recent times, than the other general causes of illness, some of which even seem to have diminished. . . . I do not hesitate to say that if they were once the rarest, they are today the most frequent."[8] And soon men regained that awareness, which had been so intense in the sixteenth century, of the precariousness of a reason that can at any moment be compromised, and definitively, by madness. Matthey, a Geneva physician very close to Rousseau's influence, formulates the prospect for all men of reason: "Do not glory in your state, if you are wise and civilized men; an instant suffices to disturb and annihilate that supposed wisdom of which you are so proud; an unexpected event, a sharp and sudden emotion of the soul will abruptly change the most reasonable and intelligent man into a raving idiot." The threat of madness resumes its place among the emergencies of the century.

This awareness, however, has a very special style. The obsession with unreason is a very affective one, involved in the movement of iconographic resurrections. The fear of madness is much freer with regard to this heritage; and while the return of unreason has the aspect of a massive repetition, connecting with itself outside of time, the awareness of madness is on the contrary accompanied by a certain analysis of modernity, which situates it from the start in a temporal, historical, and social context. In the disparity between the awareness of unreason and the awareness of madness, we have, at the end of the eighteenth century, the point of departure for a decisive movement: that by which the experience of unreason will continue, with Hölderlin, Nerval, and Nietzsche, to proceed ever deeper toward the roots of time—unreason thus becoming, *par excellence*, the world's *contratempo*—and the knowledge of madness seeking on the contrary to situate it ever more precisely within the development of nature and history. It is after this period that the time of unreason and the time of madness receive two opposing vectors: one being unconditioned return and absolute submersion; the other, on the contrary, developing according to the chronicle of a history.[9]

1. *Madness and Liberty*. For a long time, certain forms of melancholia were considered specifically English; this was a fact in medicine and a constant in literature. Montesquieu contrasted Roman suicide, which was a form of moral and political behavior, the desired effect of a concerted education, with English suicide, which had to be

considered as an illness since "the English kill themselves without any apparent reason for doing so; they kill themselves in the very lap of happiness." It is here that the milieu plays its role, for if happiness in the eighteenth century is part of the order of nature and reason, unhappiness, or at least whatever deters from happiness without reason, must be part of another order. This order was sought first in the excesses of the climate, in nature's deviation from its equilibrium and its happy mean (temperate climates are caused by nature; intemperate climates by the milieu). But this was not sufficient to explain *la maladie anglaise;* already Cheyne had declared that wealth, refined food, the abundance all the inhabitants enjoyed, the life of pleasure and ease the richest society led, were at the origin of such nervous disorders. Increasingly, a political and economic explanation was sought, in which wealth, progress, institutions appear as the determining element of madness. At the beginning of the nineteenth century, Spurzheim made a synthesis of all these analyses in one of the last texts devoted to them.[10] Madness, "more frequent in England than anywhere else," is merely the penalty of the liberty that reigns there, and of the wealth universally enjoyed. Freedom of conscience entails more dangers than authority and despotism. "Religious sentiments . . . exist without restriction; every individual is entitled to preach to anyone who will listen to him," and by listening to such different opinions, "minds are disturbed in the search for truth." Dangers of indecision, of an irresolute attention, of a vacillating soul! The danger, too, of disputes, of passions, of obstinacy: "Everything meets with opposition, and opposition excites the feelings; in religion, in politics, in science, as in everything, each man is permitted to form an opinion; but he must expect to meet with opposition." Nor does so much liberty permit a man to master time; every man is left to his own uncertainty, and the State abandons all to their fluctuations: "The English are a nation of merchants; a mind always occupied with speculations is continually agitated by fear and hope. Egotism, the soul of commerce, easily becomes envious and summons other faculties to its aid." Besides, this liberty is far from true natural liberty: on all sides it is constrained and harried by demands opposed to the most legitimate desires of individuals: this is the liberty of interests, of coalitions, of financial combinations, not of man, not of minds and hearts. For financial reasons, families are here more tyrannical than anywhere else: only wealthy girls are able to marry; "the others are reduced to other means of satisfaction that ruin the body and derange the manifestations of the soul. The same cause favors libertinage, which predisposes to madness." A mercantile liberty thus appears as the element in which opinion can never arrive at the truth, in which the immediate is necessarily subject to contradiction, in which time escapes the mastery and certainty of the seasons, in which man is dispossessed of his desires by the laws of interest. In short, liberty, far from putting man in possession of himself, ceaselessly alienates him from his essence and his world; it fascinates him in the absolute exteriority of other people and of money, in the irreversible interiority of passion and unfulfilled desire. Between man and the happiness of a world in which he recognizes himself, between man and a nature in which he finds his truth, the liberty of the mercantile state is "milieu": and to this very degree it is the determining element of madness. When Spurzheim was writing—at the height of the Holy Alliance, during the restoration of the authoritarian monarchies—liberalism was readily blamed for all the sins of the world's madness: "It is singular to see that man's greatest desire, which is his personal liberty, has its disadvantages as well." But for us, the point of such an analysis is not its critique of liberty, but its very employment of the notion that designates for Spurzheim the non-natural milieu in which the psychological and physiological mechanisms of madness are favored, amplified, and multiplied.

2. *Madness, Religion, and Time.* Religious beliefs prepare a kind of landscape of images, an illusory milieu favorable to every hallucination and every delirium. For a long time, doctors were suspicious of the effects of too strict a devotion, too strong a belief. Too much moral rigor, too much anxiety about salvation and the life to come were often thought to bring on melancholia. The *Encyclopédie* does not fail to cite such cases: "The intemperate impressions made by certain extravagant preachers, the excessive fears they inspire of the pains with which our religion threatens those who break its laws, produce astonishing revolutions in weak minds. At the hospital of Montélimar, several women were reported suffering from mania and melancholia as a result of a mission held in that city; these creatures were ceaselessly struck by the horrible images that had thoughtlessly been presented to them; they spoke of nothing but despair, revenge, punishment, etc., and one of them absolutely refused to undergo any cure, convinced that she was in Hell and that nothing could extinguish the fire she believed was devouring her." Pinel follows the line of these enlightened physicians—forbidding books of devotion to be given to "melancholics by piety," even recommending solitary confinement for "religious persons who believe themselves to be inspired and who seek to make proselytes." But this again is more of a critique than a positive analysis: the religious object or theme is suspected of arousing delirium and hallucination by the delirious and hallucinatory nature attributed to it. Pinel reports the case of a recently cured madman who had "read in a religious book . . . that each man has his guardian angel; on the following night, he thought he was surrounded by a choir of angels and imagined he heard celes-

tial music and received revelations." Religion is considered here only as an element in the transmission of error. But even before Pinel, there had been analyses of a more rigorous historical nature, in which religion appeared as a milieu of satisfaction or repression of the passions. In 1781 a German author described as happy those distant eras when priests were endowed with absolute powers: then idleness did not exist, every moment was marked by "ceremonies, religious practices, pilgrimages, visits to the poor and the sick, calendar festivals."[11] Time was thus assigned to an organized happiness, which left no leisure for empty passions, for disgust with life, for boredom. If a man felt guilty, he was subjected to real, often material punishment which occupied his mind and gave him an assurance that the transgression was redressed. And when the confessor encountered those "hypochondriacal penitents who came too often to confession," he assigned them as penance either a severe hardship that "diluted their too thick blood," or long pilgrimages: "The change of air, the length of the road, absence from home, distance from the things which upset them, their associations with other pilgrims, the slow and energetic movement of walking, had more effect upon them than the comfortable journeys . . . that in our day take the place of pilgrimages." Finally, the sacred nature of the priest gave each of his injunctions an absolute value, and no one dreamed of trying to avoid it; "usually the whims of sick people deny all this to the physician." For Moehsen, religion is the mediation between man and transgression, between man and punishment: in the form of an authoritarian synthesis, it suppresses the transgression by imposing the punishment; if, on the contrary, religion loosens its hold but maintains the ideal forms of remorse of conscience, of spiritual mortification, it leads directly to madness; only the consistency of the religious milieu can permit man to escape alienation in the excessive delirium of

transgressions. By accomplishing its rites and its requirements, man avoids both the useless idleness of his passions
before the transgression, and the vain repetition of his remorse once the transgression is committed; religion organizes all human life around fulfillment of the moment. That
old religion of happier times was the perpetual celebration
of the present. But once it was idealized in the modern age,
religion cast a temporal halo around the present, an empty
milieu—that of idleness and remorse, in which the heart of
man is abandoned to its own anxiety, in which the passions
surrender time to unconcern or to repetition in which, finally, madness can function freely.

3. *Madness, Civilization, and Sensibility*. Civilization, in
a general way, constitutes a milieu favorable to the development of madness. If the progress of knowledge dissipates
error, it also has the effect of propagating a taste and even a
mania for study; the life of the library, abstract speculations, the perpetual agitation of the mind without the exercise of the body, can have the most disastrous effects. Tissot explains that in the human body it is those parts subject
to frequent work which are first strengthened and hardened; among laborers, the muscles and fibers of the arms
harden, giving them their physical strength and the good
health they enjoy until an advanced age; "among men of
letters, the brain hardens; often they become incapable of
connecting their ideas," and so are doomed to dementia.
The more abstract or complex knowledge becomes, the
greater the risk of madness. A body of knowledge still close
to what is most immediate in the senses, requiring, according to Pressavin, only a little work on the part of the inner
sense and organs of the brain, provokes only a sort of physiological happiness: "The sciences whose objects are easily
perceived by our senses, which offer the soul agreeable relations because of the harmony of their consonance . . .
perform throughout the entire bodily machine a light ac-

tivity which is beneficial to all the functions." On the contrary, a knowledge too poor in these sensuous relations, too free with regard to the immediate, provokes a tension of the brain alone which disequilibrates the whole body; sciences "of things whose relationships are difficult to grasp because they are not readily available to our senses, or because their too complicated relations oblige us to expend great application in their study, present the soul with an exercise that greatly fatigues the inner sense by a too continuous tension upon that organ." Knowledge thus forms around feeling a milieu of abstract relationships where man risks losing the physical happiness in which his relation to the world is usually established. Knowledge multiplies, no doubt, but its cost increases too. Is it certain that there are more wise men today? One thing, at least, is certain: "there are more people who have the infirmities of wisdom." The milieu of knowledge grows faster than knowledge itself.

But it is not only knowledge that detaches man from feeling; it is sensibility itself: a sensibility that is no longer controlled by the movements of nature, but by all the habits, all the demands of social life. Modern man—but woman more than man—turns day into night and night into day: "The moment at which our women rise in Paris is far removed from that which nature has indicated; the best hours of the day have slipped away; the purest air has disappeared; no one has benefited from it. The vapors, the harmful exhalations, attracted by the sun's heat, are already rising in the atmosphere; this is the hour that beauty chooses to rise."[12] This disorder of the senses continues in the theater, where illusions are cultivated, where vain passions and the most fatal movements of the soul are aroused by artifice; women especially enjoy these spectacles "that inflame and arouse them"; their souls "are so strongly shaken that this produces a commotion in their nerves, fleeting, in truth, but whose consequences are usually serious; the momentary loss of their senses, the tears they shed at the performances of our modern tragedies are the least accidents that can result from them."[13] Novels form a still more artificial milieu, and are more dangerous to a disordered sensibility; the verisimilitude modern authors attempt to produce, and all the art they employ to imitate truth, only give more prestige to the violent and dangerous sentiments they seek to awaken in their female readers: "In the earliest epochs of French gallantry and manners, the less perfected minds of women were content with facts and events as marvelous as they were unbelievable; now they demand believable facts yet sentiments so marvelous that their own minds are disturbed and confounded by them; they then seek, in all that surrounds them, to realize the marvels by which they are enchanted; but everything seems to them without sentiment and without life, because they are trying to find what does not exist in nature."[14] The novel constitutes the milieu of perversion, *par excellence*, of all sensibility; it detaches the soul from all that is immediate and natural in feeling and leads it into an imaginary world of sentiments violent in proportion to their unreality, and less controlled by the gentle laws of nature; "The existence of so many authors has produced a host of readers, and continued reading generates every nervous complaint; perhaps of all the causes that have harmed women's health, the principal one has been the infinite multiplication of novels in the last hundred years . . . a girl who at ten reads instead of running will, at twenty, be a woman with the vapors and not a good nurse."[15]

Slowly, and still in a very scattered fashion, the eighteenth century constituted, around its awareness of madness and of its threatening spread, a whole new order of concepts. In the landscape of unreason where the sixteenth century had located it, madness concealed a meaning and an origin that were obscurely moral; its secrecy related it to sin, and the animality imminently perceived in it did not make it, paradoxically, more innocent. In the second half of the eighteenth century, madness was no longer recognized in what brings man closer to an immemorial fall or an indefinitely present animality; it was, on the contrary, situated in those distances man takes in regard to himself, to his world, to all that is offered by the immediacy of nature; madness became possible in that milieu where man's relations with his feelings, with time, with others, are altered; madness was possible because of everything which, in man's life and development, is a break with the immediate. Madness was no longer of the order of nature or of the Fall, but of a new order, in which men began to have a presentiment of history, and where there formed, in an obscure originating relationship, the "alienation" of the physicians and the "alienation" of the philosophers—two configurations in which man in any case corrupts his truth, but between which the nineteenth century, after Hegel, soon lost all trace of resemblance.

VIII

THE NEW DIVISION

EVERY psychiatrist, every historian yielded, at the beginning of the nineteenth century, to the same impulse of indignation; everywhere we find the same outrage, the same virtuous censure: "No one blushed to put the insane in prison." And Esquirol, listing the fortress of Hâ in Bordeaux, the houses of correction in Toulouse and Rennes, the "Bicêtres" still existing in Poitiers, in Caen, in Amiens, the "Château" of Angers, continues: "Moreover, there are few prisons where the raving mad are not to be found; these unfortunates are chained in dungeons beside criminals. What a monstrous association! The calm madmen are treated worse than malefactors."

The entire century echoes him; in England, it was the Tukes, who had turned historians and apologists for their ancestral occupation; in Germany, after Wagnitz, it was Reil who groaned over those wretches "thrown, like State criminals, into dungeons where the eye of humanity never penetrates." The age of positivism, for over half a century, constantly claimed to have been the first to free the mad from a lamentable confusion with the felonious, to separate the innocence of unreason from the guilt of crime.

Yet it is simple enough to show the vanity of this claim. For years the same protests had been raised; before Reil, there had been Franck: "Those who have visited the insane asylums of Germany recall with dread what they have seen. One is horrified upon entering these asylums of misery and affliction; one hears only cries of despair, yet here dwells the man distinguished by his talents and his virtues." Before Esquirol, before Pinel, there had been La Rochefoucauld-Liancourt, there had been Tenon; and before them, an incessant murmur throughout the eighteenth century, composed of insistent protests, lodged year after year even by those whom one would have thought the most indifferent, the most eager perhaps that such a confusion should subsist. Twenty-five years before the exclamations of a Pinel, we must invoke Malesherbes "visiting the State prisons with the intention of breaking down their gates. Prisoners whom he found to be insane . . . were sent to houses where the society, the exercise, and the care he had scrupulously prescribed would be sure, he said, to cure them." Still earlier in the century, and in a lower voice, there had been all those directors, those bursars, those overseers who from generation to generation always asked and sometimes achieved the same thing: the separation of madmen from convicts; there had been the Prior of La Charité in Senlis who begged the police to remove several prisoners and confine them instead in any of several fortresses; there had been that overseer of the House of Correction in Brunswick who asked—and this was only in 1713—that the madmen not be allowed to mingle with the internees assigned to the workshops. Had not what the nineteenth century formulated so ostentatiously, with all the resources of its pathos, already been whispered and indefatigably repeated by the eighteenth? Did Esquirol and Reil and the

Tukes do anything more than shout at the top of their lungs what had been, for years, commonplaces of asylum practice? The slow emigration of the mad which we have mentioned, from 1720 to the Revolution, was probably no more than the most visible effect of that practice.

And yet, let us listen to what was being said in this half-silence. When the Prior of Senlis asked that madmen be separated from certain convicts, what were his arguments? "He is deserving of mercy, as well as two or three others who would be better off in some citadel, because of the company of six others who are mad, and who torment them night and day." And the meaning of this sentence would be so clearly understood by the police that the internees in question would be set free. And the demands of the Brunswick overseer have the same meaning: the workshop is disturbed by the cries and the confusion of the insane; their frenzy is a perpetual danger, and it would be better to send them back to the cells, or to keep them in chains. And already, we can anticipate that from one century to the next, the same protests did not have, at bottom, the same value. Early in the nineteenth century, there was indignation that the mad were not treated any better than those condemned by common law or than State prisoners; throughout the eighteenth century, emphasis was placed on the fact that the prisoners deserved a better fate than one that lumped them with the insane. For Esquirol, the scandal is due to the fact that the mad are only mad; for the Prior of Senlis, to the fact that the convicts are, after all, only convicts.

A difference which is perhaps not of such significance, and which ought to have been easily perceived. And yet, it is necessary to emphasize it in order to understand how the consciousness of madness was transformed in the course of the eighteenth century. It did not evolve in the context of a humanitarian movement that gradually related it more closely to the madman's human reality, to his most affecting and most intimate aspect; nor did it evolve under the pressure of a scientific need that made it more attentive, more faithful to what madness might have to say for itself. If it slowly changed, it was within that simultaneously real and artificial space of confinement. Certain imperceptible shifts in its structures, or at times certain violent crises, gradually formed the awareness of madness contemporaneous with the Revolution. No medical advance, no humanitarian approach was responsible for the fact that the mad were gradually isolated, that the monotony of insanity was divided into rudimentary types. It was the depths of confinement itself that generated the phenomenon; it is from confinement that we must seek an account of this new awareness of madness.

A political more than a philanthropic awareness. For if the eighteenth century perceived that there were among the confined—among the libertines, the debauched, the prodigal sons—certain men whose confusion and disorder were of another nature, and whose anxiety was irreducible, this perception was the result of the confined themselves. They were the first to protest, and with the most violence. Ministers, police officers, magistrates were assailed with the same endless and tirelessly repeated complaints: one man writes to Maurepas, indignant at being "forced to mingle with madmen, some of whom are so violent that at every moment I risk suffering dangerous abuse from them"; another—the Abbé de Montcrif—makes the same complaint to Lieutenant Berryer: "This is the ninth month that I have been confined here in this dreadful place with fifteen or twenty raving madmen, pell-mell with epileptics." The farther we advance into the century, the stronger grow these protests against confinement: increasingly, madness becomes the specter of the internees, the very image of their humiliation, of their reason vanquished and reduced to silence. The day soon comes when Mirabeau recognizes in the shameful promiscuity of madness both a subtle instrument of brutality against those to be punished and the very image of despotism, bestiality triumphant. The madman is not the first and the most innocent victim of confinement, but the most obscure and the most visible, the most insistent of the symbols of the confining power. Tyranny secretly persists among the confined in this lurid presence of unreason. The struggle against the established powers, against the family, against the Church, continues at the very heart of confinement, in the saturnalia of reason. And madness so well represents these punishing powers that it effectively plays the part of an additional punishment, a further torment which maintains order in the uniform chastisement of the houses of correction. La Rochefoucauld-Liancourt bears witness to this in his report to the Committee on Mendicity: "One of the punishments inflicted upon the epileptics and upon the other patients of the wards, even upon the deserving poor, is to place them among the mad." The scandal lies only in the fact that the madmen are the brutal truth of confinement, the passive instrument of all that is worst about it. Is this not symbolized by the fact—also a commonplace of all the literature of confinement in the eighteenth century—that a sojourn in a house of correction necessarily leads to madness? Having to live in this delirious world, amid the triumph of unreason, how may one avoid joining, by the fatality of the site and the event, the very men who are its living symbol? "I observe that the majority of the insane confined in the houses of correction and the State prisons have become so, the latter through the excess of ill-treatment, the former through the horror of the solitude in which they continually encounter the harassments of an imagination sharpened by pain."[1]

The presence of madmen among the prisoners is not the

scandalous limit of confinement, but its truth; not abuse, but essence. The polemic instituted by the eighteenth century against confinement certainly dealt with the enforced mingling of the mad and the sane; but it did not deal with the basic relation acknowledged between madness and confinement. Whatever attitude is adopted, that, at least, is not in question. Mirabeau, the Friend of Man, is as severe about confinement as about the confined themselves; in his eyes, no one confined in "the celebrated State prisons" is innocent; but his place is not in these costly institutions, where he drags out a useless life; why confine "daughters of joy who, transported to provincial manufactories, could become daughters of labor"? Or "rascals who are waiting only for freedom in order to get themselves hanged? Why are these people, attached to walking fetters, not employed at those tasks which might prove harmful to voluntary workers? They would serve as an example . . ." Once this entire population was removed, who would remain in the houses of confinement? Those who could not be placed anywhere else, and who belong there by right: "Some prisoners of State whose crimes must not be revealed," to whom may be added "old men who, having consumed in debauchery and dissipation all the fruit of their life's labor, and having cherished the ambitious prospect of dying in a hospital, come there in peace"; finally, the mad, who must wallow somewhere: "These last can vegetate anywhere."[2] Mirabeau the younger conducts his demonstration in the opposite direction: "I formally defy anyone in the world to prove that State prisoners, rascals, libertines, madmen, ruined old men constitute I do not say the majority, but the third, the fourth, the tenth part of the inhabitants of fortresses, houses of correction, and State prisons." For him the scandal is thus not that the mad are mingled with the criminal, but that they do not constitute, together, the essential part of the confined population; who then can complain of being forced to mix with criminals? Not those who have lost their reason forever, but those who in their youth spent their time in wildness: "I might ask . . . why rascals and libertines are mingled together. . . . I could ask why young men with dangerous dispositions are left with men who will rapidly lead them to the last degree of corruption. . . . Finally, if this confusion of libertines and villains exists, as is all too true, why do we, by this odious, infamous, atrocious combination, make ourselves guilty of the most abominable of all crimes, that of leading men into crime?" As for madmen, what other fate could be desired for them? Neither reasonable enough not to be confined, nor wise enough not to be treated as wicked, "it is all too true that those who have lost the use of reason must be hidden from society."[3]

We see how the political critique of confinement functioned in the eighteenth century. Not in the direction of a liberation of the mad; nor can we say that it permitted a more philanthropic or a greater medical attention to the insane. On the contrary, it linked madness more firmly than ever to confinement, and this by a double tie: one which made madness the very symbol of the confining power and its absurd and obsessive representative within the world of confinement; the other which designated madness as the object *par excellence* of all the measures of confinement. Subject and object, image and goal of repression, symbol of its blind arbitrariness and justification of all that could be reasonable and deserved within it: by a paradoxical circle, madness finally appears as the only reason for a confinement whose profound unreason it symbolizes. Still so close to this eighteenth-century notion, Michelet would formulate it with an astonishing rigor; he returns to the very movement of Mirabeau's thought, apropos of the stay the latter made at Vincennes at the same time as Sade:

First, confinement causes alienation: "Prison makes men

mad. Those found in the Bastille and in Bicêtre were stupe-fied."

Secondly, what is most unreasonable, most shameful, most profoundly immoral in the tyranny of the eighteenth century is represented in the space of confinement, and by a madman: "We have seen the frenzies of La Salpêtrière. A dreadful lunatic existed at Vincennes, the poisonous de Sade, writing in the hope of corrupting the time to come."

Thirdly, it is for this one madman alone that confinement ought to have been reserved, and nothing of the kind was done: "He was soon set free, and Mirabeau kept in confinement."

Hence an abyss yawns in the middle of confinement; a void which isolates madness, denounces it for being irreducible, unbearable to reason; madness now appears with what distinguishes it from all these confined forms as well. The presence of the mad appears as an injustice; but *for others*. The undifferentiated unity of unreason had been broken. Madness was individualized, strangely twinned with crime, at least linked with it by a proximity which had not yet been called into question. In this confinement drained of a part of its content, these two figures—madness, crime—subsist alone; by themselves, they symbolize what may be necessary about it; they alone are what henceforth deserves to be confined. Having taken its distance, having finally become an assignable form in the confused world of unreason, did not liberate madness; between madness and confinement, a profound relation had been instituted, a link which was almost one of essence.

But at the same moment, confinement suffered another, still deeper crisis that called into question not only its repressive role but its very existence; a crisis which arose not from within, and which was not attached to political protests, but which slowly appeared on the entire social and economic horizon.

Poverty was gradually being freed from the old moral confusions. Men had seen unemployment assume, during crises, an aspect that could no longer be identified with that of sloth; had seen indigence and idleness forced to spread into the countryside, where men had supposed they could recognize precisely the most immediate and the purest forms of moral life; all this revealed that poverty was perhaps not only of the order of transgression: "Mendicity is the fruit of poverty, which itself is the result of accidents occurring either in the cultivation of the land or in the production of manufactures, or in the rise of commodity prices, in an excess of population, etc. . . ."[4] Poverty had become an economic phenomenon.

But not contingent—nor destined to be suppressed forever. There was a certain quantity of indigence which man would not succeed in eliminating—a kind of fatality of poverty which must accompany all the forms of society to the end of time, even where all the idle were employed: "There need be, in a well-governed state, only those poor born in indigence, or those who fall into it by accident."[5] This basic poverty was in a sense inalienable: birth or accident, it formed a part of life that could not be avoided. For a long time, it was inconceivable to have a state in which there were no paupers, so deeply did need appear to be inscribed in man's fate and in the structure of society: property, labor, and poverty are terms which remain linked in the thought of philosophers until the nineteenth century.

Necessary because it could not be suppressed, this role of poverty was necessary too because it made wealth possible. Because they labor and consume little, those who are in need permit a nation to enrich itself, to set a high value on its fields, its colonies, and its mines, to manufacture products which will be sold the world over; in short, a people would be poor which had no paupers. Indigence becomes an indispensable element in the State. In it is concealed the secret but also the real life of a society. The poor constitute the basis and the glory of nations. And their poverty, which cannot be suppressed, must be exalted and revered: "My purpose is merely to attract a share of that vigilant attention [that of the government] to the suffering portion of the People . . .; the succor it is owed derives essentially from the honor and the prosperity of an Empire, of which the Poor are everywhere the firmest support, for a sovereign cannot preserve and extend his realm without favoring the population, the cultivation of the Land, the Arts, and commerce; and the Poor are the necessary agents of these great powers which establish the true strength of a People."[6] Here is an entire moral rehabilitation of the Pauper, which designates, at a deeper level, a social and economic reintegration of his role and character. In the mercantilist economy, the Pauper, being neither producer nor consumer, had no place: idle, vagabond, unemployed, he belonged only to confinement, a measure by which he was exiled and as it were abstracted from society. With the nascent industry which needs manpower, he once again plays a part in the body of the nation.

Thus, economic thought elaborates on new foundations the notion of poverty. There had been the entire Christian tradition for which the Poor Man had had a real and concrete existence, a presence of flesh and blood: an always individual countenance of need, the symbolic passage of God in man's image. The abstraction of confinement had removed the Poor Man, had identified him with other figures, enveloping him in an ethical condemnation, but had not dissociated him from his features. The eighteenth century discovered that "the Poor" did not exist as a concrete and final reality; that in them, two realities of different natures had too long been confused.

On one hand, there was *Poverty:* scarcity of commodities and money, an economic situation linked to the state of commerce, of agriculture, of industry. On the other, there was *Population:* not a passive element subject to the fluctuations of wealth, but a force which directly contributed to the economic situation, to the production of wealth, since it is man's labor which creates—or at least transmits, shifts, and multiplies—wealth. The "Poor Man" was a vague notion in which were combined that wealth which is Man and the state of Need which is acknowledged as essential to humanity. Indeed, between Poverty and Population, there is a rigorously inverse relation.

Physiocrats and economists are in agreement on this. Population is in itself one of the elements of wealth; it forms, indeed, its certain and inexhaustible source. For François Quesnay and his disciples, man is the essential mediation between the land and wealth: "A *man is worth as much as the land,* according to an old proverb. If a man is valueless, so is the land. With men, one doubles the land one possesses; one clears it, one acquires it. God alone could from the earth make a man, whereas all over the world it has been possible to have land by means of men, or at least the product of the land, which comes down to the same thing. It follows that the first good is the possession of men, and the second, of the land."[7]

For the economists, the population is a good quite as essential, if not more so, since in their view wealth is created not only in agricultural labor, but in every industrial transformation, and even in commercial circulation. Wealth is linked to a labor actually effected by man: "The State having real wealth only in the annual products of its lands and in the industry of its inhabitants, its wealth will be at a maximum when the product of each acre of land and of the industry of each individual is raised to its maximum."[8] Paradoxically, a population will be precious in proportion to its numbers, since it will afford industry a cheap labor force, which, by lowering the cost price, will permit a development of production and of commerce. In this infinitely open labor market, the "fundamental price"—what corresponds for Turgot to the worker's subsistence—and the price determined by supply and demand ultimately coincide. A nation will therefore be favored in commercial competition to the degree that it has at its disposal the greatest potential wealth of a numerous population.

Confinement was a gross error, and an economic mistake: poverty was to be suppressed by removing and maintaining by charity a *poor population*. Actually, it was *poverty* that was being artificially masked; and a part of the *population* was being really suppressed, wealth being always constant. Was the intention to help the poor escape their provisional indigence? They were kept from doing so: the labor market was limited, which was all the more dangerous in that this was precisely a period of crisis. On the contrary, the high cost of products should have been palliated by a cheap labor force, their scarcity being compensated by a new industrial and agricultural effort. The only reasonable remedy: to restore this entire population to the circuit of production, in order to distribute it to the points where the labor force was rarest. To utilize the poor, vagabonds, exiles, and *émigrés* of all kinds, was one of the secrets of wealth, in the competition among nations: "What is the best means of weakening the neighboring states whose power and industry tend to overshadow us?" asked Josias Tucker apropos of the emigration of the Protestants. "Is it to force their subjects to remain at home by refusing to receive and incorporate them among us, or is it to attract them to us by good wages, allowing them to enjoy the advantages of the other citizens?"

Confinement is open to criticism because of the repercussions it can have on the labor market; but still more, because it constitutes, and with it the entire enterprise of traditional charity, a dangerous financing. Like the Middle Ages, the classical period had always sought to provide aid to the poor by the system of foundations. This meant that a share of land capital or income was thereby immobilized. And for good, since, in the just concern to avoid the commercialization of the charity enterprises, all juridical measures were taken so that these goods would never return to circulation. But with the passage of time, their utility diminished; the economic situation changed, poverty altered its aspect: "Society does not always have the same needs; nature and the distribution of property, the division between the different orders of the people, the opinions, the customs, the general occupations of the nation or of its different portions, the climate itself, the diseases and other accidents of human life undergo a continual variation; new needs are born; others cease to make themselves felt."[9] The definitive character of the foundation was in contradiction to the variable and indefinite rate of the accidental needs which it was supposed to satisfy. Without the wealth which it immobilized being restored to circulation, new wealth had to be created as new needs appeared. The share of funds and revenues which were set aside constantly increased, thereby diminishing the productive share. Which inevitably led to a greater poverty, hence to more numerous foundations. And the process could extend indefinitely. The moment could come when "the ever multiplying foundations would ultimately absorb all funds and all private property." Upon close scrutiny, the classical forms of aid were a cause of impoverishment, the gradual immobilization and in a sense the slow death of all productive wealth: "If all the men who ever lived had had a tomb, it would have been quite necessary, in order to find land to cultivate, to overturn these sterile monuments, and to stir the ashes of the dead in order to feed the living."[10]

What disappeared, in the course of the eighteenth century, was not the inhuman rigor with which madmen were treated, but the evident necessity of confinement, the total unity in which they were situated without difficulty, and those countless threads that wove them into the continuous texture of unreason. Madness was set free long before Pinel, not from the material constraints which kept it in the dungeon, but from a much more binding, perhaps more decisive servitude which kept it under the domination of unreason's obscure power. Even before the Revolution, madness was free: free for a perception which individualized it, free for the recognition of its unique features and for all the operations that would finally give it its status as an object.

Left alone, and detached from its former relations, within the crumbling walls of confinement, madness was a problem—raising questions it had hitherto never formulated.

Above all, it embarrassed the legislator who, unable to keep from sanctioning the end of confinement, no longer knew at what point in the social sphere to situate it—prison, hospital, or family aid. The measures taken immediately before or after the beginning of the Revolution reflect this indecision.

In his circular on the *lettres de cachet*, Breteuil asked the administrators to indicate the nature of the detention orders in the various houses of confinement, and what reasons justified them. After a year or two of detention at the most, those men were to be set free "who, having done nothing that could expose them to the severity of the punishments pronounced by the laws, had abandoned themselves to the excesses of libertinage, debauchery, and dissipation." On the other hand, those prisoners were to be kept in the houses of confinement "whose minds are deranged and whose imbecility makes them incapable of conducting themselves in a world where their rages would make them dangerous. With respect to these, all that is necessary is to ascertain whether their condition is still the same, and unfortunately it becomes indispensable to continue their detention as long as it is acknowledged that their freedom is harmful to society, or a useless benefit to themselves." This was the first stage: to reduce as much as possible the practice of confinement with regard to moral transgressions, family conflicts, the most benign aspects of libertinage, yet to leave it untouched in its principle, and with one of its major meanings intact: the internment of the mad. This is the moment when madness actually takes possession of confinement, while confinement itself is divested of its other forms of utility.

The second stage was that of the great investigations prescribed by the National Assembly and by the Constituent Assembly, immediately following the Declaration of the Rights of Man: "No man may be arrested or detained except in the cases determined by law and according to the forms therein prescribed. . . . The law must permit only the penalties strictly and evidently necessary, and no one may be punished under a law established and promulgated subsequent to the crime." The era of confinement was over. There remained only an imprisonment shared for the moment by condemned or presumed criminals and the mad. The Committee on Mendicity of the Constituent Assembly designated five persons to visit the houses of confinement in Paris. The Duke de la Rochefoucauld-Liancourt presented the report (December 1789); he declared that the presence of madmen gave the houses of correction a degrading aspect and was likely to reduce the inmates to a state unworthy of humanity; the *mélange* tolerated there proved a great frivolity on the part of the authorities and the magistrates: "This carelessness is far from the enlightened and scrupulous pity for misfortune whereby it receives all possible alleviation and consolation . . . ; in seeking to succor poverty, can one ever consent to appear to degrade humanity?"

If the mad defile those with whom they have been imprudently confined, a special internment must be reserved for them; a confinement that is not medical, but that ought to be the most efficacious and the easiest form of aid: "Of all the misfortunes that afflict humanity, the condition of madness is still one of those that with most reason call for pity and respect; it is for this condition that our attentions must with most reason be prodigal; when there is no hope of a cure, how many means still remain that can afford these unfortunates at least a tolerable existence." In this text, the status of madness appears in all its ambiguity: it is necessary both to protect the confined population from its dangers, and to grant it the benefits of a special aid.

The third stage was the great series of decrees issued between the twelfth and the sixteenth of March 1790. In them, the Declaration of the Rights of Man received a concrete application: "In the space of six weeks, beginning with the present decree, all persons detained in fortresses, religious houses, houses of correction, police houses, or other prisons whatsoever, by *lettres de cachet* or by order of the agents of the executive power, so long as they are not convicted, or under arrest, or not charged with major crimes, or confined by reason of madness, will be set at liberty." Confinement is thus definitively reserved for certain categories of convicted criminals and for madmen. But for the latter, a special arrangement is in order: "Persons detained for reasons of dementia will be, for the space of three months, starting from the day of publication of the present decree, at the suit of our procurators, interrogated by the magistrates in the usual manner, and by virtue of their disposition visited by physicians who, under the supervision of the directors of the district, will pronounce upon the true circumstances of the patients in order that, after the sentence that will have certified as to their condition, they may be released or cared for in hospitals indicated for that purpose." It appears that the choice is henceforth made. On March 29, 1790, Bailly, Duport-Dutertre, and a police administrator went to La Salpêtrière to determine in what manner this decree could be carried out; they then made a similar visit to Bicêtre. The difficulties were numerous; to begin with, there existed no hospitals intended or at least reserved for the mad.

In the face of these material difficulties, to which were added certain theoretical uncertainties, a long phase of hesitation was to begin. From all sides, the Assembly was asked to provide a text which would grant protection from madmen even before the promised creation of the hospitals. And by a regression, which was to be of great importance for the future, madmen were brought under the sway of immediate and unchecked measures adopted not even against dangerous criminals, but against marauding beasts. The Law of August 16–24, 1790, "entrusts to the vigilance and authority of the municipal bodies . . . the care of obviating and remedying the disagreeable events that may be occasioned by madmen set at liberty, and by the wandering of vicious and dangerous animals." The law of July 22, 1791, reinforces this arrangement, making families responsible for the supervision of the insane, and permitting the municipal authorities to take all measures that might prove useful: "The relatives of the insane must care for them, prevent them from straying, and see that they do not commit offenses or disorders. The municipal authority must obviate the inconvenience that may result from the negligence with which private persons fulfill this duty." By this detour around their liberation, madmen regained, but this time within the law itself, that animal status in which confinement had seemed to isolate them; they again became wild beasts at the very period when doctors began to attribute to them a gentle animality. But even though this legal disposition was put in the hands of the authorities, the problems were not solved thereby; hospitals for the insane still did not exist.

Countless requests flooded the Ministry of the Interior. Delessart answered one of them, for example: "I feel as you do, Monsieur, how important it is that we labor without respite toward the establishment of houses designed to serve as retreats for the unfortunate class of the insane. . . . With regard to those insane persons whom the lack of such an establishment has relegated to the various prisons of your department, I do not see any other means at present of removing them from those places so unsuited to their state, except to transfer them temporarily, if possible, to Bicêtre. It would therefore be appropriate for the Directory to write to the Paris establishment in order to ascertain a way to have them admitted to that house, where the costs of their upkeep will be paid by your department or by the communes where these unfortunates reside, if their families are not in a position to assume that expense." Bicêtre thus became the great center to which all the insane were sent, especially once Saint-Lazare was closed. The same was true for the women at La Salpêtrière: in 1792, two hundred madwomen were taken there who had been installed five years previously in the former novitiate of the Capucines on the Rue Saint-Jacques. But in the remote provinces, there was no question of sending the insane to the former *hôpitaux généraux*. Generally, they were detained in the prisons, as was the case for example at the fortress of Hâ, at the Château of Angers, or at Bellevaux. The disorder in such places was indescribable, and continued for a long time—until the Empire. Antoine Nodier gives some details about Bellevaux: "Every day, the uproar warns the neighborhood that those confined are fighting and persecuting one another. The guards rush upon them. Constituted as they are today, the prison guards are the laughingstock of the combatants. The municipal administrators are implored to intervene in order to re-establish peace and quiet; their authority is flouted; they are shamed and insulted; this is no longer a house of justice and detention."

The disorders are as great, greater perhaps, at Bicêtre; political prisoners are kept there; hunted suspects are hidden there; poverty and famine keep many people hungry. The administration never ceases to protest; it asks that criminals be kept separate; and—it is important to note— some people still suggest that, in their place of detention, madmen be confined as well. On the ninth Brumaire, Year III, the bursar of Bicêtre writes to "Citizens Grandpré and Osmond, members of the Committee on Administration and Tribunals": "I submit that at a moment when humanity is decidedly the order of the day, there is no one who does not experience an impulse of horror upon seeing crime and indigence united in the same asylum." Was it necessary to recall the September massacres, the continual escapes, and, for so many innocent eyes, the sight of strangled prisoners, of swinging chains? The indigent and the old "have before their eyes nothing but chains, bars, and bolts. Add to this the groans of the prisoners that sometimes reach them. . . . It is on this basis that I urgently ask either that the prisoners be removed from Bicêtre, leaving only the indigent there, or that the indigent be removed, leaving only the prisoners." And here, finally, is the decisive point, if we remember that this letter was written in the middle of the Revolution, long before the reports of Georges Cabanis, and several months after Pinel, according to tradition, had "liberated" the insane of Bicêtre: "We could perhaps in this latter case leave the madmen there, another class of unfortunates who cause horrible suffering to humanity. . . . Make haste, then, citizens who cherish humanity, to realize such a beautiful dream, and be persuaded in advance that you will thereupon have deserved well of it." So great was the confusion of those years; so difficult was it, at the moment when "humanity" was being re-evaluated, to determine the place madness was to occupy within it; so difficult was it to situate madness in a social sphere that was being restructured.

IX

THE BIRTH OF
THE ASYLUM

WE know the images. They are familiar in all histories of
psychiatry, where their function is to illustrate that happy
age when madness was finally recognized and treated according to a truth to which we had too long remained blind.

"The worthy Society of Friends . . . sought to assure
those of its members who might have the misfortune to lose
their reason without a sufficient fortune to resort to expen-
sive establishments all the resources of medicine and all the
comforts of life compatible with their state; a voluntary
subscription furnished the funds, and for the last two years,
an establishment that seems to unite many advantages with
all possible economy has been founded near the city of
York. If the soul momentarily quails at the sight of that
dread disease which seems created to humiliate human reason, it subsequently experiences gentler emotions when it

considers all that an ingenious benevolence has been able to invent for its care and cure.

"This house is situated a mile from York, in the midst of a fertile and smiling countryside; it is not at all the idea of a prison that it suggests, but rather that of a large farm; it is surrounded by a great, walled garden. No bars, no grilles on the windows."[1]

As for the liberation of the insane at Bicêtre, the story is famous: the decision to remove the chains from the prisoners in the dungeons; Couthon visiting the hospital to find out whether any suspects were being hidden; Pinel courageously going to meet him, while everyone trembled at the sight of the "invalid carried in men's arms." The confrontation of the wise, firm philanthropist and the paralytic monster. "Pinel immediately led him to the section for the deranged, where the sight of the cells made a painful impression on him. He asked to interrogate all the patients. From most, he received only insults and obscene apostrophes. It was useless to prolong the interview. Turning to Pinel: 'Now, citizen, are you mad yourself to seek to unchain such beasts?' Pinel replied calmly: 'Citizen, I am convinced that these madmen are so intractable only because they have been deprived of air and liberty.'

" 'Well, do as you like with them, but I fear you may become the victim of your own presumption.' Whereupon, Couthon was taken to his carriage. His departure was a relief; everyone breathed again; the great philanthropist immediately set to work."[2]

These are images, at least insofar as each of the stories derives the essence of its power from imaginary forms: the patriarchal calm of Tuke's home, where the heart's passions and the mind's disorders slowly subside; the lucid firmness of Pinel, who masters in a word and a gesture the two animal frenzies that roar against him as they hunt him down; and the wisdom that could distinguish, between the raving madman and the bloodthirsty member of the Convention, which was the true danger: images that will carry far—to our own day—their weight of legend.

The legends of Pinel and Tuke transmit mythical values, which nineteenth-century psychiatry would accept as obvious in nature. But beneath the myths themselves, there was an operation, or rather a series of operations, which silently organized the world of the asylum, the methods of cure, and at the same time the concrete experience of madness.

Tuke's gesture, first of all. Because it is contemporary with Pinel's, because he is known to have been borne along by a whole current of "philanthropy," this gesture is regarded as an act of "liberation." The truth was quite different:" . . . there has also been particular occasion to observe the great loss, which individuals of our society have sustained, by being put under the care of those who are not only strangers to our principles, but by whom they are frequently mixed with other patients, who may indulge themselves in ill language, and other exceptionable practices. This often seems to leave an unprofitable effect upon the patients' minds after they are restored to the use of their reason, alienating them from those religious attachments which they had before experienced; and sometimes, even corrupting them with vicious habits to which they had been strangers."[3] The Retreat would serve as an instrument of segregation: a moral and religious segregation which sought to reconstruct around madness a milieu as much as possible like that of the Community of Quakers. And this for two reasons: first, the sight of evil is for every sensitive soul the cause of suffering, the origin of all those strong and untoward passions such as horror, hate, and disgust which engender or perpetuate madness: "It was thought, very justly, that the indiscriminate mixture, which must occur in large public establishments, of persons of opposite religious sentiments and practices; of the profligate and the virtuous; the profane and the serious; was calculated to check the progress of returning reason, and to fix, still deeper, the melancholy and misanthropic train of ideas . . ."[4] But the principal reason lies elsewhere: it is that religion can play the double role of nature and of rule, since it has assumed the depth of nature in ancestral habit, in education, in everyday exercise, and since it is at the same time a constant principle of coercion. It is both spontaneity and constraint, and to this degree it controls the only forces that can, in reason's eclipse, counterbalance the measureless violence of madness; its precepts, "where these have been strongly imbued in early life . . . become little less than principles of our nature; and their restraining power is frequently felt, even under the delirious excitement of insanity. To encourage the influence of religious principles over the mind of the insane is considered of great consequence, as a means of cure."[5] In the dialectic of insanity where reason hides without abolishing itself, religion constitutes the concrete form of what cannot go mad; it bears what is invincible in reason, it bears what subsists beneath madness as quasi-nature and around it as the constant solicitation of a milieu "where, during lucid intervals, or the state of convalescence, the patient might enjoy the society of those who were of similar habits and opinions." Religion safeguards the old secret of reason in the presence of madness, thus making closer, more immediate, the constraint that was already rampant in classical confinement. There, the religious and moral milieu was imposed from without, in such a way that madness was controlled, not cured. At the Retreat, religion was part of the movement which indicated in spite of everything the presence of reason in madness, and which led from insanity to health. Religious segregation has a very precise meaning: it does not attempt to preserve the sufferers from the profane presence of non-Quakers, but to place the insane individual within a moral element where he will be in debate with himself and his surroundings: to constitute for him a milieu where, far from being protected, he will be kept in a perpetual anxiety, ceaselessly threatened by Law and Transgression.

"The principle of fear, which is rarely decreased by insanity, is considered as of great importance in the management of the patients."[6] Fear appears as an essential presence in the asylum. Already an ancient figure, no doubt, if we think of the terrors of confinement. But these terrors surrounded madness from the outside, marking the boundary of reason and unreason, and enjoying a double power: over the violence of fury in order to contain it, and over reason itself to hold it at a distance; such fear was entirely on the surface. The fear instituted at the Retreat is of great depth; it passes between reason and madness like a mediation, like an evocation of a common nature they still share, and by which it could link them together. The terror that once reigned was the most visible sign of the alienation of madness in the classical period; fear was now endowed with a power of disalienation, which permitted it to restore a primitive complicity between the madman and the man of reason. It re-established a solidarity between them. Now madness would never—could never—cause fear again; it would *be afraid*, without recourse or return, thus entirely in the hands of the pedagogy of good sense, of truth, and of morality.

Samuel Tuke tells how he received at the Retreat a maniac, young and prodigiously strong, whose seizures caused panic in those around him and even among his guards. When he entered the Retreat he was loaded with chains; he wore handcuffs; his clothes were attached by ropes. He had no sooner arrived than all his shackles were removed, and he was permitted to dine with the keepers;

his agitation immediately ceased; "his attention appeared to be arrested by his new situation." He was taken to his room; the keeper explained that the entire house was organized in terms of the greatest liberty and the greatest comfort for all, and that he would not be subject to any constraint so long as he did nothing against the rules of the house or the general principles of human morality. For his part, the keeper declared he had no desire to use the means of coercion at his disposal. "The maniac was sensible of the kindness of his treatment. *He promised to restrain himself*." He sometimes still raged, shouted, and frightened his companions. The keeper reminded him of the threats and promises of the first day; if he did not control himself, it would be necessary to go back to the old ways. The patient's agitation would then increase for a while, and then rapidly decline. "He would listen with attention to the persuasions and arguments of his friendly visitor. After such conversations, the patient was generally better for some days or a week." At the end of four months, he left the Retreat, entirely cured. Here fear is addressed to the invalid directly, not by instruments but in speech; there is no question of limiting a liberty that rages beyond its bounds, but of marking out and glorifying a region of simple responsibility where any manifestation of madness will be linked to punishment. The obscure guilt that once linked transgression and unreason is thus shifted; the madman, as a human being originally endowed with reason, is no longer guilty of being mad; but the madman, as a madman, and in the interior of that disease of which he is no longer guilty, must feel morally responsible for everything within him that may disturb morality and society, and must hold no one but himself responsible for the punishment he receives. The assignation of guilt is no longer the mode of relation that obtains between the madman and the sane man in their generality; it becomes both the concrete form of coexistence of each madman with his keeper, and the form of awareness that the madman must have of his own madness.

We must therefore re-evaluate the meanings assigned to Tuke's work: liberation of the insane, abolition of constraint, constitution of a human milieu—these are only justifications. The real operations were different. In fact Tuke created an asylum where he substituted for the free terror of madness the stifling anguish of responsibility; fear no longer reigned on the other side of the prison gates, it now raged under the seals of conscience. Tuke now transferred the age-old terrors in which the insane had been trapped to the very heart of madness. The asylum no longer punished the madman's guilt, it is true; but it did more, it organized that guilt; it organized it for the madman as a consciousness of himself, and as a non-reciprocal relation to the keeper; it organized it for the man of reason as an awareness of the Other, a therapeutic intervention in the madman's existence. In other words, by this guilt the madman became an object of punishment always vulnerable to himself and to the Other; and, from the acknowledgment of his status as object, from the awareness of his guilt, the madman was to return to his awareness of himself as a free and responsible subject, and consequently to reason. This movement by which, objectifying himself for the Other, the madman thus returned to his liberty, was to be found as much in Work as in Observation.

Let us not forget that we are in a Quaker world where God blesses men in the signs of their prosperity. Work comes first in "moral treatment" as practiced at the Retreat. In itself, work possesses a constraining power superior to all forms of physical coercion, in that the regularity of the hours, the requirements of attention, the obligation to produce a result detach the sufferer from a liberty of mind that would be fatal and engage him in a system of responsibilities: "Regular employment is perhaps the most generally efficacious; and those kinds of employment are doubtless to be preferred, both on a moral and physical account, which are accompanied by considerable bodily action; that are most agreeable to the patient and which are most opposite to the illusions of his disease."[7] Through work, man returns to the order of God's commandments; he submits his liberty to laws that are those of both morality and reality. Hence mental work is not to be rejected; yet with absolute rigor, all exercises of the imagination must be excluded as being in complicity with the passions, the desires, or all delirious illusions. On the contrary, the study of what is eternal in nature and most in accord with the wisdom and goodness of Providence has the greatest efficacity in reducing the madman's immoderate liberties and bringing him to discover the forms of his responsibility. "The various branches of the mathematics and natural science furnish the most useful class of subjects on which to employ the minds of the insane." In the asylum, work is deprived of any productive value; it is imposed only as a moral rule; a limitation of liberty, a submission to order, an engagement of responsibility, with the single aim of disalienating the mind lost in the excess of a liberty which physical constraint limits only in appearance.

Even more efficacious than work, than the observation of others, is what Tuke calls "the need for esteem": "This principle in the human mind, which doubtless influences in a great degree, though often secretly, our general manners; and which operates with peculiar force on our introduction into a new circle of acquaintance." In classical confinement, the madman was also vulnerable to observation, but such observation did not, basically, involve him; it involved only his monstrous surface, his visible animality; and it included at least one form of reciprocity, since the sane man could read in the madman, as in a mirror, the imminent movement of his downfall. The observation Tuke now instituted as one of the great elements of asylum existence was both deeper and less reciprocal. It pursued in the madman the least perceptible signs of his madness, in the place where madness becomes secretly distinct from reason, begins to detach itself from it; and the madman cannot return this observation in any form, since he is merely observed; he is a kind of new arrival, a latecomer in the world of reason. Tuke organized an entire ceremonial around these observations. There were social occasions in the English manner, where everyone was obliged to imitate all the formal requirements of social existence; nothing else circulated except the observation that would spy out any incongruity, any disorder, any awkwardness where madness might betray itself. The directors and staff of the Retreat thus regularly invited several patients to "tea-parties"; the guests "dress in their best clothes, and vie with each other in politeness and propriety. The best fare is provided, and the visitors are treated with all the attention of strangers. The evening generally passes with the greatest harmony and enjoyment. It rarely happens that any unpleasant circumstance occurs; the patients control, to a wonderful degree, their different propensities; and the scene is at once curious and affectingly gratifying." Curiously, this rite is not one of intimacy, of dialogue, of mutual acquaintance; it is the organization around the madman of a world where everything would be like and near him, but in which he himself would remain a stranger, the Stranger *par excellence* who is judged not only by appearances but by all that they may betray and reveal in spite of themselves. Incessantly cast in this empty role of unknown visitor, and challenged in everything that can be known about him, drawn to the surface of himself by a social personality silently imposed by observation, by form and mask, the madman is obliged to objectify himself in the eyes of reason as the perfect stranger, that is, as the man whose strangeness does not reveal itself. The city of reason welcomes him only with this qualification and at the price of this surrender to anonymity.

We see that at the Retreat the partial suppression of physical constraint was part of a system whose essential element was the constitution of a "self-restraint" in which the patient's freedom, engaged by work and the observation of others, was ceaselessly threatened by the recognition of guilt. Instead of submitting to a simple negative operation that loosened bonds and delivered one's deepest nature from madness, it must be recognized that one was in the grip of a positive operation that confined madness in a system of rewards and punishments, and included it in the movement of moral consciousness. A passage from a world of Censure to a universe of Judgment. But thereby a psychology of madness becomes possible, for under observation madness is constantly required, at the surface of itself, to deny its dissimulation. It is judged only by its acts; it is not accused of intentions, nor are its secrets to be fathomed. Madness is responsible only for that part of itself which is visible. All the rest is reduced to silence. Madness no longer exists except as *seen*. The proximity instituted by the asylum, an intimacy neither chains nor bars would ever violate again, does not allow reciprocity: only the nearness of observation that watches, that spies, that comes closer in order to see better, but moves ever farther away, since it accepts and acknowledges only the values of the Stranger. The science of mental disease, as it would develop in the asylum, would always be only of the order of observation and classification. It would not be a dialogue. It could not be that until psychoanalysis had exorcised this phenomenon of observation, essential to the nineteenth-century asylum, and substituted for its silent magic the powers of language. It would be fairer to say that psychoanalysis doubled the absolute observation of the watcher with the endless monologue of the person watched—thus preserving the old asylum structure of non-reciprocal observation but balancing it, in a non-symmetrical reciprocity, by the new structure of language without response.

Surveillance and Judgment: already the outline appears of a new personage who will be essential in the nineteenth-century asylum. Tuke himself suggests this personage, when he tells the story of a maniac subject to seizures of irrepressible violence. One day while he was walking in the garden of the asylum with the keeper, this patient suddenly entered a phase of excitation, moved several steps away, picked up a large stone, and made the gesture of throwing it at his companion. The keeper stopped, looked the patient in the eyes; then advanced several steps toward him and "in a resolute tone of voice . . . commanded him to lay down the stone"; as he approached, the patient lowered his hand, then dropped his weapon; "he then submitted to be quietly led to his apartment." Something had been born, which was no longer repression, but authority. Until the end of the eighteenth century, the world of madmen was peopled only by the abstract, faceless power which kept them confined; within these limits, it was empty, empty of all that was not madness itself; the guards were often recruited among the inmates themselves. Tuke established, on the contrary, a mediating element between guards and patients, between reason and madness. The space reserved by society for insanity would now be haunted by those who were "from the other side" and who represented both the prestige of the authority that confines and the rigor of the reason that judges. The keeper intervenes, without weapons, without instruments of constraint, with observation and language only; he advances upon madness, deprived of all that could protect him or make him seem threatening, risking an immediate confrontation without recourse. In fact, though, it is not as a concrete person that he confronts madness, but as a reasonable being, invested by that very fact, and before any combat takes place, with the authority that is his for not being mad. Reason's victory over unreason was once assured only by material force, and in a sort of real combat. Now the combat was always decided beforehand, unreason's defeat inscribed in advance in the concrete situation where madman and man of reason meet. The absence of constraint in the nineteenth-century asylum is not unreason liberated, but madness long since mastered.

For this new reason which reigns in the asylum, madness does not represent the absolute form of contradiction, but instead a minority status, an aspect of itself that does not have the right to autonomy, and can live only grafted onto the world of reason. Madness is childhood. Everything at the Retreat is organized so that the insane are transformed into minors. They are regarded "as children who have an overabundance of strength and make dangerous use of it. They must be given immediate punishments and rewards; whatever is remote has no effect on them. A new system of education must be applied, a new direction given to their ideas; they must first be subjugated, then encouraged, then applied to work, and this work made agreeable by attractive means."[8] For a long time already, the law had regarded the insane as minors, but this was a juridical situation, abstractly defined by interdiction and trusteeship; it was not a concrete mode of relation between man and man. Minority status became for Tuke a style of existence to be applied to the mad, and for the guards a mode of sovereignty. Great emphasis was placed on the concept of the "family" which organized the community of the insane and their keepers at the Retreat. Apparently this "family" placed the patient in a milieu both normal and natural; in reality it alienated him still more: the juridical minority assigned to the madman was intended to protect him as a subject of law; this ancient structure, by becoming a form of coexistence, delivered him entirely, as a psychological subject, to the authority and prestige of the man of reason, who assumed for him the concrete figure of an adult, in other words, both domination and destination.

In the great reorganization of relations between madness and reason, the family, at the end of the eighteenth century, played a decisive part—simultaneously imaginary landscape and real social structure; it is from the family that Tuke starts out, and toward it that he progresses. Lending it the prestige of primitive values not yet compromised in the social, Tuke makes the family play a role of disalienation; it was, in his myth, the antithesis of that "milieu" which the eighteenth century saw as the origin of all madness. But he introduced it as well, in a very real way, into the world of the asylum, where it appears both as truth and as norm for all relations that may obtain between the madman and the man of reason. Thus minority under family tutelage, a juridical status in which the madman's civil status is alienated, becomes a concrete situation in which his concrete liberty is alienated. The entire existence of madness, in the world now being prepared for it, was enveloped in what we may call, in anticipation, a "parental complex." The prestige of patriarchy is revived around madness in the bourgeois family. It is this historical sedimentation which psychoanalysis would later bring to light, according it through a new myth the meaning of a destiny that supposedly marked all of Western culture and perhaps all civilization, whereas it had been slowly deposited by it and only solidified quite recently at the turn of this century, when madness was doubly alienated within the family—by the myth of a disalienation in patriarchal purity, and by a truly alienating situation in an asylum constituted in the family mode. Henceforth, and for a period of time the end of which it is not yet possible to predict, the discourse of unreason will be indissociably linked with the half-real, half-imaginary dialectic of the Family. So that what, in their violence, it was once obligatory to interpret as profanations or blasphemies, it would henceforth be necessary to see as an incessant attack against the Father. Thus in the modern world, what had been the great, irreparable confrontation of reason and unreason became the secret thrust of instincts against the solidity of the family institution and against its most archaic symbols.

There is an astonishing convergence of the movement of fundamental institutions and this evolution of madness in the world of confinement. The liberal economy, as we have seen, tended to entrust the care of the poor and the sick to the family rather than to the State: the family thus became the site of social responsibility. But if the patient can be entrusted to the family, he is nonetheless mad, which is too strange and inhuman. Tuke, precisely, reconstitutes around madness a simulated family, which is an institutional parody but a real psychological situation. Where the family is inadequate, he substitutes for it a fictitious family decor of signs and attitudes. But by a very curious intersection, the day would come when the family was relieved of its responsibility to care for the patient in general, while it kept the fictitious values that concern madness; and long after the diseases of the poor had again become an affair of state, the asylum would keep the insane in the imperative fiction of the family; the madman remains a minor, and for a long time reason will retain for him the aspect of the Father.

Closed upon these fictitious values, the asylum was protected from history and from social evolution. In Tuke's mind, the problem was to constitute a milieu which would imitate the oldest, the purest, the most natural forms of coexistence: the most human milieu possible, while being the least social one possible. In fact, he isolated the social structure of the bourgeois family, reconstituted it symbolically in the asylum, and set it adrift in history. The asylum, always oriented to anachronistic structures and symbols, would be, *par excellence*, inadapted and out of time. And exactly where animality manifested a presence without history, an eternal return, would slowly reappear the immemorial scars of old hatreds, old family profanations, the forgotten signs of incest and punishment.

Pinel advocates no religious segregation. Or rather, a segregation that functions in the opposite direction from that practiced by Tuke. The benefits of the renovated asylum were offered to all, or almost all, except the fanatics "who believe themselves inspired and seek to make converts." Bicêtre and La Salpêtrière, according to Pinel's intention, form a complementary figure to the Retreat.

Religion must not be the moral substratum of life in the asylum, but purely and simply a medical object: "Religious opinions in a hospital for the insane must be considered only in a strictly medical relation, that is, one must set aside all other considerations of public worship and political belief, and investigate only whether it is necessary to oppose the exaltation of ideas and feelings that may originate in this source, in order to effect the cure of certain alienated minds."[9] A source of strong emotions and terrifying images which it arouses through fears of the Beyond, Catholicism frequently provokes madness; it generates delirious beliefs, entertains hallucinations, leads men to despair and to melancholia. We must not be surprised if, "examining the registers of the insane asylum at Bicêtre, we find inscribed there many priests and monks, as well as country people maddened by a frightening picture of the future." Still less surprising is it to see the number of religious madnesses vary. Under the Old Regime and during the Revolution, the strength of superstitious beliefs, or the violence of the struggles in which the Republic opposed the Catholic

Church, multiplied melancholias of religious origin. With the return of peace, the Concordat having erased the struggles, these forms of delirium disappeared; in the Year X, 50 per cent of the melancholics in Bicêtre were suffering from religious madness, 33 per cent the following year, and only 18 per cent in the Year XII. The asylum must thus be freed from religion and from all its iconographic connections; "melancholics by devotion" must not be allowed their pious books; experience "teaches that this is the surest means of perpetuating insanity or even of making it incurable, and the more such permission is granted, the less we manage to calm anxiety and scruples." Nothing takes us further from Tuke and his dreams of a religious community that would at the same time be a privileged site of mental cures, than this notion of a neutralized asylum, purified of those images and passions to which Christianity gave birth and which made the mind wander toward illusion, toward error, and soon toward delirium and hallucinations.

But Pinel's problem was to reduce the iconographic forms, not the moral content of religion. Once "filtered," religion possesses a disalienating power that dissipates the images, calms the passions, and restores man to what is most immediate and essential: it can bring him closer to his moral truth. And it is here that religion is often capable of effecting cures. Pinel relates several Voltairean stories. One, for example, of a woman of twenty-five, "of strong constitution, united in wedlock to a weak and delicate man"; she suffered "quite violent fits of hysteria, imagining she was possessed by a demon who followed her in different shapes, sometimes emitting bird noises, sometimes mournful sounds and piercing cries." Happily, the local curé was more concerned with natural religion than learned in the techniques of exorcism; he believed in curing through the benevolence of nature; this "enlightened man, of kindly and persuasive character, gained ascendancy over the patient's mind and managed to induce her to leave her bed, to resume her domestic tasks, and even to spade her garden. . . . This was followed by the most fortunate effects, and by a cure that lasted three years." Restored to the extreme simplicity of this moral content, religion could not help conniving with philosophy and with medicine, with all the forms of wisdom and science that can restore the reason in a disturbed mind. There are even instances of religion serving as a preliminary treatment, preparing for what will be done in the asylum: take the case of the young girl "of an ardent temperament, though very docile and pious" who was torn between "the inclinations of her heart and the severe principles of her conduct"; her confessor, after having vainly counseled her to attach herself to God, proposed examples of a firm and measured holiness, and "offered her the best remedy against high passions: patience and time." Taken to La Salpêtrière, she was treated, on Pinel's orders, "according to the same moral principles," and her illness proved "of very short duration." Thus the asylum assimilates not the social theme of a religion in which men feel themselves brothers in the same communion and the same community, but the moral power of consolation, of confidence, and a docile fidelity to nature. It must resume the moral enterprise of religion, exclusive of its fantastic text, exclusively on the level of virtue, labor, and social life.

The asylum is a religious domain without religion, a domain of pure morality, of ethical uniformity. Everything that might retain the signs of the old differences was eliminated. The last vestiges of rite were extinguished. Formerly the house of confinement had inherited, in the social sphere, the almost absolute limits of the lazar house; it was a foreign country. Now the asylum must represent the great continuity of social morality. The values of family and work, all the acknowledged virtues, now reign in the asylum. But their reign is a double one. First, they prevail in fact, at the heart of madness itself; beneath the violence and disorder of insanity, the solid nature of the essential virtues is not disrupted. There is a primitive morality which is ordinarily not affected even by the worst dementia; it is this morality which both appears and functions in the cure: "I can generally testify to the pure virtues and severe principles often manifested by the cure. Nowhere except in novels have I seen spouses more worthy of being cherished, parents more tender, lovers more passionate, or persons more attached to their duties than the majority of the insane fortunately brought to the period of convalescence."[10] This inalienable virtue is both the truth and the resolution of madness. Which is why, if it reigns, it *must* reign as well. The asylum reduces differences, represses vice, eliminates irregularities. It denounces everything that opposes the essential virtues of society: celibacy—"the number of girls fallen into idiocy is seven times greater than the number of married women for the Year XI and the Year XIII; for dementia, the proportion is two to four times greater; we can thus deduce that marriage constitutes for women a kind of preservative against the two sorts of insanity which are most inveterate and most often incurable"; debauchery, misconduct, and "extreme perversity of habits"—"vicious habits such as drunkenness, limitless promiscuity, an apathetic lack of concern can gradually degrade the reason and end in outright insanity"; laziness—"it is the most constant and unanimous result of experience that in all public asylums, as in prisons and hospitals, the surest and perhaps the sole guarantee of the maintenance of health and good habits and order is the law of rigorously executed mechanical work." The asylum sets itself the task of the homogeneous rule of morality, its rigorous extension to all those who tend to escape from it.

But it thereby generates an indifference; if the law does

not reign universally, it is because there are men who do not recognize it, a class of society that lives in disorder, in negligence, and almost in illegality: "If on the one hand we see families prosper for a long series of years in the bosom of harmony and order and concord, how many others, especially in the lower classes, afflict the eye with a repulsive spectacle of debauchery, of dissensions, and shameful distress! That, according to my daily notes, is the most fertile source of the insanity we treat in the hospitals."[11]

In one and the same movement, the asylum becomes, in Pinel's hands, an instrument of moral uniformity and of social denunciation. The problem is to impose, in a universal form, a morality that will prevail from within upon those who are strangers to it and in whom insanity is already present before it has made itself manifest. In the first case, the asylum must act as an awakening and a reminder, invoking a forgotten nature; in the second, it must act by means of a social shift in order to snatch the individual from his condition. The operation as practiced at the Retreat was still simple: religious segregation for purposes of moral purification. The operation as practiced by Pinel was relatively complex: to effect moral syntheses, assuring an ethical continuity between the world of madness and the world of reason, but by practicing a social segregation that would guarantee bourgeois morality a universality of fact and permit it to be imposed as a law upon all forms of insanity.

In the classical period, indigence, laziness, vice, and madness mingled in an equal guilt within unreason; madmen were caught in the great confinement of poverty and unemployment, but all had been promoted, in the proximity of transgression, to the essence of a Fall. Now madness belonged to social failure, which appeared without distinction as its cause, model, and limit. Half a century later, mental disease would become degeneracy. Henceforth, the essential madness, and the really dangerous one, was that which rose from the lower depths of society.

Pinel's asylum would never be, as a retreat from the world, a space of nature and immediate truth like Tuke's, but a uniform domain of legislation, a site of moral syntheses where insanities born on the outer limits of society were eliminated. The entire life of the inmates, the entire conduct of their keepers and doctors, were organized by Pinel so that these moral syntheses would function. And this by three principal means:

1. *Silence.* The fifth chained prisoner released by Pinel was a former ecclesiastic whose madness had caused him to be excommunicated; suffering from delusions of grandeur, he believed he was Christ; this was "the height of human arrogance in delirium." Sent to Bicêtre in 1782, he had been in chains for twelve years. For the pride of his bearing, the grandiloquence of his ideas, he was one of the most celebrated spectacles of the entire hospital, but as he knew that he was reliving Christ's Passion, "he endured with patience this long martyrdom and the continual sarcasms his mania exposed him to." Pinel chose him as one of the first twelve to be released, though his delirium was still acute. But Pinel did not treat him as he did the others; without a word, he had his chains struck off, and "ordered expressly that everyone imitate his own reserve and not address a word to this poor madman. This prohibition, which was rigorously observed, produced upon this self-intoxicated creature an effect much more perceptible than irons and the dungeon; he felt humiliated in an abandon and an isolation so new to him amid his freedom. Finally, after long hesitations, they saw him come of his own accord to join the society of the other patients; henceforth, he returned to more sensible and true ideas."[12]

Deliverance here has a paradoxical meaning. The dungeon, the chains, the continual spectacle, the sarcasms were, to the sufferer in his delirium, the very element of his liberty. Acknowledged in that very fact and fascinated from without by so much complicity, he could not be dislodged from his immediate truth. But the chains that fell, the indifference and silence of all those around him confined him in the limited use of an empty liberty; he was delivered in silence to a truth which was not acknowledged and which he would demonstrate in vain, since he was no longer a spectacle, and from which he could derive no exaltation, since he was not even humiliated. It was the man himself, not his projection in a delirium, who was now humiliated: for physical constraint yielded to a liberty that constantly touched the limits of solitude; the dialogue of delirium and insult gave way to a monologue in a language which exhausted itself in the silence of others; the entire show of presumption and outrage was replaced by indifference. Henceforth, more genuinely confined than he could have been in a dungeon and chains, a prisoner of nothing but himself, the sufferer was caught in a relation to himself that was of the order of transgression, and in a nonrelation to others that was of the order of shame. The others are made innocent, they are no longer persecutors; the guilt is shifted inside, showing the madman that he was fascinated by nothing but his own presumption; the enemy faces disappear; he no longer feels their presence as observation, but as a denial of attention, as observation deflected; the others are now nothing but a limit that ceaselessly recedes as he advances. Delivered from his chains, he is now chained, by silence, to transgression and to shame. He feels himself punished, and he sees the sign of his innocence in that fact; free from all physical punishment, he must prove himself guilty. His torment was his glory; his deliverance must humiliate him.

Compared to the incessant dialogue of reason and madness during the Renaissance, classical internment had been a silencing. But it was not total: language was engaged in things rather than really suppressed. Confinement, prisons, dungeons, even tortures, engaged in a mute dialogue between reason and unreason—the dialogue of struggle. This dialogue itself was now disengaged; silence was absolute; there was no longer any common language between madness and reason; the language of delirium can be answered only by an absence of language, for delirium is not a fragment of dialogue with reason, it is not language at all; it refers, in an ultimately silent awareness, only to transgression. And it is only at this point that a common language becomes possible again, insofar as it will be one of acknowledged guilt. "Finally, after long hesitations, they saw him come of his own accord to join the society of the other patients . . ." The absence of language, as a fundamental structure of asylum life, has its correlative in the exposure of confession. When Freud, in psychoanalysis, cautiously reinstitutes exchange, or rather begins once again to listen to this language, henceforth eroded into monologue, should we be astonished that the formulations he hears are always those of transgression? In this inveterate silence, transgression has taken over the very sources of speech.

2. *Recognition by Mirror.* At the Retreat, the madman was observed, and knew he was observed; but except for that direct observation which permitted only an indirect apprehension of itself, madness had no immediate grasp of its own character. With Pinel, on the contrary, observation operated only within the space defined by madness, without surface or exterior limits. Madness would see itself, would be seen by itself—pure spectacle and absolute subject.

"Three insane persons, each of whom believed himself to be a king, and each of whom took the title Louis XVI, quarreled one day over the prerogatives of royalty, and defended them somewhat too energetically. The keeper approached one of them, and drawing him aside, asked: 'Why do you argue with these men who are evidently mad? Doesn't everyone know that you should be recognized as Louis XVI?' Flattered by this homage, the madman immediately withdrew, glancing at the others with a disdainful hauteur. The same trick worked with the second patient. And thus in an instant there no longer remained any trace of an argument."[13] This is the first phase, that of exaltation. Madness is made to observe itself, but in others: it appears in them as a baseless pretense—in other words, as absurd. However, in this observation that condemns others, the madman assures his own justification and the certainty of being adequate to his delirium. The rift between presumption and reality allows itself to be recognized only in the object. It is entirely masked, on the contrary, in the subject, which becomes immediate truth and absolute judge: the exalted sovereignty that denounces the others' false sovereignty dispossesses them and thus confirms itself in the unfailing plenitude of presumption. Madness, as simple delirium, is projected onto others; as perfect unconsciousness, it is entirely accepted.

It is at this point that the mirror, as an accomplice, becomes an agent of demystification. Another inmate of Bicêtre, also believing himself a king, always expressed himself "in a tone of command and with supreme authority." One day when he was calmer, the keeper approached him and asked why, if he were a sovereign, he did not put an end to his detention, and why he remained mingled with madmen of all kinds. Resuming this speech the following days, "he made him see, little by little, the absurdity of his pretensions, showed him another madman who had also been long convinced that he possessed supreme power and had become an object of mockery. At first the maniac felt shaken, soon he cast doubts upon his title of sovereign, and finally he came to realize his chimerical vagaries. It was in two weeks that this unexpected moral revolution took place, and after several months of tests, this worthy father was restored to his family."[14] This, then, is the phase of abasement: presumptuously identified with the object of his delirium, the madman recognizes himself as in a mirror in this madness whose absurd pretensions he has denounced; his solid sovereignty as a subject dissolves in this object he has demystified by accepting it. He is now pitilessly observed by himself. And in the silence of those who represent reason, and who have done nothing but hold up the perilous mirror, he recognizes himself as objectively mad.

We have seen by what means—and by what mystifications—eighteenth-century therapeutics tried to persuade the madman of his madness in order to release him from it. Here the movement is of an entirely different nature; it is not a question of dissipating error by the impressive spectacle of a truth, even a pretended truth; but of treating madness in its arrogance rather than in its aberration. The classical mind condemned in madness a certain blindness to the truth; from Pinel on, madness would be regarded rather as an impulse from the depths which exceeds the juridical limits of the individual, ignores the moral limits fixed for him, and tends to an apotheosis of the self. For the nineteenth century, the initial model of madness would be to believe oneself to be God, while for the preceding centuries it had been to deny God. Thus madness, in the spectacle of itself as unreason humiliated, was able to find its salvation when, imprisoned in the absolute subjectivity of its delirium, it surprised the absurd and objective image of that delirium in the identical madman. Truth insinuated itself, as if by surprise (and not by violence, in the eighteenth-century mode), in this play of reciprocal observations where it never saw anything but itself. But the asylum, in this community of madmen, placed the mirrors in such a way that the madman, when all was said and done, inevitably surprised himself, despite himself, *as a madman*. Freed from the chains that made it a purely observed object, madness lost, paradoxically, the essence of its liberty, which was solitary exaltation; it became responsible for what it knew of its truth; it imprisoned itself in an infinitely self-referring observation; it was finally chained to the humiliation of being its own object. Awareness was now linked to the shame of being identical to that other, of being compromised in him, and of already despising oneself before being able to recognize or to know oneself.

3. *Perpetual Judgment*. By this play of mirrors, as by silence, madness is ceaselessly called upon to judge itself. But beyond this, it is at every moment judged from without; judged not by moral or scientific conscience, but by a sort of invisible tribunal in permanent session. The asylum Pinel dreamed of and partly realized at Bicêtre, but especially at La Salpêtrière, is a juridical microcosm. To be efficacious, this judgment must be redoubtable in aspect; all the iconographic apanage of the judge and the executioner must be present in the mind of the madman, so that he understands what universe of judgment he now belongs to. The decor of justice, in all its terror and implacability, will thus be part of the treatment. One of the inmates at Bicêtre suffered from a religious delirium animated by a fear of hell; he believed that the only way he could escape eternal damnation was by rigorous abstinence. It was necessary to compensate this fear of a remote justice by the presence of a more immediate and still more redoubtable one: "Could the irresistible curse of his sinister ideas be counterbalanced other than by the impression of a strong and deep fear?" One evening, the director came to the patient's door "with matter likely to produce fear—an angry eye, a thundering tone of voice, a group of the staff armed with strong chains that they shook noisily. They set some soup beside

the madman and gave him precise orders to eat it during the night, or else suffer the most cruel treatment. They retired, and left the madman in the most distressed state of indecision between the punishment with which he was threatened and the frightening prospect of the torments in the life to come. After an inner combat of several hours, the former idea prevailed, and he decided to take some nourishment."[15]

The asylum as a juridical instance recognized no other. It judged immediately, and without appeal. It possessed its own instruments of punishment, and used them as it saw fit. The old confinement had generally been practiced outside of normal juridical forms, but it imitated the punishment of criminals, using the same prisons, the same dungeons, the same physical brutality. The justice that reigned in Pinel's asylum did not borrow its modes of repression from the other justice, but invented its own. Or rather, it used the therapeutic methods that had become known in the eighteenth century, but used them as chastisements. And this is not the least of the paradoxes of Pinel's "philanthropic" and "liberating" enterprise, this conversion of medicine into justice, of therapeutics into repression. In the medicine of the classical period, baths and showers were used as remedies as a result of the physicians' vagaries about the nature of the nervous system: the intention was to refresh the organism, to relax the desiccated fibers; it is true that they also added, among the happy consequences of the cold shower, the psychological effect of the unpleasant surprise which interrupted the course of ideas and changed the nature of sentiments; but we were still in the landscape of medical speculation. With Pinel, the use of the shower became frankly juridical; the shower was the habitual punishment of the ordinary police tribunal that sat permanently at the asylum: "Considered as a means of repression, it often suffices to subject to the general law of manual labor a madman who is susceptible to it, in order to conquer an obstinate refusal to take nourishment, and to subjugate insane persons carried away by a sort of turbulent and reasoned humor."

Everything was organized so that the madman would recognize himself in a world of judgment that enveloped him on all sides; he must know that he is watched, judged, and condemned; from transgression to punishment, the connection must be evident, as a guilt recognized by all: "We profit from the circumstance of the bath, remind him of the transgression, or of the omission of an important duty, and with the aid of a faucet suddenly release a shower of cold water upon his head, which often disconcerts the madman or drives out a predominant idea by a strong and unexpected impression; if the idea persists, the shower is repeated, but care is taken to avoid the hard tone and the shocking terms that would cause rebellion; on the contrary, the madman is made to understand that it is for his sake and reluctantly that we resort to such violent measures; sometimes we add a joke, taking care not to go too far with it."[16] This almost arithmetical obviousness of punishment, repeated as often as necessary, the recognition of transgression by its repression—all this must end in the internalization of the juridical instance, and the birth of remorse in the inmate's mind: it is only at this point that the judges agree to stop the punishment, certain that it will continue indefinitely in the inmate's conscience. One maniac had the habit of tearing her clothes and breaking any object that came into her hands; she was given showers, she was put into a straitjacket, she finally appeared "humiliated and dismayed"; but fearing that this shame might be transitory and this remorse too superficial, "the director, in order to impress a feeling of terror upon her, spoke to her with the most energetic firmness, but without anger, and announced to her that she would henceforth be treated with the greatest severity." The desired result was not long in coming: "Her repentance was announced by a torrent of tears which she shed for almost two hours." The cycle is complete twice over: the transgression is punished and its author recognizes her guilt.

There were, however, madmen who escaped from this movement and resisted the moral synthesis it brought about. These latter would be set apart in the heart of the asylum, forming a new confined population, which could not even relate to justice. When we speak of Pinel and his work of liberation, we too often omit this second reclusion. We have already seen that he denied the benefits of asylum reform to "fanatics who believe themselves inspired and seek to make converts, and who take a perfidious pleasure in inciting the other madmen to disobedience on the pretext that it is better to obey God than man." But confinement and the dungeon will be equally obligatory for "those who cannot be subjected to the general law of work and who, in malicious activity, enjoy tormenting the other inmates, provoking and ceaselessly inciting them to subjects of discord," and for women "who during their seizures have an irresistible propensity to steal anything they can lay their hands on." Disobedience by religious fanaticism, resistance to work, and theft, the three great transgressions against bourgeois society, the three major offenses against its essential values, are not excusable, even by madness; they deserve imprisonment pure and simple, exclusion in the most rigorous sense of the term, since they all manifest the same resistance to the moral and social uniformity that forms the *raison d'être* of Pinel's asylum.

Formerly, unreason was set outside of judgment, to be delivered, arbitrarily, to the powers of reason. Now it is judged, and not only upon entering the asylum, in order to be recognized, classified, and made innocent forever; it is caught, on the contrary, in a perpetual judgment, which never ceases to pursue it and to apply sanctions, to proclaim its transgressions, to require honorable amends, to exclude, finally, those whose transgressions risk compromising the social order. Madness escaped from the arbitrary only in order to enter a kind of endless trial for which the asylum furnished simultaneously police, magistrates, and torturers; a trial whereby any transgression in life, by a virtue proper to life in the asylum, becomes a social crime, observed, condemned, and punished; a trial which has no outcome but in a perpetual recommencement in the internalized form of remorse. The madmen "delivered" by Pinel and, after him, the madmen of modern confinement are under arraignment; if they have the privilege of no longer being associated or identified with convicts, they are condemned, at every moment, to be subject to an accusation whose text is never given, for it is their entire life in the asylum which constitutes it. The asylum of the age of positivism, which it is Pinel's glory to have founded, is not a free realm of observation, diagnosis, and therapeutics; it is a juridical space where one is accused, judged, and condemned, and from which one is never released except by the version of this trial in psychological depth—that is, by remorse. Madness will be punished in the asylum, even if it is innocent outside of it. For a long time to come, and until our own day at least, it is imprisoned in a moral world.

To silence, to recognition in the mirror, to perpetual judgment, we must add a fourth structure peculiar to the world of the asylum as it was constituted at the end of the eighteenth century: this is the apotheosis of the *medical personage*. Of them all, it is doubtless the most important, since it would authorize not only new contacts between doctor and patient, but a new relation between insanity and medical thought, and ultimately command the whole modern experience of madness. Hitherto, we find in the asylums only the same structures of confinement, but displaced and deformed. With the new status of the medical personage, the deepest meaning of confinement is abolished: mental disease, with the meanings we now give it, is made possible.

The work of Tuke and of Pinel, whose spirit and values are so different, meet in this transformation of the medical personage. The physician, as we have seen, played no part in the life of confinement. Now he becomes the essential figure of the asylum. He is in charge of entry. The ruling at the Retreat is precise: "On the admission of patients, the committee should, in general, require a certificate signed by a medical person. . . . It should also be stated whether the patient is afflicted with any complaint independent of insanity. It is also desirable that some account should be sent, how long the patient has been disordered; whether any, or what sort of medical means have been used."[17] From the end of the eighteenth century, the medical certificate becomes almost obligatory for the confinement of madmen. But within the asylum itself, the doctor takes a preponderant place, insofar as he converts it into a medical space. However, and this is the essential point, the doctor's intervention is not made by virtue of a medical skill or power that he possesses in himself and that would be justified by a body of objective knowledge. It is not as a scientist that *homo medicus* has authority in the asylum, but as a wise man. If the medical profession is required, it is as a juridical and moral guarantee, not in the name of science. A man of great probity, of utter virtue and scruple, who had had long experience in the asylum would do as well. For the medical enterprise is only a part of an enormous moral task that must be accomplished at the asylum, and which alone can ensure the cure of the insane: "Must it not be an inviolable law in the administration of any establishment for the insane, whether public or private, to grant the maniac all the liberty that the safety of his person and of that of others permits, and to proportion his repression to the greater or lesser seriousness of danger of his deviations . . . , to gather all the facts that can serve to enlighten the physician in treatment, to study with care the particular varieties of behavior and temperament, and accordingly to use gentleness or firmness, conciliatory terms or the tone of authority and an inflexible severity?"[18] According to Samuel Tuke, the first doctor appointed at the Retreat was recommended by his "indefatigable perseverance"; doubtless he had no particular knowledge of mental illnesses when he entered the asylum, but "he entered on his office with the anxiety and ardor of a feeling mind, upon the exertion of whose skill, depended the dearest interest of many of his fellow-creatures." He tried the various remedies that his own common sense and the experience of his predecessors suggested. But he was soon disappointed, not because the results were bad, or that the number of cures was minimal: "Yet the medical means were so imperfectly connected with the progress of recovery, that he could not avoid suspecting them, to be rather concomitants than causes." He then realized that there was little to be done using the medical methods known up to that time. The concern for humanity prevailed within him, and he decided to use no medicament that would be too disagreeable to the patient. But it must not be thought that the doctor's role had little importance at the Retreat: by the visits he paid regularly to the patients, by the authority he exercised in the house over all the staff, "the physician . . . sometimes possesses more influence over the patients' minds, than the other attendants."

It is thought that Tuke and Pinel opened the asylum to medical knowledge. They did not introduce science, but a personality, whose powers borrowed from science only their disguise, or at most their justification. These powers, by their nature, were of a moral and social order; they took root in the madman's minority status, in the insanity of his person, not of his mind. If the medical personage could isolate madness, it was not because he knew it, but because he mastered it; and what for positivism would be an image of objectivity was only the other side of this domination. "It is a very important object to win the confidence of these sufferers, and to arouse in them feelings of respect and obedience, which can only be the fruit of superior discernment, distinguished education, and dignity of tone and manner. Stupidity, ignorance, and the lack of principles, sustained by a tyrannical harshness, may incite fear, but always inspire distrust. The keeper of madmen who has obtained domination over them directs and rules their conduct as he pleases; he must be endowed with a firm character, and on occasion display an imposing strength. He must threaten little but carry out his threats, and if he is disobeyed, punishment must immediately ensue."[19] The physician could exercise his absolute authority in the world of the asylum only insofar as, from the beginning, he was Father and Judge, Family and Law—his medical practice being for a long time no more than a complement to the old rites of Order, Authority, and Punishment. And Pinel was well aware that the doctor cures when, exclusive of modern therapeutics, he brings into play these immemorial figures.

Pinel cites the case of a girl of seventeen who had been raised by her parents with "extreme indulgence"; she had fallen into a "giddy, mad delirium without any cause that could be determined"; at the hospital she was treated with great gentleness, but she always showed a certain "haughtiness" which could not be tolerated at the asylum; she spoke "of her parents with nothing but bitterness." It was decided to subject her to a regime of strict authority; "the keeper, in order to tame this inflexible character, seized the moment of the bath and expressed himself forcibly concerning certain unnatural persons who dared oppose their parents and disdain their authority. He warned the girl she would henceforth be treated with all the severity she deserved, for she herself was opposed to her cure and dissimulated with insurmountable obstinacy the basic cause of her illness." Through this new rigor and these threats, the sick girl felt "profoundly moved . . . she ended by acknowledging her wrongs and making a frank confession that she had suffered a loss of reason as the result of a forbidden romantic attachment, naming the person who had been its object." After this first confession, the cure became easy: "a most favorable alteration occurred . . . she was henceforth soothed and could not sufficiently express her gratitude toward the keeper who had brought an end to her continual agitation, and had restored tranquillity and calm to her heart." There is not a moment of the story that could not be transcribed in psychoanalytical terms. To such a degree was it true that the medical personage, according to Pinel, had to act not as the result of an objective definition of the disease or a specific classifying diagnosis, but by relying upon that prestige which envelops the secrets of the Family, of Authority, of Punishment, and of Love; it is by bringing such powers into play, by wearing the mask of Father and of Judge, that the physician, by one of those abrupt short cuts that leave aside mere medical competence, became the almost magic perpetrator of the cure, and assumed the aspect of a Thaumaturge; it was enough that he observed and spoke, to cause secret faults to appear, insane presumptions to vanish, and madness at last to yield to reason. His presence and his words were gifted with that power of disalienation, which at one blow revealed the transgression and restored the order of morality.

It is a curious paradox to see medical practice enter the uncertain domain of the quasi-miraculous at the very moment when the knowledge of mental illness tries to assume a positive meaning. On the one hand, madness puts itself at a distance in an objective field where the threats of unreason disappear; but at this same moment, the madman tends to form with the doctor, in an unbroken unity, a "couple" whose complicity dates back to very old links. Life in the asylum as Tuke and Pinel constituted it permitted the birth of that delicate structure which would become the essential nucleus of madness—a structure that formed a kind of microcosm in which were symbolized the massive structures of bourgeois society and its values: Family-Child relations, centered on the theme of paternal authority; Transgression-Punishment relations, centered on the theme of immediate justice; Madness-Disorder relations, centered on the theme of social and moral order. It is from these that the physician derives his power to cure; and it is to the degree that the patient finds himself, by so many old links, already alienated in the doctor, within the doctor-patient couple, that the doctor has the almost miraculous power to cure him.

In the time of Pinel and Tuke, this power had nothing extraordinary about it; it was explained and demonstrated in the efficacity, simply, of moral behavior; it was no more mysterious than the power of the eighteenth-century doctor when he diluted fluids or relaxed fibers. But very soon the meaning of this moral practice escaped the physician, to the very extent that he enclosed his knowledge in the norms of positivism: from the beginning of the nineteenth century, the psychiatrist no longer quite knew what was the nature of the power he had inherited from the great reformers, and whose efficacity seemed so foreign to his idea of mental illness and to the practice of all other doctors.

This psychiatric practice, mysterious even to those who used it, is very important in the situation of the madman within the medical world. First because medicine of the mind for the first time in the history of Western science was to assume almost complete autonomy: from the time of the Greeks, it had been no more than a chapter of medicine, and we have seen Willis study madness under the rubric "diseases of the head"; after Pinel and Tuke, psychiatry would become a medicine of a particular style: those most eager to discover the origin of madness in organic causes or in hereditary dispositions would not be able to avoid this style. They would be all the more unable to avoid it in that this particular style—bringing into play increasingly obscure moral powers—would originally be a sort of bad conscience; they would increasingly confine themselves in positivism, the more they felt their practice slipping out of it.

As positivism imposes itself upon medicine and psychiatry, this practice becomes more and more obscure, the psychiatrist's power more and more miraculous, and the doctor-patient couple sinks deeper into a strange world. In the patient's eyes, the doctor becomes a thaumaturge; the authority he has borrowed from order, morality, and the family now seems to derive from himself; it is because he is a doctor that he is believed to possess these powers, and while Pinel, with Tuke, strongly asserted that his moral action was not necessarily linked to any scientific competence, it was thought, and by the patient first of all, that it was in the esotericism of his knowledge, in some almost daemonic secret of knowledge, that the doctor had found the power to unravel insanity; and increasingly the patient would accept this self-surrender to a doctor both divine and satanic, beyond human measure in any case; increasingly he would alienate himself in the physician, accepting entirely and in advance all his prestige, submitting from the very first to a will he experienced as magic, and to a science he regarded as prescience and divination, thus becoming the ideal and perfect correlative of those powers he projected upon the doctor, pure object without any resistance except his own inertia, quite ready to become precisely that hysteric in whom Charcot exalted the doctor's marvelous powers. If we wanted to analyze the profound structures of objectivity in the knowledge and practice of nineteenth-century psychiatry from Pinel to Freud,[20] we should have to show in fact that such objectivity was from the start a reification of a magical nature, which could only be accomplished with the complicity of the patient himself, and beginning from a transparent and clear moral practice, gradually forgotten as positivism imposed its myths of scientific objectivity; a practice forgotten in its origins and its meaning, but always used and always present. What we call psychiatric practice is a certain moral tactic contemporary with the end of the eighteenth century, preserved in the rites of asylum life, and overlaid by the myths of positivism.

But if the doctor soon became a thaumaturge for the patient, he could not be one in his own positivist doctor's eyes. That obscure power whose origin he no longer knew, in which he could not decipher the patient's complicity, and in which he would not consent to acknowledge the ancient powers which constituted it, nevertheless had to be given some status; and since nothing in positivist understanding could justify such a transfer of will or similar remote-control operations, the moment would soon come when madness itself would be held responsible for such anomalies. These cures without basis, which must be recognized as not being false cures, would soon become the true cures of false illnesses. Madness was not what one believed, nor what it believed itself to be; it was infinitely less than itself: a combination of persuasion and mystification. We can see here the genesis of Babinski's pithiatism. And by a strange reversal, thought leaped back almost two centuries to the era when between madness, false madness, and the simulation of madness, the limit was indistinct—identical symptoms confused to the point where transgression replaced unity; further still, medical thought finally effected an identification over which all Western thought since Greek medicine had hesitated: the identification of madness with madness—that is, of the medical concept with the critical concept of madness. At the end of the nineteenth century, and in the thought of Babinski's contemporaries, we find that prodigious postulate, which no medicine had yet dared formulate: that madness, after all, was only madness.

Thus while the victim of mental illness is entirely alienated in the real person of his doctor, the doctor dissipates the reality of the mental illness in the critical concept of madness. So that there remains, beyond the empty forms of positivist thought, only a single concrete reality: the doctor-patient couple in which all alienations are summarized, linked, and loosened. And it is to this degree that all nineteenth-century psychiatry really converges on Freud, the first man to accept in all its seriousness the reality of the physician-patient couple, the first to consent not to look away nor to investigate elsewhere, the first not to attempt to hide it in a psychiatric theory that more or less harmonized with the rest of medical knowledge; the first to follow its consequences with absolute rigor. Freud demystified all the other asylum structures: he abolished silence and observation, he eliminated madness's recognition of itself in the mirror of its own spectacle, he silenced the instances of condemnation. But on the other hand he exploited the structure that enveloped the medical personage; he amplified its thaumaturgical virtues, preparing for its omnipotence a quasi-divine status. He focussed upon this single presence—concealed behind the patient and above him, in an absence that is also a total presence—all the powers that had been distributed in the collective existence of the asylum; he transformed this into an absolute Observation, a pure and circumspect Silence, a Judge who punishes and rewards in a judgment that does not even condescend to language; he made it the Mirror in which madness, in an almost motionless movement, clings to and casts off itself.

To the doctor, Freud transferred all the structures Pinel and Tuke had set up within confinement. He did deliver the patient from the existence of the asylum within which his "liberators" had alienated him; but he did not deliver him from what was essential in this existence; he regrouped its powers, extended them to the maximum by uniting them in the doctor's hands; he created the psychoanalytical situation where, by an inspired short-circuit, alienation becomes disalienating because, in the doctor, it becomes a subject.

The doctor, as an alienating figure, remains the key to psychoanalysis. It is perhaps because it did not suppress this ultimate structure, and because it referred all the others to it, that psychoanalysis has not been able, will not be able, to hear the voices of unreason, nor to decipher in themselves the signs of the madman. Psychoanalysis can unravel some of the forms of madness; it remains a stranger to the sovereign enterprise of unreason. It can neither liberate nor transcribe, nor most certainly explain, what is essential in this enterprise.

Since the end of the eighteenth century, the life of unreason no longer manifests itself except in the lightning-flash of works such as those of Hölderlin, of Nerval, of Nietzsche, or of Artaud—forever irreducible to those alienations that can be cured, resisting by their own strength that gigantic moral imprisonment which we are in the habit of calling, doubtless by antiphrasis, the liberation of the insane by Pinel and Tuke.

CONCLUSION

THE Goya who painted *The Madhouse* must have experienced before that grovel of flesh in the void, that nakedness among bare walls, something related to a contemporary pathos: the symbolic tinsel that crowned the insane kings left in full view suppliant bodies, bodies vulnerable to chains and whips, which contradicted the delirium of the faces, less by the poverty of these trappings than by the human truth which radiated from all that unprofaned flesh. The man in the tricorne is not mad because he has stuck an old hat upon his nakedness; but within this madman in a hat rises—by the inarticulate power of his muscular body, of his savage and marvelously unconstricted youth—a human presence already liberated and somehow free since the beginning of time, by his birthright. *The Madhouse* is less concerned with madness and those strange faces one finds elsewhere in the *Caprichos*, moreover, than with the vast monotony of these new bodies, shown in all their vigor, and whose gestures, if they invoke their dreams, celebrate especially their dark freedom: its language is close to the world of Pinel.

The Goya of the *Disparates* and the Quinta del Sordo addresses himself to another madness. Not that of madmen cast into prison, but that of man cast into darkness. Does Goya not link us, by memory, with the old world of enchantments, of fantastic rides, of witches perched on the branches of dead trees? Is not the monster whispering its secrets into the ears of the *Monk* related to the gnome who fascinated Bosch's *Saint Anthony?* But they are different for Goya, and their prestige, which overshadows all his later work, derives from another power. For Bosch or Brueghel, these forms are generated by the world itself; through the fissures of a strange poetry, they rise from stones and plants, they well out of an animal howl; the whole complicity of nature is not too much for their dance. Goya's forms are born out of nothing: they have no background, in the double sense that they are silhouetted against only the most monotonous darkness, and that nothing can assign them their origin, their limit, and their nature. The *Disparates* are without landscape, without walls, without setting—and this is still a further difference from the *Caprichos;* there is not a star in the night sky of the great human bats we see in the *Way of Flying.* The branch on which these witches jabber—out of what tree does it grow? Does it fly? Toward what sabbath, and what clearing? Nothing in all this deals with a world, neither this one nor any other. It is indeed a question of that *Sleep of Reason* which Goya, in 1797, had already made the first image of the "universal idiom"; it is a question of a night which is doubtless that of classical unreason, that triple night into which Orestes sank. But in that night, man communicates with what is deepest in himself, and with what is most solitary. The desert of Bosch's Saint Anthony was infinitely populous; and even if it was a product of her imagination, the landscape that Dulle Griet moved through was marked by a whole human language. Goya's Monk, with that hot beast against his back, its paws on his shoulders and its mouth panting at his ear, remains alone: no secret is revealed. All that is present is the most internal, and at the same time the most savagely free, of forces: the power which hacks apart the bodies in the *Gran Disparate*, which breaks free and assaults our eyes in the *Raging Madness*. Beyond that point, the faces themselves decompose; this is no longer the madness of the *Caprichos*, which tied on masks truer than the truth of faces; this is a madness *beneath* the mask, a madness that eats away faces, corrodes features; there are no longer eyes or mouths, but glances shot from nowhere and staring at nothing (as in the *Witches' Sabbath*); or screams from black holes (as in the *Pilgrimage of Saint Isidore*). Madness has become man's possibility of abolishing both man and the world—and even those images that challenge the world and deform man. It is, far beyond dreams, beyond the nightmare of bestiality, the last recourse: the end and the beginning of everything. Not because it is a promise, as in German lyricism, but because it is the ambiguity of chaos and apocalypse: Goya's *Idiot* who shrieks and twists his shoulder to escape from the nothingness that imprisons him—is this the birth of the first man and his first movement toward liberty, or the last convulsion of the last dying man?

And this madness that links and divides time, that twists the world into the ring of a single night, this madness so foreign to the experience of its contemporaries, does it not transmit—to those able to receive it, to Nietzsche and to Artaud—those barely audible voices of classical unreason, in which it was always a question of nothingness and night, but amplifying them now to shrieks and frenzy? But giving them for the first time an expression, a *droit de cité*, and a hold on Western culture which makes possible all contestations, as well as *total* contestation? But restoring their primitive savagery?

Sade's calm, patient language also gathers up the final words of unreason and also gives them, for the future, a remoter meaning. Between Goya's broken drawings and that uninterrupted stream of words continuing from the first volume of *Justine* to the tenth of *Juliette*, there is doubtless nothing in common except a certain movement that retraces the course of contemporary lyricism, drying up its sources, rediscovering the secret of unreason's nothingness.

Within the château where Sade's hero confines himself, within the convents, the forests, the dungeons where he endlessly pursues the agony of his victims, it seems at first glance that nature can act with utter freedom. There man rediscovers a truth he had forgotten, though it was manifest: what desire can be contrary to nature, since it was given to man by nature itself? And since it was taught by nature in the great lesson of life and death which never stops repeating itself in the world? The madness of desire, insane murders, the most unreasonable passions—all are wisdom and reason, since they are a part of the order of nature. Everything that morality and religion, everything that a clumsy society has stifled in man, revives in the castle of murders. There man is finally attuned to his own nature; or rather, by an ethic peculiar to this strange confinement, man must scrupulously maintain, without deviation, his fidelity to nature: a strict task, a total enterprise: "You will know nothing unless you have known everything; if you are timid enough to stop with Nature, she will escape you forever."[1] Conversely, if man has wounded or changed nature, it is man's task to repair the damage through the mathematics of a sovereign vengeance: "Nature caused us all to be born equal; if fate is pleased to disturb this plan of the general law, it is our responsibility to correct its caprice, and to repair by our attention the usurpations of the stronger."[2] The slowness of revenge, like the insolence of desire, belongs to nature. There is nothing that the madness of men invents which is not either nature made manifest or nature restored.

But this is only the first phase of Sade's thought: the ironic justification, both rational and lyrical, the gigantic *pastiche*, of Rousseau. Beyond this demonstration-by-absurdity of the inanity of contemporary philosophy, beyond all its verbiage about man and nature, the real decisions are still to be made: decisions that are also breaks, in which the links between man and his natural being disappear.[3] The famous Society of the Friends of Crime, the project of a Swedish Constitution, once we remove their stinging references to the *Social Contract* and to the proposed constitutions for Poland or Corsica, establish nothing but the sovereign rigor of subjectivity in the rejection of all natural liberty and all natural equality: uncontrolled disposal of one member by the other, the unconditional exercise of violence, the limitless application of the right of death—this entire society, whose only link is the very rejection of a link, appears to be a dismissal of nature—the only cohesion asked of individuals is intended to protect, not a natural existence, but the free exercise of sovereignty over and against nature.[4] The relation established by Rousseau is precisely reversed; sovereignty no longer transposes the natural existence; the latter is only an object for the sovereign, which permits him to measure his total liberty. Followed to its logical conclusion, desire leads only in appearance to the rediscovery of nature. Actually, for Sade there is no return to the natal terrain, no hope that the first rejection of social order may surreptitiously become the re-established order of happiness, through a dialectic of nature renouncing and thus confirming itself. The solitary madness of desire that still for Hegel, as for the eighteenth-century philosophers, plunges man into a natural world that is immediately resumed in a social world, for Sade merely casts man into a void that dominates nature in a total absence of proportion and community, into the endlessly repeated nonexistence of gratification. The night of madness is thus limitless; what might have been supposed to be man's violent nature was only the infinity of non-nature.

Here is the source of Sade's great monotony: as he advances, the settings dissolve; the surprises, the incidents, the pathetic or dramatic links of the scenes vanish. What was still vicissitude in *Justine*—an event experienced, hence new—becomes in *Juliette* a sovereign game, always triumphant, without negativity, and whose perfection is such that its novelty can only be its similarity to itself. As with Goya, there are no longer any backgrounds for these meticulous *Disparates*. And yet in this absence of decor, which can as easily be total night as absolute day (there are no shadows in Sade), we advance slowly toward a goal: the death of Justine. Her innocence had exhausted even the desire to torment it. We cannot say that crime had not overcome her virtue; we must say inversely that her natural virtue had brought her to the point of having exhausted all the possible means of being an object for crime. And at this point, when crime can do nothing more than drive her from the domain of its sovereignty (Juliette expels her from the Château de Noirceuil), Nature in her turn, so long dominated, scorned, profaned,[5] submits entirely to that which contradicted her: Nature in turn enters madness, and there, in an instant, but for an instant only, restores her omnipotence. The storm that is unleashed, the lightning that strikes and consumes Justine, is Nature become criminal subjectivity. This death that seems to escape from the insane domain of Juliette belongs to Nature more profoundly than any other; the night of storm, of thunder and lightning, is a sufficient sign that Nature is lacerating herself, that she has reached the extreme point of her dissension, and that she is revealing in this golden flash a sovereignty which is both herself and something quite outside herself: the sovereignty of a mad heart that has attained, in its solitude, the limits of the world that wounds it, that turns it against itself and abolishes it at the moment when to have mastered it so well gives it the right to identify itself with that world. That lightning-flash which Nature drew from herself in order to strike Justine was identical with the long existence of Juliette, who would also disappear in solitude, leaving no trace or corpse or anything upon which Nature could claim her due. The nothingness of unreason, in which the language of Nature had died forever, has become a violence of Nature and against Nature, to the point of the savage abolition of itself.[6]

For Sade as for Goya, unreason continues to watch by night; but in this vigil it joins with fresh powers. The nonbeing it once was now becomes the power to annihilate. Through Sade and Goya, the Western world received the possibility of transcending its reason in violence, and of recovering tragic experience beyond the promises of dialectic.

After Sade and Goya, and since them, unreason has belonged to whatever is decisive, for the modern world, in any work of art: that is, whatever any work of art contains that is both murderous and constraining.

The madness of Tasso, the melancholia of Swift, the delirium of Rousseau belong to their works, just as these works belong to their authors. Here in the texts, there in the lives of the men, the same violence spoke, or the same bitterness; visions certainly were exchanged; language and delirium interlaced. But further, the work of art and madness, in classical experience, were more profoundly united at another level: paradoxically, at the point where they limited one another. For there existed a region where madness challenged the work of art, reduced it ironically, made of

its iconographic landscape a pathological world of hallucinations; that language which was delirium was not a
work of art. And conversely, delirium was robbed of its
meager truth as madness if it was called a work of art. But
by admitting this very fact, there was no reduction of one
by the other, but rather (remembering Montaigne) a discovery of the central incertitude where the work of art is
born, at the moment when it stops being born and is truly a
work of art. In this opposition, to which Tasso and Swift
bore witness after Lucretius—and which it was vain to attempt to separate into lucid intervals and crises—was disclosed a distance where the very truth of a work of art
raised a problem: was it madness, or a work of art? Inspiration, or hallucination? A spontaneous babble of words, or
the pure origins of language? Must its truth, even before its
birth, be taken from the wretched truth of men, or discovered far beyond its origin, in the being that it presumes?
The madness of the writer was, for other men, the chance
to see being born, over and over again, in the discouragement of repetition and disease, the truth of the work of
art.

The madness of Nietzsche, the madness of Van Gogh or
of Artaud, belongs to their work perhaps neither more nor
less profoundly, but in quite another way. The frequency
in the modern world of works of art that explode out of
madness no doubt proves nothing about the reason of that
world, about the meaning of such works, or even about the
relations formed and broken between the real world and
the artists who produced such works. And yet this frequency must be taken seriously, as if it were the insistence
of a question: from the time of Hölderlin and Nerval, the
number of writers, painters, and musicians who have "suc-
cumbed" to madness has increased; but let us make no mistake here; between madness and the work of art, there has
been no accommodation, no more constant exchange, no

communication of languages; their opposition is much more dangerous than formerly; and their competition now allows no quarter; theirs is a game of life and death. Artaud's madness does not slip through the fissures of the work of art; his madness is precisely the *absence of the work of art*, the reiterated presence of that absence, its central void experienced and measured in all its endless dimensions. Nietzsche's last cry, proclaiming himself both Christ and Dionysos, is not on the border of reason and unreason, in the perspective of the work of art, their common dream, finally realized and immediately vanishing, of a reconciliation of the "shepherds of Arcady and the fishermen of Tiberias"; it is the very annihilation of the work of art, the point where it becomes impossible and where it must fall silent; the hammer has just fallen from the philosopher's hands. And Van Gogh, who did not want to ask "permission from doctors to paint pictures," knew quite well that his work and his madness were incompatible.

Madness is the absolute break with the work of art; it forms the constitutive moment of abolition, which dissolves in time the truth of the work of art; it draws the exterior edge, the line of dissolution, the contour against the void. Artaud's *oeuvre* experiences its own absence in madness, but that experience, the fresh courage of that ordeal, all those words hurled against a fundamental absence of language, all that space of physical suffering and terror which surrounds or rather coincides with the void—that is the work of art itself: the sheer cliff over the abyss of the work's absence. Madness is no longer the space of indecision through which it was possible to glimpse the original truth of the work of art, but the decision beyond which this truth ceases irrevocably, and hangs forever over history. It is of little importance on exactly which day in the autumn of 1888 Nietzsche went mad for good, and after which his texts no longer afford philosophy but psychiatry: all of

them, including the postcard to Strindberg, belong to
Nietzsche, and all are related to *The Birth of Tragedy*. But
we must not think of this continuity in terms of a system,
of a thematics, or even of an existence: Nietzsche's madness—that is, the dissolution of his thought—is that by
which his thought opens out onto the modern world. What
made it impossible makes it immediate for us; what took it
from Nietzsche offers it to us. This does not mean that
madness is the only language common to the work of art
and the modern world (dangers of the pathos of maledic-
tion, inverse and symmetrical danger of psychoanalyses);
but it means that, through madness, a work that seems to
drown in the world, to reveal there its non-sense, and to
transfigure itself with the features of pathology alone, actually engages within itself the world's time, masters it, and
leads it; by the madness which interrupts it, a work of art
opens a void, a moment of silence, a question without answer, provokes a breach without reconciliation where the
world is forced to question itself. What is necessarily a
profanation in the work of art returns to that point, and, in
the time of that work swamped in madness, the world is
made aware of its guilt. Henceforth, and through the mediation of madness, it is the world that becomes culpable
(for the first time in the Western world) in relation to the
work of art; it is now arraigned by the work of art, obliged
to order itself by its language, compelled by it to a task of
recognition, of reparation, to the task of restoring reason
from that unreason and *to* that unreason. The madness in
which the work of art is engulfed is the space of our enterprise, it is the endless path to fulfillment, it is our mixed vocation of apostle and exegete. This is why it makes little
difference when the first voice of madness insinuated itself
into Nietzsche's pride, into Van Gogh's humility. There is
no madness except as the final instant of the work of art—
the work endlessly drives madness to its limits; *where there*

is a work of art, there is no madness; and yet madness is contemporary with the work of art, since it inaugurates the time of its truth. The moment when, together, the work of art and madness are born and fulfilled is the beginning of the time when the world finds itself arraigned by that work of art and responsible before it for what it is.

Ruse and new triumph of madness: the world that thought to measure and justify madness through psychology must justify itself before madness, since in its struggles and agonies it measures itself by the excess of works like those of Nietzsche, of Van Gogh, of Artaud. And nothing in itself, especially not what it can know of madness, assures the world that it is justified by such works of madness.

NOTES

CHAPTER I. "STULTIFERA NAVIS"

1. Cf. J. Lebeuf, *Histoire de la ville et de tout le diocèse de Paris* (Paris, 1754–58).
2. *Tristan et Iseut*, Bossuat edition, pp. 219–22.
3. Pierre de Lancre, *Tableau de l'inconstance des mauvais anges* (Paris, 1612).
4. In this sense, the experience of madness exhibits a rigorous continuity with the experience of leprosy. The ritual of the leper's exclusion showed that he was, as a living man, the very presence of death.
5. Erasmus, *Praise of Folly*, §9.
6. Louise Labé, *Débat de folie et d'amour* (Lyons, 1566), p. 98.
7. Sebastian Brant, *Stultifera navis*, Latin translation of 1497, fol. 11.
8. Saint-Évremond, *Sir Politik would be*, act V, scene ii.
9. Cervantes, *Don Quixote*, Part II, Chap. 1.
10. T. Gazoni, *L'Ospedale di passi incurabili* (Ferrara, 1586). Cf. Charles de Beys, *L'Ospital des fous* (1635).
11. Mathurin Régnier, *Satire XIV*, vv. 7–10.

CHAPTER II. THE GREAT CONFINEMENT

1. Edict of 1656, article IV. Later the Saint-Esprit and the Enfants-Trouvés would be added, and the Savonnerie withdrawn.
2. *Ibid.*, article XII.
3. La Rochefoucauld-Liancourt's report in the name of the Committee on Mendicity to the Constituent Assembly (*Procès verbaux de l'Assemblée nationale*, Vol. XXI).

4. From a spiritual point of view, poverty at the end of the sixteenth and the beginning of the seventeenth century was experienced as an apocalyptic threat. "One of the most evident signs that the coming of the Son of God and the end of time are at hand is the extreme of both spiritual and temporal poverty to which the world is reduced. These are evil days . . . afflictions have multiplied because of the multitude of transgressions, pain being the inseparable shadow of evil." (Jean-Pierre Camus, *De la mendicité légitime des pauvres* [Douai, 1634], pp. 3–4.)

5. Musquinet de la Pagne, *Bicêtre réformé ou établissement d'une maison de discipline* (Paris, 1790), p. 22.

6. Bossuet, *Élevations sur les mystères*, Sixth Week, Twelfth Elevation.

7. "We seek that God should serve our mad appetites, and that He should be as though subject to ourselves." Calvin, *Forty-ninth Sermon on Deuteronomy*, July 3, 1555.

8. Regulations of the Hôpital Général, articles XII and XIII.

9. Jean-Jacques Rousseau, *Discours sur les sciences et les arts.*

10. John Howard, *The State of the Prisons in England and Wales* (London, 1784), p. 73.

11. Sermon cited in Pierre Collet, *Vie de saint Vincent de Paul* (Paris, 1818).

CHAPTER III. THE INSANE

1. François Ravaisson, *Les Archives de la Bastille* (Paris, 1866–1904), Vol. XIII, pp. 161–62.

2. Bibliothèque national, Fonds Clairambault, 986.

3. It did happen, but very late, and doubtless under the influence of the practice which concerned madmen, that those afflicted with venereal disease were also exhibited. Père Richard, in his *Mémoires*, tells of the visit the Prince de Condé made to them with the Duke d'Enghien in order to "inspire him with a horror of vice." (*Mémoires du Père Richard*, manuscript in the Bibliothèque de la Ville de Paris, fol. 25.)

4. Ned Ward, in *The London Spy* (London, 1700), cites the figure of twopence.

5. "Everyone used to be admitted to visit Bicêtre, and in good weather you might see at least two thousand persons a day. After paying your money, you were led by a guide into the section for the insane." (*Mémoires du Père Richard, loc. cit.,* fol. 61). The visit included an Irish priest "who slept on straw," a ship's captain whom the sight of men made furious, "for it was the injustice of men that had driven him mad," a young man "who sang in a ravishing fashion" (*ibid.*).

6. Mirabeau (H.), *Observations d'un voyageur anglais* (Paris, 1788), p. 213, n. 1.

7. Jean-Étienne-Dominique Esquirol, "Mémoire historique et statistique sur la Maison Royale de Charenton," in *Des maladies mentales* (Paris, 1838), Vol. II, p. 212.

8. Pascal, *Pensées* (Brunschvicg edition), no. 339.

9. Bossuet, *Panégyrique de saint Bernard,* Preamble.

10. Saint Vincent here alludes to the text of Saint Paul (I Cor., I, 23): "to the Jews, indeed, a stumbling-block and to the Gentiles foolishness."

11. *Correspondance de saint Vincent de Paul,* Coste edition (Paris, 1920–24), Vol. V, p. 146.

CHAPTER IV. PASSION AND DELIRIUM

1. François Boissier de Sauvages, *Nosologie méthodique* (Lyons, 1772), Vol. VII, p. 12.

2. F. Bayle and H. Grangeon, *Relation de l'état de quelques personnes prétendues possédées faite d'autorité au Parlement de Toulouse* (Toulouse, 1682), pp. 26–27.

3. Malebranche, *Recherche de la vérité,* Book V, Chap. 3.

4. Sauvages, *op. cit.,* Vol. VII, p. 291.

5. Robert Whytt, *Traité des maladies nerveuses* (French trans., Paris, 1777), Vol. II, pp. 288–91.

6. Charles-Gaspard de la Rive, "Sur un établissement pour la guérison des aliénés," *Bibliothèque britannique,* Vol. VIII, p. 304.

7. *Encyclopédie*, article on Mania.

8. *L'Ame matérielle, ou nouveau système sur les purs principes des philosophes anciens et modernes qui soutiennent son immatérialité*. Arsenal, manuscript no. 2239, p. 169.

9. Paul Zacchias, *Quaestiones medico-legales* (Avignon, 1660–61), Book II, Vol. II, question 4, p. 119.

10. Sauvages, *op. cit.*, Vol. VII, p. 15.

11. *Ibid.*, p. 20.

12. Ysbrand van Diemerbroek, *Disputationes practicae, de morbis capitis*, in *Opera omnia anatomica et medica* (Utrecht, 1685), Historia III, pp. 4–5.

13. J.-D.-T. Bienville, *De la nymphomanie* (Amsterdam, 1771), pp. 140–53.

14. Robert James, *Dictionnaire universel de médecine* (French trans., Paris, 1746–48), Vol. III, p. 977.

15. *Ibid.*

16. Zacchias, *op. cit.*, Book I, Vol. II, question 4, p. 118.

17. Archibald Pitcairne, quoted by Sauvages, *op. cit.*, Vol. VII, pp. 33 and 301.

18. *Encyclopédie*, article on Madness.

19. We should add Andromache herself, widow, and bride, and widow again, in her mourning garments and festive garb which ultimately mingle and say the same thing; and the luster of her royalty in the night of her slavery.

20. Cf. for example annotations like the following, apropos of a madman confined for seventeen years at Saint-Lazare: "His health is fading greatly; it is to be hoped that he will soon die." (Bibliothèque national, Fonds Clairambault, 986, fol. 113)

CHAPTER V. ASPECTS OF MADNESS

1. Johann Weyer, *De praestigiis daemonum* (1563).

2. *Ibid.*

3. *Apologie pour Monsieur Duncan*.

4. *Ibid.*

5. Hippolyte-Jules la Mesnardière, *Traité de la mélancolie* (La Flèche, 1635), p. 10.

6. *Apologie pour Monsieur Duncan.*
7. Thomas Willis, *Opera omnia* (Lyons, 1681), Vol. II, p. 242.
8. "A soldier became melancholic because of his parents' rejection of a girl he desperately loved. He was distracted, complained of a severe headache, and of a continual heaviness in that part. He grew visibly thinner; his face turned pale and he became so weak that he voided his excrement without noticing it. . . . There was no delirium, although the patient gave no positive answers and seemed to be entirely absorbed. He never asked for either food or drink." (*Gazette salutaire*, March 17, 1763)
9. Robert James, *Dictionnaire universel de médecine* (French trans., Paris, 1746–48), Vol. IV, p. 1215.
10. *Encyclopédie*, article on Mania.
11. William Cullen, *Institutions de médecine pratique* (French trans., 2 vols., Paris, 1785), Vol. II, p. 315.
12. M. Flemyng, *Nevropathia sive de morbis hypochondriacis et hystericis* (Amsterdam, 1741), pp. i–ii.
13. Thomas Sydenham, *Médecine pratique* (French trans., Paris, 1784), pp. 400–404.
14. *Ibid.*, pp. 395–96.
15. *Ibid.*, p. 394.
16. *Ibid.*, p. 394.
17. Jean-Baptiste Pressavin, *Nouveau traité des vapeurs* (Lyons, 1770), pp. 2–3.
18. Robert Whytt, *Traité des maladies nerveuses* (French trans., Paris, 1777), Vol. I, pp. 23–24, 50–51.
19. *Ibid.*, pp. 47, 126–27, 166–67.
20. Simon-André Tissot, *Traité des nerfs et de leurs maladies* (Paris, 1778–80), Vol. I, Part 2, p. 302.
21. *Ibid.*, pp. 278–79, 302–3.
22. Pressavin, *op. cit.*, p. 65.
23. Louis-Sébastien Mercier, *Tableau de Paris* (Amsterdam, 1783), Vol. III, p. 199.

CHAPTER VI. DOCTORS AND PATIENTS

1. Madame de Sévigné used it a great deal, finding it "good against sadness" (cf. letters of October 16 and 20, 1675).

2. Lange, *Traité des vapeurs* (Paris, 1689), p. 251.

3. Consultation de la Closure, Arsenal, manuscript no. 4528, fol. 119.

4. Joseph Raulin, *Traité des affections vaporeuses du sexe* (Paris, 1758), p. 339.

5. Jean-Baptiste Pressavin, *Nouveau Traité des vapeurs* (Lyons, 1770), Foreword, not paginated.

6. A. Rostaing, *Réflexions sur les affections vaporeuses* (Paris, 1778), p. 75.

7. Jean-Étienne-Dominique Esquirol, *Des maladies mentales* (Paris, 1838), Vol. II, p. 225.

8. Thomas Sydenham, "Dissertation sur l'affection hystérique," *Médecine pratique* (French trans., Paris, 1784), p. 425.

9. William Cullen, *Institutions de médecine pratique* (French trans., Paris, 1785), Vol. II, p. 317.

10. There is still some question whether the inventor of the rotatory machine was Maupertuis, Darwin, or the Dane Katzenstein.

11. *Encyclopédie*, article on Music.

12. Alexander Crichton, *On Mental Diseases*, cited in Élias Regnault, *Du dégré de compétence des médecins* (Paris, 1828), pp. 187–88.

13. Cullen, *op. cit.*, p. 307.

14. François Leuret, *Fragments psychologiques sur la folie* (Paris, 1834), pp. 308–21.

15. Cited by Robert Whytt, *Traité des maladies nerveuses* (French trans., Paris, 1777), Vol. I, p. 296.

16. Thomas Willis, *Opera omnia* (Lyons, 1681), Vol. II, p. 261.

17. M. Hulshorff, *Discours sur les penchants*, read at the Academy of Berlin. Cited in the *Gazette salutaire*, August 17, 1769.

18. *Ibid., loc. cit.*

19. *Encyclopédie*, article on Melancholy.

20. Bernardin de Saint-Pierre, *Préambule de L'Arcadie. Oeuvres* (Paris, 1818), Vol. VII, pp. 11–14.

21. Simon-André Tissot, *Avis aux gens de lettres sur leur santé* (Lausanne, 1767), pp. 90–94.

22. Philippe Pinel, *Traité médico-philosophique sur l'aliénation mentale* (Paris, 1801), pp. 238–39.

CHAPTER VII. THE GREAT FEAR

1. Denis Diderot, *Le Neveu de Rameau. Oeuvres* (Pléiade edition), p. 435.
2. Louis-Sébastien Mercier, *Tableau de Paris* (Amsterdam, 1783), Vol. I, pp. 233–34.
3. *Ibid.*, Vol. VIII, p. 1.
4. *Ibid.*, p. 2.
5. Musquinet de la Pagne, *Bicêtre réformé ou établissement d'une maison de discipline* (Paris, 1790), p. 16.
6. "I knew, as did everyone, that Bicêtre was both hospital and prison; but I did not know that the hospital had been built to nurture sickness, the prison to nurture crime." (Mirabeau [H.], *Observations d'un voyageur anglais* [Paris, 1788], p. 6.)
7. Mirabeau, *op. cit.*, p. 14.
8. Simon-André Tissot, *Traité des nerfs et de leurs maladies* (Paris, 1778–80), Vol. I, pp. iii–iv.
9. In nineteenth-century evolutionism, madness is indeed a return, but along a chronological *path;* it is not the absolute collapse of time. It is a question of time turned back, not of repetition in the strict sense. Psychoanalysis, which has tried to confront madness and unreason again, has found itself faced with this problem of time; fixation, death-wish, collective unconscious, archetype define more or less happily this heterogeneity of two temporal structures: that which is proper to the experience of Unreason and to the knowledge it envelops; that which is proper to the knowledge of madness, and to the science it authorizes.
10. Johann Christoph Spurzheim, *Observations sur la folie* (Paris, 1818).
11. J. C. N. Moehsen, *Geschichte der Wissenschaften in der Mark Brandenburg* (Berlin and Leipzig, 1781).
12. Edmé-Pierre Beauchesne, *De l'influence des affections de l'âme dans les maladies nerveuses des femmes* (Paris, 1783), p. 31.

13. *Ibid.*, p. 33.
14. *Ibid.*, pp. 37–38.
15. "Causes physiques et morales des maux des nerfs," *Gazette salutaire*, October 6, 1768 (anonymous article).

CHAPTER VIII. THE NEW DIVISION

1. Mirabeau (H.), *Des lettres de cachet et des prisons d'état*, Chap. 11. *Oeuvres* (Merilhou edition), Vol. I, p. 264.
2. Mirabeau (V.), *L'Ami des hommes* (Paris, 1758), Vol. II, pp. 414 ff.
3. Mirabeau, *Des lettres de cachet*, p. 264.
4. Jean-Pierre Brissot de Warville, *Théorie des lois criminelles* (Paris, 1781), Vol. I, p. 79.
5. *Encyclopédie*, article on Hospital.
6. Abbé de Récalde, *Traité sur les abus qui subsistent dans les hôpitaux du royaume* (Paris, 1786), pp. ii, iii.
7. Mirabeau, *L'Ami des hommes*, Vol. I, p. 22.
8. Turgot, "Éloge de Gournay," *Oeuvres* (Schelle edition), Vol. I, p. 607.
9. Turgot, article on Foundation in the *Encyclopédie*.
10. Turgot, "Lettre à Trudaine sur le Limousin," *Oeuvres* (Schelle edition), Vol. II, pp. 478–95.

CHAPTER IX. THE BIRTH OF THE ASYLUM

1. Charles-Gaspard de la Rive, letter to the editors of the *Bibliothèque britannique* concerning a new establishment for the cure of the insane. This text appeared in the *Bibliothèque britannique*, then in a separate brochure. De la Rive's visit to the Retreat dates from 1798.
2. Scipion Pinel, *Traité complet du régime sanitaire des aliénés* (Paris, 1836), p. 56.
3. Samuel Tuke, *Description of the Retreat, an Institution near York for Insane Persons of the Society of Friends* (York, 1813), p. 50.
4. *Ibid.*, p. 23.
5. *Ibid.*, p. 121.
6. *Ibid.*, p. 141.

7. *Ibid.*, p. 156.
8. De la Rive, *loc. cit.*, p. 30.
9. Philippe Pinel, *Traité médico-philosophique sur l'aliéna-tion mentale* (Paris, 1801), p. 265.
10. *Ibid.*, p. 141.
11. *Ibid.*, pp. 29–30.
12. Scipion Pinel, *op. cit.*, p. 63.
13. Cited in René Sémelaigne, *Aliénistes et philanthropes* (Paris, 1912), Appendix, p. 502.
14. Philippe Pinel, *op. cit.*, p. 256.
15. *Ibid.*, pp. 207–8.
16. *Ibid.*, p. 205.
17. Cited in Tuke, *op. cit.*, pp. 89–90.
18. Philippe Pinel, *op. cit.*, pp. 292–93.
19. John Haslam, *Observations on Insanity with Practical Re-marks on This Disease* (London, 1798), cited by Philippe Pinel, *op. cit.*, pp. 253–54.
20. These structures still persist in non-psychoanalytic psy-chiatry, and in many aspects of psychoanalysis itself.

Conclusion

1. *Cent vingt journées de Sodome*, quoted by Maurice Blanchot, *Lautréamont et Sade* (Paris, 1949), p. 235.
2. *Ibid.*, *loc. cit.*, p. 225.
3. Infamy must be able to go as far as "to dismember nature and dislocate the universe." *Cent vingt journées de Sodome* (Paris, 1935), Vol. II, p. 369.
4. This cohesion imposed on the *socii* consists, in effect, of not admitting among themselves the validity of the right of death, which they can exercise over others, but of rec-ognizing among themselves an absolute right of free dis-posal; each must be able to *belong* to the other.
5. Cf. the episode of the volcano at the end of *Juliette* (Pau-vert edition, Paris, 1954), Vol. VI, pp. 31–33.
6. "One would have said that Nature, weary of her own works, was ready to mingle all the elements together in order to force them into new forms." *Ibid.*, p. 270.

Michel Foucault studied at the Sorbonne, earning his Licence de Philosophie in 1948, his Licence de Psychologie in 1950, and the Diplôme de Psycho-Pathologie from the Université de Paris in 1952. He was a lecturer at the University of Upsala, Sweden, for four years, and in 1959–60 he was the Director of the Institut Français in Hamburg, Germany. He then became a Professor and the Director of the Institut de Philosophie at the Faculté des Lettres in Clermont, France.

Dr. Foucault has lectured in many universities, including those in Copenhagen, Oslo, Lisbon, Madrid, Istanbul, Naples, and Brussels. He writes frequently for French newspapers and reviews and is an editor of *Critique*.

His three other books, published in France in 1962–63, deal with psychology and medical history. *Madness and Civilization*, his first book, was published in France in 1961 and won the Medal of the Centre de la Recherche Scientifique. It is his first work to appear in English.

VINTAGE WORKS OF SCIENCE
AND PSYCHOLOGY